Ernest Kevan

Ernest F. Kevan

Ernest Kevan

LEADER IN TWENTIETH CENTURY BRITISH EVANGELICALISM

Paul E. Brown

THE BANNER OF TRUTH TRUST

THE BANNER OF TRUTH TRUST
3 Murrayfield Road, Edinburgh, EH12 6EL, UK
P.O. Box 621, Carlisle, PA 17013, USA

*

*

ISBN: 978 1 84871 156 3

*

Typeset in 11/15 Sabon Oldstyle Figures at
The Banner of Truth Trust, Edinburgh

Printed in the USA by
Versa Press, Inc.,
East Peoria, IL

For the students of
London Bible College, 1943-1965
who owe so much to
Dr Ernest Kevan

We need to live our lives, as Ernest Kevan lived his life, in the presence of God and in anticipation of the coming of Christ. Then by God's grace we shall grow in strong biblical convictions... and in the gentle courtesy of Christ as we defend and proclaim our convictions.

Dr John R. W. Stott
(At Dr Kevan's memorial service in 1965)

'Of whom the world was not worthy' (Heb. 11:38) is also an apt description of Ernest Kevan, who as pastor, theologian and leader had a profound impact on post-War evangelicalism. I am therefore grateful for this extraordinarily detailed and careful biography that preserves these accomplishments for the church's memory.

Dr David F. Wells
Distinguished Research Professor
Gordon-Conwell Theological Seminary

As one who served for a number of years under Dr Kevan's leadership when Principal of London Bible College, I am delighted to commend this well-researched, well-written book. It is a full and balanced account of a remarkable man whose very full life was lived to the glory of God and whom God used to play a significant part in the post-World War II revival of evangelicalism. In my judgment it brings to life a very private man in a way that I would hardly have thought possible. Somewhat unusual and very useful are appendices 1 and 2 which summarise The Grace of Law, *Dr Kevan's magnum opus, and give extracts from a wide variety of his writings, respectively. Here is a worthy portrait of a worthy man.*

Dr Harold Rowdon
Lecturer in Church History at
London Bible College, 1954-1991

Contents

	List of Illustrations	ix
	Acknowledgements	xi
	Introduction	xv
1.	A Godly Family	1
2.	Called by Grace	15
3.	An Unexpected Turn of Events	23
4.	Church Hill Baptist Church, Walthamstow	33
5.	Enlarging the Work	43
6.	A Notable Anniversary	57
7.	'Zion', New Cross	73
8.	Doctrine and Development	91
9.	The Second World War	101
10.	Two Invitations	113
11.	Trinity Road Chapel	125
12.	The Beginning of London Bible College	135
13.	The College Principal	147
14.	'Uncle Ernie'	167

15. Prepared for Service 179
16. BD or not BD 187
17. An Interdenominational College 199
18. The Wider Ministry: 1949-1953 209
19. The Wider Ministry: 1954-1960 221
20. Glory 229
21. Strength and Gentleness 239
22. In Retrospect 249

APPENDICES

1. *The Grace of Law* 257
2. Selection of Writings 267
3. Documents 277

Select Bibliography 285
Index 289

Illustrations

Between pages 178 and 179

1. Frederick Kevan as a younger man.
2. Frederick and Kate Kevan in 1935.
3. Ernest Kevan in 1917.
4. Kevan aged 30.
5. Church Hill Baptist Chapel, Walthamstow.
6. Zion Chapel, New Cross.
7. Interior of Zion Chapel.
8. Mrs Kevan, at an unknown church occasion.
9. The beginning of the full-time College in January 1946.
10. The old London Bible College premises at 19 Marylebone Road.
11. London Bible College students with the Principal and his wife in 1948.
12. The new London Bible College premises completed in 1958.
13. The field conference of the Strict Baptist Mission in India, 1960.
14. The staff wheelbarrow race at the College sports day in 1958.
15. A victorious Principal takes first place.
16. Kevan during his time as Principal of London Bible College.

Acknowledgements

THREE BOOKS HAVE BEEN indispensable in writing this biography. *Ernest Kevan: Pastor and Principal*, by Gilbert Kirby (Eastbourne: Victory Press, 1968), was published three years after the death of Dr Kevan. In the same year, *London Bible College: The First 25 Years*, appeared. Published by Henry E. Walter Ltd, this was written by Dr Harold Rowdon, Lecturer in Church History at London Bible College from 1954 to 1991. I must also acknowledge the help received from Dr Rowdon in answering a number of questions as I prepared to deliver a paper on Dr Kevan at the Westminster Conference. Thirdly, there is Ian Randall's *Educating Evangelicalism: The Origins, Development and Impact of London Bible College*, published by Paternoster Press in 2000.

It is impossible to mention by name all those who have responded to my appeals for information and who have given me help, but many must be included. Phil Arthur, my pastor now, first put my name forward to give a paper on Dr Kevan and has continued to encourage. Iain Murray has been a great encouragement to me and I am very grateful for his advice. In a busy life he has looked and commented on earlier drafts; his experience and wisdom have been invaluable. I have been glad to renew contact with Tim Buckley and Dr Ralph Martin from the staff of London Bible College, and especially Donald Baker, for thirteen years Secretary of the College, who has supplied me with important details. I am grateful to Dr Steer, the Principal at the time of what is now called the London School of Theology, for allowing me to visit the School and look at material kept there; and in particular to Jenny Aston, his PA, for her help.

The Rev. Professor Anthony Thiselton, Dr Kevan's nephew, who was at London Bible College when I arrived there, allowed me to borrow his grandmother's diary and supplied me with photographs and provided other details. I am very grateful to him. Mrs Calista Lucy, the Keeper of the Archives at Dulwich College, gave information about Dr Kevan's time at the College. Dr Kenneth Dix, who has recently been called to glory, helped me greatly with extracts from *The Gospel Herald* and other magazines, and I am grateful to the Strict Baptist Historical Society Library which has all the old Minute Books from Church Hill Baptist Church, Walthamstow. Pastor Ray Pulman and Miss Muriel Squires of Zion, New Cross have helped me with information from that church and allowed me to examine the Church Books. Among Grace Baptists who have given me information I must include Clifford Pond, Douglas Dawson, John Field, Philip Grist and John Appleby. Among those from Trinity Road Chapel, or at least connected with that church in the past, are Reg Warner, Paul Ebling, Mrs Sheila Paterson, Mrs Mary Levell (*née* Walden), Mrs Kath Paterson (*née* Walden), and Margaret Wilson. Dennis Arnold was a great help in tracking down some of Dr Kevan's books second hand and Paul Cook answered a number of questions for me. Among College students, mainly my contemporaries, Brian Edwards has supplied me with various college magazines, prospectuses and lecture notes. Alan Gibson,

David Lucke, Mike Perrin have all supplied information and Andrew Anderson read most of the chapters in the first draft for me. My daughter, Elisabeth Aguilera, helped in revising the early chapters.

For all these and those whose names have not been included I am truly grateful. Without your help the book could scarcely have been written and would have been far poorer. My wife, Mary, who was also at the College, has read every page and commented and corrected where necessary. I owe her the greatest debt.

While greatly valuing the contribution of others I have also relied in some measure on my own memories of him. I have had to draw my own conclusions about events in his life and have drawn my own picture of his character. I do not claim an objectivity which would belong to someone who never knew Kevan. The final responsibility is mine.

Introduction

If you look up Dr Ernest F. Kevan on the internet you are likely to think that he is only known for writing a book entitled *The Grace of Law*. Certainly he did write this important book, but he was much more than an author. He was the first Principal of the London Bible College (now called the London School of Theology), but before that he had gained a reputation as the pastor of three churches in London: Church Hill Baptist Church, Walthamstow; Zion Baptist Church, New Cross; then Trinity Road Chapel, Tooting, during the time when he was waiting to see what would come of plans for London Bible College.

His life spans virtually the first sixty-five years of the twentieth century and for the last twenty years of that period he was at the centre of evangelical life in London, and in some respects in Britain as a whole. As the twentieth century recedes into history, church historians will increasingly look back over it in order to understand and assess the state of the Christian churches. They will want to consider the contribution of evangelicalism and the men and movements that were influential. I would like to hope that this book might make some small contribution towards that.

It is now over a century since Kevan was born and the changes that have taken place are greater than any that have taken place in any comparable period of time. I have tried to give some brief idea of the historical and cultural background; and also hope that quotations will give some flavour of the evangelicalism of the first half of the twentieth century. Kevan was born and bred a Londoner; he lived in London all his life, he understood its ethos and, I think, shared in many of its values. Someone brought up in the London of his day was not likely to be parochial, simply because it was the hub of empire and to a large degree the centre of world trade. He had also been tested by fire through two world wars.

It has been an advantage that my own father lived two or three miles from where Kevan was brought up and his early life parallels Kevan's in a number of respects; in particular they both had identical experiences in 1920 which suddenly changed the course of their lives. My father was a year younger than Kevan and I have all his diaries from 1921 and these have been a help in understanding the character and difficulties of those days. Our family also lived in London for three years during the Second World War when my father was pastor of a Baptist church.

I have tried to let Dr Kevan speak for himself. This is particularly so when it comes to events in his own life. He mentioned a number of these in his book of children's talks entitled, *Let's Talk*, and I have quoted from several of them because he has his own way of speaking and drawing lessons from his experience. I have also quoted fairly extensively from other books and articles for the same reason; and there is an appendix with extracts from some of his writings.

Some people have been unsure about the pronunciation of his name. He was once introduced by a church secretary who pronounced his name 'Key-van'. When Kevan gave his talk to the children he said, 'My name is Mr Kevan, you can always remember it because it rhymes with "heaven"'!

While it may be true that his name is not known by many contemporary Christians it would be a great loss for it to be forgotten altogether. He was known both as a preacher and a theologian, but first and most important of all he was a Christian man of great faith, wisdom and graciousness. He deserves to be remembered supremely because of his integrity and godliness and his commitment to the work to which God had called him, and in these things he is an example to all.

PAUL E. BROWN

Halton, nr. Lancaster
November 2011

1

A Godly Family

As the nineteenth century came to its close, the Victorian era was also slipping away, the Queen's life finally ending in January 1901. A new century, and with it a new era bringing terrible wars and many changes, was opening up. When on 5 September 1899 Frederick William Kevan married Kate Mason, it is unlikely that they were thinking of what the future might hold in political and national terms. They might well, however, have been hoping that the Lord would bless their union with children, and the advancement of the kingdom of Jesus Christ was never far from their minds. In God's good purpose, their only son would play a significant part in the service of Christ as the twentieth century proceeded; the influence of his ministry spreading out across the world.

At the time of their marriage Frederick Kevan was twenty-five and his bride was nineteen, though less than three months away from her twentieth birthday. They were married and began their life together in the borough of Wandsworth, London, just south of the river Thames. Their first child, Ethel, was born in the August of 1900, and she was followed on 11 January 1903, by Ernest Frederick. Another girl, Hilda, would be born two years later.

The census of 1901 reveals that Frederick, his wife and daughter were living in three rooms at 69 Sisters Avenue, Battersea. At that time Battersea was a separate borough adjacent to Wandsworth, but has been part of Wandsworth since 1965. 'Three rooms' probably means that the kitchen and bathroom were shared with the family with whom they lodged; Mr and Mrs Bralwright, who were in their seventies, and their unmarried daughter. Most bedrooms of the period had a large earthenware bowl and jug, so that hot water could be brought up from the kitchen for washing. It was not unusual in those days for families to lodge in this way. It is possible that this was where Frederick had lived before his marriage. Their circumstances were humble enough at the beginning of their life together.

Frederick was the youngest of four sons born to Samuel and Ann Kevan; his mother was forty-eight at the time of his birth, which makes it remarkable for those days. Samuel had been born in 1829 in Southwark, still south of the Thames, but several miles east of Wandsworth. At that time Southwark was located as being in Surrey; though the leafy connotations frequently associated with the word 'Surrey' today are certainly not applicable.

Samuel Kevan, Ernest Kevan's grandfather, was both a printer and a Strict Baptist minister. He did not enter the pastorate until he was thirty-six years old, and it may well be that in some of his churches he was able to turn to printing to supplement his income. There was a great deal of poverty in the nineteenth century and, although we cannot generalize, not a few Strict Baptist churches were made up primarily of members who were poor. His first church was in Colnbrook, near Slough, to which he was called in 1865. In replying to the invitation he had received he wrote: 'Dear Brothers and Sisters, pray for me, that the good Holy Spirit of God may compassionately help and fit me for so important a work.' He was described as: 'A kind man and a good preacher, and there was a close bond of Christian love between the pastor and his church which continued for many years after he left Colnbrook.'[1]

Samuel Kevan's second pastorate was in Waterside; now known as West Hill Baptist Church in Wandsworth. After that it seems he ministered in a second church in Wandsworth before he moved to Halstead, in Essex, and finally Ramsey in Huntingdonshire.

Although brought up in a godly family, Frederick Kevan did not come to know the Lord until after he had left home. He was converted under the ministry of Mr R. Thompson in Providence Chapel, Meyrick Road, Clapham Junction. This was the area just north of the railway station of that name; the railway dividing what was then the industrial and working class area of Battersea from the more prosperous locality leading to Clapham Common and Wandsworth Common to the south. Frederick was baptized in 1892, the year in which he reached the age of seventeen. He became extremely active in the church, in due course becoming a deacon, church secretary and, for some years, superintendent of the Sunday School with about three hundred and fifty to four hundred children.[2]

Battersea was originally a village and has a long past. In the sixteenth century Huguenot refugees from France began to set up industries near the confluence of the river Wandle (hence Wandsworth) and the Thames. These included mills, breweries and factories for dying, bleaching and calico printing. In the middle of the eighteenth century, wharves and more factories extended further and further eastwards along the Thames. Among these were a number of chemical works. Around the industrial buildings large numbers of houses were built for workers and the whole area continued growing right up into

[1]David J. Kerridge, *'He Leadeth Me Beside Still Waters', The Story of the Particular Baptists in Colnbrook from 1645* (published privately, 1997), pp. 33, 34.

[2]Details from *The Gospel Herald* (March 1936), p. 56.

the twentieth century. Somewhat further south, beyond the railway, larger houses were built for more prosperous citizens.

Sisters Avenue, where the Kevan family was living in 1901, was situated in this district, running roughly in a southerly direction towards Clapham Common. The householders near to number 69 included an art teacher, a bank accountant and an engineer. Some households included servants, number 73 having two. On the other hand next door the householder was a 'lodging housekeeper' and number 83 is also described as 'letting apartments'. This was an area for people rising in status. By the time Ernest was born the family had moved a couple of streets away to Elspeth Road.

Frederick Kevan's occupation in the 1901 and 1911 census is given as a Chemical Merchants Clerk, which indicates the administrative side of the business and the opportunity for promotion. He was a man of energy and ability and his advancement in business was accompanied by moving house. In 1911 they were living in Wroughton Road in Wandsworth Common, but three years later in Mayford Road; such frequent moves almost certainly indicating that they were renting, rather than buying. In that year, 1914, his wife wrote in her diary:

> The Lord of Hosts has marvellously appeared for us today in connection with my dear husband's business and was better to us than all our years. 'Bless the Lord, O my soul, and forget not all his benefits.'

It may be that this marked Frederick's promotion to general manager of Bowen's Chemical Works. Some time after 1917 they moved to a larger house – 17 Blenkarne Road – still in the same area.

Wandsworth Common is some distance from Battersea and Frederick travelled by hansom cab to his work, though this may have been when his health was beginning to deteriorate.

It was also quite some way from the Meyrick Road chapel and so the Kevans transferred their membership to a nearer chapel in Chatham Road and Frederick became a deacon there. It was this chapel that the young Ernest Kevan was to attend as he grew up.

C. H. Spurgeon, pastor of the large Metropolitan Tabernacle in the previous century, wrote in 1878 in his magazine *The Sword and the Trowel*: 'Chatham Road, Wandsworth Common. Here a chapel, accommodating 240, has been erected and paid for through the efforts of our two sons, C. and T. Spurgeon. This is purely a mission chapel, in the midst of a neighbourhood greatly needing the gospel, but far from eager to hear it. It is a light in a dark place.'[3] When the Kevan children were older and presumably able to travel the required distance easily, a move was made back to the church in Meyrick Road. It is uncertain when this took place, though it was after 1917.

Frederick Kevan not only prospered in business; he was also very active in Christian work. An appreciation of him in the *Gospel Herald* after his death in 1936 says that 'he was unusually well read in Strict Baptist history, and discovered much accurate information for Dr Whitley's *Baptists of London*.[4] Dr Whitley, who was Secretary of The Baptist Historical Society, was the leading Baptist historian of his day, so this indicates the quality of Frederick Kevan's knowledge and study.

He also served on the committee of the Metropolitan Association of Strict Baptist Churches and the committee of the South India Strict Baptist Missionary Society before its amalgamation with the Strict Baptist Mission. Both the

[3]Printed in the 'Annual Paper Descriptive of the Work Connected with the Pastors' College', as a supplement to *The Sword and the Trowel* (May 1878).
[4]*Gospel Herald* (March 1936), p. 56.

qualities and interests of Frederick Kevan were to be repeated in his son. The Strict Baptist Mission was later replaced by Grace Baptist Mission and the churches of the Metropolitan Association now come under the Association of Grace Baptist Churches South East.

Sunday School work was one of Frederick Kevan's greatest interests and he collaborated in the production of a new magazine called *Seed Thoughts* for Sunday School teachers, writing the preface for the first issue in 1914. Pastor E. Rose, his pastor at Chatham Road, was the first editor, but by 1923 this role had been taken by Frederick. 'He thought, planned, and wrote for it, possessing an able and ready pen, with a great gift for detail and organization.' He gave himself wholeheartedly to this work and a contribution from his pen appeared in the very month in which he died.[5]

Kate Kevan was a lady of strong character. She taught in Sunday School, but she was also in great demand as a speaker at Women's Meetings in many parts of London. On a lighter note Ernest said that she liked puzzles, especially jigsaw puzzles. What gives us a real insight into the family, however, is the fact that she kept a diary. This was not the usual sort of diary; it was actually entitled, *The Christian's Log Book*.[6] On the left hand pages are quotations for the day, the first always being a verse from the Bible. The right hand pages are simply dated January 1st etc. and are lined and blank for diary notes to be made. So it is not for any particular year. The first entry is in 1913, and her daughter, Hilda, added some entries after her mother's death. So it spans many years but is by no means a comprehensive account, as many pages are blank.

[5]*Gospel Herald* (March 1936), p. 56; also *Seed Thoughts* (March 1936), p. 41.

[6]The full title is: *The Christian's Log Book or Precious Pearls from Master Minds for Every Day Wear*, by Mary E. H. Peat (London: Jarrold & Sons Ltd., n.d.). The Preface is dated, Gisleham Rectory, 1904.

One phrase recurs throughout the diary: 'Praise the Lord', and this sets the tone for Mrs Kevan's life, even in times of difficulty. Occasionally she expresses some deep emotion; one example reads like this: 'Thank God for the beauty of Christ and the Bible, and may the Holy Spirit shew me so much more of Christ that I may be more like him.' She comments: 'Baxter's *Saints' Rest* is a book which, next to the Word of God, I have found most helpful', and she also recommends *Kept for the Master's Use* by Frances Ridley Havergal.

Her spiritual experience had its fluctuations of feeling. In 1919, on 30 November, her birthday, she recalls that this is also the date of her baptism and adds, ''Tis grace which kept me to this day and will not let me go!' Her baptism appears to have been some twenty years earlier but it is not possible to decipher the exact number. However, on 28 December 1913, she had written: 'My new life began on this Lord's Day, when I saw my Saviour by the eye of faith.' The following November, on her birthday, she wrote: 'My first anniversary of my natural birth that I have had full assurance of my birth into the family of God. Bless the Lord Oh my soul.'

If we let the second diary entry interpret the first, this would mean that she was given a great sense of assurance in 1913 such as she had not known before. Although she had been baptized much earlier she had nevertheless suffered from some uncertainty about her salvation. Such uncertainty is not altogether unusual in believers, and tended to be much more marked in Strict Baptist circles. In her case, she was brought out of this into 'full assurance' as a child of God.

Growing up

It is clear that Ernest was greatly blessed in his parents and their help and example must have made a deep impression on him. Family life in the Kevan home was strict, but it was also very happy. In his book of children's talks on the Bible entitled *Let's Talk*, Ernest Kevan several times mentions his early life, and these excerpts give an insight into his upbringing as well as illustrating the way he spoke to children. He says, for example:

> I had two sisters, one older and one younger than myself; so I must leave you to judge whether I was fortunate or unfortunate. We were very good friends and used to have a lot of fun up in the top room of the house, which we called the play-room. We were allowed to do just what we liked there – even to make as much noise as we liked. You should have seen us sometimes. We dressed up in all sorts of curious clothes, sometimes imagining we were wild Indians, and sometimes pretending we were kings and queens. Quite often, when we were very small, we played at 'mothers and fathers'. As I was the only boy, I had to be 'father', and my elder sister was 'mother'. I rather think this game was not very popular with our younger sister. Then at another time we played 'schools'. In this we all had a turn at being 'teacher', but I think we who were 'children' had the best of the fun.[7]

As other children have done who were brought up in Christian homes they used to play at 'church' on Sunday evenings before they were old enough to go to the services themselves. The pulpit was an armchair with the back turned towards the 'congregation' and the 'preacher' stood on the seat. Ernest claimed this position for himself as he was the only 'man' available. As there were not enough 'people' for a 'proper service' there was a lot of argument about who should do what.

Later the children would go with their parents to the Sunday services, and doubtless also to Sunday School. Every

[7]Ernest Kevan, *Let's Talk: Talks About the Bible* (London: Henry E. Walter, 1965), p. 93.

day family prayers were held, and on Sunday evenings after the evening service the family would gather round the piano to sing hymns. The children had tasks assigned to them in the home. Ernest did the washing up, Ethel, the older sister, did the drying and Hilda put things away. It was also Ernest's task to clean the shoes on a Saturday evening, so that they were ready for Sunday, when only a minimum of work was done. Theirs was a very orderly house and their parents had an unusual way of calling for their children; they used a bell. One ring of the bell meant that the elder daughter was required, two indicated that Ernest was being called, whereas three was the signal for Hilda, the youngest. As soon as the bell sounded, the children would stop their play, and count to see how many rings there would be and who was needed.

Although he was strict in the way he brought up his family, Mr Kevan was adored by his children. Ernest probably saw more of his father than did either of his sisters. Somewhat to their envy he would often have long sessions in his father's study.[8] Ernest clearly had a high regard for his father and would later write of the way he 'taught me so much theology'.[9] During these sessions with his father he would be introduced to books and as he grew older they would doubtless discuss theology and church history together.

We should not think that Ernest was different from any other boy. One of his earliest memories was when he had scarlet fever and was in hospital. He was getting better and a nurse took some of the children out for a walk in the

[8]Details in Gilbert Kirby, *Ernest Kevan: Pastor and Principal* (Eastbourne: Victory Press, 1968), p. 11.

[9]Ernest Kevan, *The Grace of Law*, (London: Carey Kingsgate Press, 1964). The dedication reads: 'This book is gratefully dedicated to MY WIFE without whose sacrifice the production of this book would not have been possible, and to the memory of MY FATHER who taught me so much theology'.

afternoon. However, he made himself dirty by playing with soot and as a result had to go without jam for his tea. Rather more serious was some of his behaviour at school. In one of his talks he asked: 'Do you ever have to write 'a hundred lines' at school? I am sorry to tell you that on more than one occasion when I was at school I had to write, "I must not talk in school", a hundred times.' He also added, 'I can well remember being "kept in", as you call it. In my school it was called "extra lesson" for two hours on the school half-holiday. Even now I can almost catch the sound of the friendly crack of the cricket bat as I used to hear it through the window of the "extra lesson" room…' He enjoyed cricket and swimming but his favourite sport was rugby, or 'rugger', as it was generally known then. He sometimes practised tackling on his sisters, which suggests it was not their favourite!

There was a lady called Mrs Back who used to look after them when they were small and their parents needed to be out in the evenings. Kevan recalls: 'I'm afraid that sometimes we had been very unkind to her and gave her a most worrying time. We were *very* naughty on some occasions.' In spite of that she would invariably say to them, as she put them to bed, 'Now! my dears, go to sleep quickly and I'll tell your Mother you've been very good.'[10] Kevan knew that he was a sinner and concern over the state of his soul was to come while he was still quite young.

School days

Kevan's first secondary school was Battersea Grammar School, but it was evident that he was an able student and his father was by this time in a financial position to pay for his son's education. So Ernest took an entrance

[10]Kevan, *Let's Talk*, pp. 59, 63, 66, 145.

examination and was accepted by Dulwich College, a well-known Public School about four miles away from his home. 'Public School', of course, actually means a school which is privately run. When he and his father went for an interview with the Master (as the Headmaster was known), his father, being rather concerned about his son attending Anglican worship, asked if he could be excused chapel attendance. The Master replied that this would be no problem; there was a special room for those who did not attend chapel where Jews, Muslims, Hindus and others went! Kevan senior was rather taken aback at this and changed his mind. Ernest would smile about it later.

He entered Dulwich College at the beginning of the summer term in 1917, when he was fourteen, going into the Senior School on the Science and Engineering side. After his first term he concentrated on engineering, though he also continued to take French. At Dulwich he was brought into contact with young men of academic and sporting ability, many of them from a different background to his own. He appreciated and enjoyed his time at Dulwich and flourished there, as his own description of his commencement reveals:

> When I was a boy my father took me from a smaller school where I was, and sent me to a fine large school. (It is the finest school in England. I am sure all the old boys, who wear the same 'old school tie' as I do, think the same!) It was all very exciting, and I can remember still the new 'togs' (that means clothes) I had. How proud I was to be wearing the new cap with the red-and-white badge and the blue stripes. In the school term in which I started, there were about forty other new boys. We were sorted out for our various 'houses', and had all kinds of mysteries explained to us, were told about the school tuck-shop, and a hundred and one other things. Then we were all filed off by a prefect

> to a room where there was a piano and one of the masters. The truth then came out. We would all have to sing, 'Doh, ray, me fah, soh…', and the singing master would listen to see if he could find any recruits for the school choir. My voice was at the cracked stage then, and so I was soon dismissed. Since I have become a man I have often wished I had gone into the choir; but when I was at school, and saw all the 'chumps' who belonged to the choir having to stay late for practices, it seemed much better fun to go out and play rugger. But there were days when the choir had its own back, because at the School Concerts and on Speech Day they used to do jolly well.[11]

In fact, before his voice broke he was a very good soprano, and his party piece was: 'O pilot, 'tis a fearful night'.

Kevan gained a reputation later on for his diligence and hard work, and these showed themselves early in life. It was not so much that he was intellectually brilliant, but he had a good mind and was able to apply himself wholeheartedly to his work. His exam results show that he was generally in the top half of his class and they also improved during his time at Dulwich as he settled in. At the end of the autumn term of 1919 he took an exam in the matriculation class. Matriculation was an examination that qualified a person for university at that time. Even if it was not his definite intention to go to university, once he had matriculated that would be an option for him after he had finished his school days. A good career in engineering seemed to be before him.

At home he had a great delight in making things and spent a good deal of time doing carpentry. He made a bridge for his model railway and stood on it to see if it was strong enough. He was also interested in chemistry, which is not surprising in view of his father's employment, and set up an improvised

[11]Kevan, *Let's Talk*, p. 41.

laboratory at home where he conducted experiments. However, 'he was not too popular when, shaking up some acid in a test tube, his thumb slipped and the contents of the test tube spilled down the front of his sister's new dress.'[12] When he was still quite young he put on a show of conjuring at Christmas time for the rest of the family, something that he would develop and use later for children's parties. He was also quite adept in the use of a catapult!

[12]Kirby, *Pastor and Principal*, p. 11.

2

Called by Grace

IN ORDER TO UNDERSTAND Kevan's upbringing it is necessary to know about the character of the churches that his family belonged to. The largest body of Baptist churches in Great Britain is the Baptist Union. This was formed in 1832 of Particular, or Calvinistic, Baptists, but a Calvinistic basis of faith was replaced simply by a declaration of adherence to 'the sentiments usually denominated evangelical'.[1] By the 1880s there was significant evidence of theological liberalism within that Union. The Strict Baptists consisted of groupings of Calvinistic Baptists that remained outside of the Union.

The Strict Baptists

The title 'Strict Baptist' is really shorthand for 'Strict and Particular Baptist', and the full name was often used on noticeboards. 'Particular' refers to particular redemption, Christ died for and saves those chosen by God; and this is a matter of faith. 'Strict' refers to restricted communion. 'Communion' originally meant 'church communion'; that is, membership of the church with all its privileges including, of course, attendance at the Lord's Supper. In practice, however, the word 'communion' was generally used simply to refer to the Lord's Supper. So 'particular' is a matter of faith, and 'strict'

[1]The Baptist Union was originally formed in 1813 but had ceased to function; it was reconstituted in 1832. See Robert Oliver, *History of the English Calvinistic Baptists, 1771-1892* (Edinburgh: Banner of Truth Trust, 2006), p. 261.

is a matter of order, and these words were used in the phrase 'the same faith and order'. It is a fact that sometimes people would grow up in such churches without knowing at all the intended meaning of 'strict and particular'. All Strict Baptist churches held to restricted communion but there were differences over 'transient communion', that is, whether visitors from a different group of Baptist churches could attend the Lord's Supper.

It would be possible to make a rough and ready division of Strict Baptist churches in the early twentieth century into three groupings, each sponsoring a different magazine. Those churches which took the *Gospel Standard* tended to hyper-Calvinism and restricted communion to members of churches which were on the Gospel Standard list. Churches that took the *Christian's Pathway* were probably what might be termed High Calvinist; they did not accept the Articles that the Gospel Standard churches had added to a basic Calvinistic confession.[2] They restricted communion to those 'of the same faith and order'; that is to those who had been baptized and were members of Calvinistic Baptist churches.

The third group originally took a magazine called the *Earthen Vessel* but this became subsumed under the *Gospel Herald*. This became the magazine of churches in the London area belonging to the Metropolitan Association of Strict Baptist Churches. This Association had been formed in 1871 with twenty-three churches. The Metropolitan Association churches were generally somewhat 'wider' – the term that was used – than the other two groups. They were Calvinistic in doctrine but in some cases communion might be open to all baptized believers, that is, they could include those from Baptist

[2]For the 'added articles', see Kenneth Dix, *Strict and Particular* (Didcot: The Baptist Historical Society for the Strict Baptist Historical Society, 2001), Appendix 3, esp. pp. 309-10.

churches that were neither Calvinistic nor Strict, though this was a matter which was hotly debated.

In 1939 there were five hundred and sixty Strict Baptist churches in England. Two hundred and fifty-six of these were Gospel Standard. Forty-eight churches belonged to the Metropolitan Association. This Association had close links both with the Norfolk and Suffolk Association, which had thirty-nine churches, and the Cambridgeshire and East Midlands Union, which had nineteen churches. Kevan was to say: 'From the early days of my childhood the Metropolitan Association became part of my thinking. It was my father's meat and drink. How he loved the Association no-one ever fully knew.'[3]

It is scarcely possible to be precise about the ethos of the churches in the Metropolitan Association as they were strongly Independent in their belief regarding church order. This meant that there was some variety of understanding and practice among the churches and little actual co-operation at church level. Thus organizations tended to be started and supported by individuals rather than churches. Churches that were 'going wide' might have young people's meetings, a choir, or 'Christian Endeavour'. Very popular and influential in that period, Christian Endeavour is a movement for encouraging service and prayer in the local church, especially among young people.

Because of their high view of baptism and communion the proportion of members to 'adherents' in the congregations of Strict Baptist churches could be relatively small. One result of this seems to have been that Sunday School teachers and other workers may not always have been members. Church anniversaries, when special preachers would be invited to minister, were very popular and were a principal means of fellowship between churches, but the numbers attending these

[3]Ernest Kevan, *Doctrine and Development*, p. 1.

gatherings and the interest they aroused were probably no real indication of the spiritual state of the churches themselves.

Years later, in 1938, Ernest Kevan was to say of the Metropolitan Association:

> I know that there are some fine examples of consecrated Christianity among our members, and we thank God for such noble souls. They are a tonic to all who have the privilege of working with them. But individually and collectively there is much to confess. The standard of our denominational spiritual life is nothing to be proud of; and closer inspection reveals many things which fill us with sorrow of heart. We are not without our worldly elements. The spirit of the age has forced its sinister way into our Strict Baptist churches quite as truly as in other communions. In some quarters denominational pride has reached such a degree that it exasperates us; but when we see it combined with worldliness and inconsistent living, it becomes nauseating. May God give us such grace that our conduct may conform to our creed! May God send us a mighty revival! May God send the mighty, rushing wind of the Holy Spirit, removing all the cobwebs of pride and prejudice, and sweetening all our ways![4]

Seeking and being found

When he was a boy Ernest Kevan was always greatly concerned in case, having been brought up in a Christian home, he would be accepted as a Christian without ever having come to a personal knowledge of Jesus Christ as Saviour and Lord. Often he would pray, 'O God, please make me a *real* Christian.'[5] Such an experience is by no means unusual for someone brought up in a Christian home, but it is probably

[4]Kevan, *Doctrine and Development*, pp. 4-5.
[5]Kirby, *Pastor and Principal*, p. 14.

even more likely for someone brought up in the Christian environment in which Kevan found himself. It is likely that he would have heard preaching which set out the marks of a Christian and the experiences through which a person would usually pass in coming to faith, and this could raise the question, 'Has this happened to me?' It is also likely that he would have heard of the possibility of people making an impulsive profession of faith, or a profession of faith which would later prove to be false by sin and departing from the Christian life.

About the time that he was ten years old he entered a period of spiritual concern. Doubtless there were times when he was more anxious, and occasions when he either forgot his concern or felt that perhaps he was a true Christian. During this period a number of verses of Scripture were a help to him, especially John 6:37, 'All that the Father giveth me shall come to me; and him that cometh to me I will in no wise cast out'; and there were other significant milestones on his pilgrimage. There was a preacher who told him that the sort of desires he had must be the result of the work of the Holy Spirit within him and this proved to be an encouragement to him. He was greatly helped, too, at the age of about eleven or twelve, by a sermon preached by Rev. H. Tydeman Chilvers, who became pastor of the Metropolitan Tabernacle in 1919 and ministered there until 1935.

There are some words from Kevan himself about this period in his life. An extract from his book *Going On*, later entitled *Now That I Am a Christian*, reads:

> When I was a boy seeking the assurance of salvation for my own heart, I remember speaking with an old lady who had been a Christian for many, many years. She was able to read my boyish heart like an open book. In reply to her questions I told her that my position was that if only I could 'feel' saved I would then be able to believe in the Saviour. To

> which she so wisely and promptly replied that I was putting the cart before the horse. The Scripture says that we have 'joy and peace in believing' (*Rom.* 15:13).[6]

Gilbert Kirby in his brief biography of Kevan believes that conversation meant a great deal to him; it taught him to look out of himself to Christ and not into himself to his feelings.

Kevan tells us more about his experience in his book *The Lord's Supper*. He begins by quoting these verses: 'Every one that loveth him that begat loveth him also that is begotten of him' and 'We know that we have passed from death unto life, because we love the brethren', and continues, referring to the second verse:

> When I was a boy and longing for the assurance of salvation, one of the passages of comfort that came to me was that verse. I did greatly love the Lord's people. I used to go to our Monday night prayer meeting. Only about ten or a dozen of us met in the little church where I was brought up, and some of the old people prayed long, long prayers! The seats got harder and harder; but in spite of the long prayers and the hardness of the seats, I knew I was where I belonged. I knew that here were my best friends and here was my Saviour and Lord, and one day the light of this just burst upon my longing heart. Although this was not the foundation of my faith, the basis of my salvation, it was nevertheless one of those auxiliary testimonies that the Lord gave to me in my own heart. Here was an evidence that I had passed from death unto life, because I loved the brethren.[7]

On Ernest's fourteenth birthday his mother wrote in her diary: 'God has been graciously pleased to spare our darling son to us to see his 14th birthday and Oh that his NEW

[6]Ernest Kevan, *Going On* (London: Marshall, Morgan & Scott, 1964), p. 17.
[7]Ernest Kevan, *The Lord's Supper* (London: Evangelical Press, 1966), p. 49.

BIRTH may be realized 'ere another year ended, for Christ's sake. Amen.' We ought not to think that the phrase 'God has been graciously pleased to spare' was merely conventional language. Infant and child mortality were not a thing of the past in those days, even though conditions had been improving. Underneath this fervent prayer are the words: '*This prayer has been answered*'. The answer had come only five days later: 'Our dear son has told us that he loves Jesus and wants to follow him in baptism. Praise ye the Lord for answered prayer.'

A sermon by Pastor W. Chisnall, then the secretary of the Strict Baptist Mission, seems to have been the final word that brought him to faith and assurance. He was baptized shortly after this on 25 February 1917 in the Chatham Road chapel, five weeks after his birthday on 11 January. A fortnight later he was received into the membership of the church, having given at a church members' meeting a testimony of the Lord's dealings with him. This chapel was completely destroyed during the Second World War, but the Sunday School building was repaired and made into the chapel. After the war Kevan was present at an induction service in the new chapel and at the tea table said a few words referring to the place where the old baptistry had been: 'As I walked up the path I passed a grave, and in that grave I was buried with my Lord in baptism.' By this he showed his appreciation of the significance of his baptism. Baptism for him was the *public* union of Jesus Christ and the believer, an event to be remembered through the years.

Some of those who knew him well have suggested that he was converted at the age of eleven, but his mother's words, and what he wrote himself, show that he did not come to an assured sense of salvation and acceptance by Christ until he was fourteen.[8] The way in which Kevan wrote of this early experience, and also spoke of it later, indicates that it had a great influence on him. It affected the way he came to understand regeneration and conversion, and influenced his pastoral care of young people and others struggling with assurance.

What is remarkable is that by the end of this year, 1917, both his sisters had also been brought to faith in Jesus Christ, were baptized and joined to the church. Eleven years later, on the anniversary of her wedding, his mother wrote:

> Truly God our heavenly Father has been with us all the way of our 29 years, and we are 'lost in wonder, love and praise!' And the most precious gift he has bestowed upon us has been the salvation of our 3 beloved children, for 'we have no greater joy than to know that our children walk in truth', i.e. Jesus who is the truth.

However, though a year of great joy for the Kevans, the year 1917 also had its dangers. This, of course, was during the Great War, the First World War. After several diary references to air raids on the city the family left for Bournemouth in October: 'We do not want to run from danger but to "know what the will of the Lord is" – and to *do it*.' They remained there for about three weeks and then returned with thankfulness to their home.

[8]For example: Timothy Buckley, who knew Kevan well, wrote this in an appreciation of him in *The Christian* (30 September 1965) after his death. J. Clement Connell also has the same in the memoir that he wrote for the Baptist Union *Memoir of Ministers and Missionaries*.

3

An Unexpected Turn of Events

IT WAS NOT LONG before the new life that Ernest Kevan had received began to manifest itself. A month after he joined the church his voice was heard for the first time in the prayer meeting. In the summer of that year, 1917, while the family was on holiday in Worthing he took part in a service on the beach; this may have been part of a beach mission for children or an open-air service, possibly on the Lord's Day. A considerable amount of open-air witness took place at that period; churches and individual Christians viewed it as an important means of evangelism.

As Kevan grew older he became involved with the Strict Baptist Open Air Mission[1] and spent a good deal of his spare time speaking in the open-air in and around London, usually on Saturdays. This Mission was founded in 1920 by a group of young men, Kevan being an early committee member. These young men would often cycle out to villages where there were local churches. After distributing tracts in an area on a Saturday afternoon they would finish with an evening rally. Kevan's conversion thus led to action in evangelism. On his fifteenth birthday he wrote in his mother's diary: 'God has saved and kept me', signing his name.

His life changed dramatically, however, when he was seventeen. On 20 August 1920, Kate Kevan wrote: 'Dear Father

[1]See 'The Strict Baptist Open Air Mission' at http://www.strictbaptisthistory.org.uk/articles.htm (accessed 8 February 2012).

ordered to give up business. (Behind a frowning providence He hides a smiling face.)' Frederick Kevan had seriously damaged his heart when lifting a window box and was never able to work again. The evidence indicates that Frederick's health had not been good for some time, though he was only forty-five in that year. In May 1918 he had been called for a medical examination to see if he was fit for military service but 'God opened the eyes of the examiners to see his weakness and he has final discharge. Praise the Lord!' In March the following year he was away from work for five weeks through illness.

With the breadwinner now a permanent invalid there were very serious financial implications for the family. It was out of the question for Ernest to continue at Dulwich College. Rather, it became imperative for him to get employment and bring in an income. He commenced work in the tea-tasting department of the Home and Colonial Stores in Mincing Lane, in the City of London[2], his mother noting that he brought home his first earnings on 30 August. Frederick's breakdown in health must actually have taken place several weeks before the doctor's verdict put an end to his working life as Ernest did not remain at Dulwich College in order to take his exams at the end of the summer term.

This sad and disappointing turn of events affected the family in many ways, though it is true that people of that generation were more used to serious setbacks than those of today. In the case of the Kevan family, faith saw them through and they were assured that God's ways were perfect. Ernest's parents had been intending to give him the best education they could, but they had to recognize that God purposed a different path for him than the one that they had anticipated.

Whatever plans Kevan may have made in his own mind were suddenly brought to an end and this unexpected change

[2]Kirby, *Pastor and Principal*, p. 13.

must have had a profound effect upon him. He would surely have asked himself what significance it had in the will of the Lord for him. He would not now be able go to university, if that had been his hope, and tea-tasting is not quite what would have been expected of someone whose academic interests lay in a different direction. Presumably he took the best job available as quickly as he could, putting his family's needs before his own aspirations. This was a very testing experience for a young believer which doubtless had spiritual benefits for him.

Although Kirby speaks of Ernest Kevan being born 'into what was in many respects a typically middle-class home,'[3] the evidence shows Frederick Kevan coming from a good home but not one that was particularly well off, prospering and climbing socially for some years, and then having to depend to an unknown extent on the earnings of his son. Years later a tribute to Ernest Kevan spoke of him rising 'from humble beginnings',[4] and that seems more accurate. Of course it was due to a gifted father that he spent three years at a public school, but life must have been very difficult for him and the family in the years immediately after 1920.

In the early decades of the twentieth century a family's way of life could change quickly and quite dramatically. What happened to the Kevans was not unusual. Social security and insurance were very limited compared with what we have today. Pensions were only introduced in 1908, with small weekly sums for those over seventy years of age and there was no significant change to this until the Pensions Act of 1946. After 1920 Frederick Kevan occasionally made a little money by typing, but that was all. His health

[3]Kirby, *Pastor and Principal*, p. 9.
[4]London Bible College, Annual Report of the Governors and Accounts of the College for the year ending 30 September 1965, p. 3.

continued to be very poor and he seems to have given himself as much as he could to his work on *Seed Thoughts*. As a later editor of these Sunday School lesson helps said:

> Words cannot describe the devoted zeal which Brother Kevan put into his editorial labours. Again, and again he had been laid low, and then sufficiently restored to pursue again his good works.[5]

On the last day of that traumatic year Kate Kevan wrote: 'Thank God for *all* the way He has led me through 1920, for mercies both spiritual and temporal. Ebenezer.'

The Londoner

Ernest Kevan was a Londoner born and bred, and his home would always be in London. When he began his working life London was a growing city, dynamic and vibrant. It was the largest city in the world with a population of 7,419,704 in 1914. New York came second with a population some one hundred thousand fewer – though this was an estimated figure and New Yorkers might have demurred. No other city exceeded three million and there were only thirteen other cities in the world which exceeded one million. London was not only the capital of Great Britain but also of the British Empire, the largest empire the world has ever seen. With the peace settlement of Versailles after the First World War the Empire had reached its greatest ever extent, covering a quarter of the world. *The Business Man's Diaries*, published in the 1920s, list Calcutta, Bombay, Sydney, Melbourne and Dublin as British cities![6]

Peter Ackroyd, in his 2001 book entitled *London: The Biography*, writes:

[5]*Seed Thoughts* (March 1936), p. 41.
[6]I have all my father's diaries from 1921 onwards.

> By the last decades of the nineteenth century London had become the city of empire; the public spaces, the railway termini, the hotels, the great docks, the new thoroughfares, the rebuilt markets, all were the visible expression of a city of unrivalled strength and immensity. It had become the centre of international finance and the engine of imperial power; it teemed with life and expectancy.

He also tells us: 'Almost one half of the world's merchant shipping was controlled, directly or indirectly, by the institutions of the City.'[7]

London grew to over eight and a half million people by 1939 when a fifth of the British population lived within its expanding boundaries. Six days a week, including Saturday mornings, two and a half million people were on the move to and from their work.[8] It is likely that most Londoners thought of their city as the capital of the world, and in certain respects it may have been. London traded with the whole world and though its population was more homogenous than it is today, people from all over the world constantly came and went. A dynamic London looked out to the whole world; among Christians, with their spiritual concern, that tended to mean a worldwide missionary vision.

The Business Man's Diary for 1921 includes several pages of information that are a great help in capturing a sense of the period and something of the religious scene. A 'Lamp-lighting Table' in the diary enabled the owner to work out the time the gas lamps would be lit in the major towns and cities of Britain, although this is the last year in which such a Table was included as electric light was gradually taking over. A 'Daily Wants Dictionary' offered various useful items of information. A cab fare in London was six pence for one

[7]Peter Ackroyd, *London: The Biography* (London: Vintage, 2001), pp. 717.
[8]Ackroyd, *London*, pp. 723, 733.

mile or twelve minutes, but a taxicab fare with a petrol-driven engine was twice as much. Basic income tax was six shillings in the pound after the first £150 for single persons and £250 for a married person; dog tax was seven shillings and sixpence each and a male servant's licence cost fifteen shillings.

These annual diaries contained 'improving thoughts' for each week – including this intriguing comment: 'Class hatred is going; inefficiency is going; small wages with resulting bad workmanship are going; individual selfishness is going; and we are beginning to get a glimmering of the fact that Christianity is not only sound ethics, but sound business'!

Other maxims read: 'There's nothing like a good day's work, for keeping fit and fine; it's tonic and it's antidote – it warms the heart like wine.' This reflects a dictum of Kevan's that he would be fond of repeating: 'Man was made for work; he is never happier than when he is doing it.' He would have believed in another similar one: 'To a normal man or woman, work stimulates and invigorates. It is a tonic; just as idleness is a disintegrating disease.' Yet another says: 'It pays to look neat. A crease in one's trousers often means an increase in one's business!' There is little doubt that Kevan was influenced by his environment and by the business ethic of the City of London. However, his view of life was more an expression of the Protestant work ethic, which he derived from the Bible, his Strict Baptist heritage and the example of his father.

Ackroyd's monumental book covers almost all aspects of London life over the centuries, but it says virtually nothing about the religious life of the city. The first few years of the twentieth century saw Nonconformity attain to its largest numbers and its greatest influence. About thirty-three percent of British people were members of a Christian church and in London about one in five of the population were regular worshippers. In the capital more people attended free churches than the Church of England and among these the Baptists had the largest number of worshippers with more than one hundred and sixty thousand. The Metropolitan Tabernacle still drew over two thousand and East London Tabernacle one thousand.[9] Such figures, of course, do not indicate the number of true Christians, and they hide the fact that theological liberalism was influencing large numbers of ministers through the theological colleges.

The rest of the century, however, was to be marked by almost continual decline. In the first half especially, great efforts were made to reach children and encourage young people in the hope that this would stem the tide. There may, in fact, have been an over-emphasis here which was detrimental to other forms of church work and witness. The churches in the Metropolitan Association were included among those that followed this pattern.

The 1921 *Diary*, already referred to, illustrates another facet of the religious life of the period. Though identical to the other *Business Man's Diaries* in nearly every respect this particular one was produced by The Alliance of Honour, which had twenty-four bishops among its vice-presidents, as well as many other ministers and well-known figures, including prominent evangelicals such as F. B. Meyer, W. H. Griffith Thomas and Dinsdale Young. At the beginning it states: 'The object of the Alliance is to impress upon men the necessity of leading pure lives; to unite them in a world-wide effort on behalf of purity and a chivalrous respect for woman-hood; and to promote the welfare of young men by the circulation of literature and the delivery of addresses, with a view to counteracting the manifold temptations to impurity in thought, word and deed.' There were many different Christian organizations

[9]Details in Ian M. Randall, *The English Baptists of the 20th Century* (Didcot: The Baptist Historical Society, 2005), pp. 2, 14-15.

for young men to join, some located particularly in the City. Whether Kevan would have joined any of these is debatable; he probably found enough to do through his local church and various Strict Baptist organizations.

Called into ministry

At fourteen Ernest Kevan was a fine-looking young man giving the appearance of being much older than he was. The First World War was still raging then and on one occasion as he was walking across Wandsworth Common two elderly ladies asked him sharply why he was not at the front.[10] In a few years he had filled out and become the well-built man at the top end of medium height that he would remain for the rest of his life. He had a full face with hair swept back and the set of his jaw indicates a man of conviction and decisiveness; a man of character, able to gain the confidence of others and lead them.

He also grew in grace and Christian service. One story from this period has its amusing side, but indicates his desire to give spiritual help. It seems to imply that he was teaching a Sunday School class at the time as well. When he was fifteen, he had been 'on the door' at his chapel greeting people as they arrived, and then took his seat in the back row. Next to him was a rather grubby child from his Sunday School class. The reading from the Bible was about one of the Lord's miracles of healing. The 'long prayer', as it was often called, seemed rather longer than usual. So the little boy whispered to Ernest: 'My little brother has got a bad ear; can Jesus make him better?' Immediately the reply came, 'Yes, let us ask him now.' So while the minister continued his prayer from the pulpit, a whispered prayer was offered in the back row for a little brother's bad ear![11]

On Ernest's nineteenth birthday in 1922 his mother's diary

[10]Kirby, *Pastor and Principal*, p. 12.
[11]Kirby, *Pastor and Principal*, pp. 14-15.

notes that he had been called by the Lord into his service. This probably means no more than that he felt called to preach, though it may indicate an openness and perhaps a desire for pastoral ministry if this should prove to be the Lord's will. Soon after, on a Wednesday evening in February, Kevan preached his first sermon back in the chapel in Chatham Road in which he had been brought up, for by this time the family had returned to Providence Chapel, Clapham Junction. His first Sunday service was on 16 April of the same year in the Strict Baptist Chapel in Bond Street, Brighton.

4

Church Hill Baptist Church, Walthamstow

On 17 September 1923, there was a church meeting at Church Hill Baptist Church, Walthamstow.[1] This church had been without a pastor for a year and a vote was taken to hear Ernest Kevan preach for a three month period. This was the method that was often used at that time when a man was being considered for the pastorate; though not if the man was already a pastor in another church. By this time Kevan was twenty years old and had been preaching for only a little over eighteen months. Presumably he had preached to the church on some occasions already and its members must have been impressed by his preaching, his spiritual maturity and evident godliness. An extended period of preaching would not only give the church ample opportunity to assess a man's abilities and character, it would also give a young man like Kevan time to consider prayerfully whether God was calling him to pastoral ministry.

Kevan had no formal training for the ministry, but it needs to be realised that this tended to be the norm amongst Strict Baptists of the period. In fact they were much more likely to be suspicious of 'lettered men', as those with college training were called. In any case it was only in this year, 1923, that a Strict Baptist Bible

[1]Details from Minutes of the Church Meetings. The Church books of Church Hill Baptist Church, together with a scrapbook containing excerpts from the *Walthamstow Guardian* and other material, are kept in the library of the Strict Baptist Historical Society.

Institute[2] came into being – not without some controversy – so prior to this there would have been nowhere for him to train, at least among the Strict Baptists, even if circumstances had allowed. However, no doubt his father was a great help to him in developing his knowledge of theology and providing books for him to read.

It is not clear when the three month period actually began, but it must have been before his next birthday in 1924. Father and mother together recorded the following: 'On January 11th 1924 we celebrated our dear son's 21st birthday, praising God for His grace in calling him to faith and to service in the Lord.' Ernest added his own comment: 'Paul thanked God and took courage – and so do I.'

As the three months drew to a close the church invited him to preach for a further three month period. At a church meeting on 22 May 1924, three candidates were accepted for baptism and they all spoke of having experienced blessing from Kevan's ministry. A month later, 23 June, the church voted, by twenty-three for and one against, to invite him to the pastorate. These are remarkably low figures for such an important decision. In 1926 the membership stood at eighty-nine and in the two years that Kevan had by then been pastor there had been a number of baptisms and new members, so it was probably around the seventy mark two years earlier. No explanation is available for the small number of members who took the decision. So Kevan preached for six months before his call, exactly the same time as his grandfather, Samuel, before his call into the ministry.

The church minute book still retains Kevan's handwritten letter of acceptance, sent to the secretary. His handwriting is almost exactly the same as it would be for the rest of his life. The letter is brief and to the point:

[2]Philip Grist, 'Strict Baptist Bible Institute', at http://www.strictbaptisthistory.org.uk/_private/sbbi.htm (accessed 8 February 2012).

17, Blenkarne Road
Wandsworth Common
S.W. 11
5-7-24

My dear brother,

Thank you very much for your very kind letter from the church with the invitation to the Pastorate. Will you please convey my hearty thanks to all the members?

Trusting in the power of our Master I am led to accept the Church invitation and I earnestly pray, & desire you all to pray, for God's richest blessing.

May I ask all the members to bear me up in prayer *especially* in view of the fact that I shall be continuing in business for the present?

May God make us all 'workers together with Him' for the glory of His name and the salvation of precious souls.

With hearty Christian love to all,
I remain,
Yours in Christ,
Ernest F. Kevan

Church Hill Baptist Church still continues under the same name and on the same site, though with a new building. It is London's oldest existing Baptist church.[3] The first Baptist church to be established in London comprised a group of General or Arminian Baptists led by Thomas Helwys which returned from exile in Holland in 1612. In the course of time a second General Baptist church was formed, but after some years both of these churches ceased to exist. The first Calvinistic or Particular Baptist church was established in 1633 and its first pastor was a man called John Spilsbury. Its founding members had seceded from an Independent church known as

[3]See Ernest Kevan, *London's Oldest Baptist Church* (London: The Kingsgate Press, 1933).

the Jacob-Lathrop-Jessey church, having become convinced of believers' baptism. The first building in which the church met was situated in Wapping and by 1670 there were around three hundred regularly attending its services.

In 1855 the church moved to Commercial Street, Whitechapel, to a large chapel capable of holding twelve hundred people. For fifty-one years its pastor was Charles Stovel, but the church struggled in the area where it was situated and decline set in towards the last years of his ministry. Until the end of the nineteenth century the church belonged to the Baptist Union, but in 1898 it joined the Metropolitan Association. In 1914 another move was made to Church Hill, Walthamstow, the building being called Commercial Street Memorial Strict Baptist Chapel, though it became more generally known as Church Hill Baptist Church. Soon afterwards another nearby Strict Baptist Church, known as Zion, closed down and some forty members joined the Church Hill church. The first pastor of the church after the move resigned three years later, and Ernest Wightman became pastor in 1919.

There were real difficulties in the church but their exact nature is not clear. In June 1921 the church was overdrawn at the bank and the treasurer had to appeal for funds to pay the pastor's salary. Some time later a number of deacons resigned but no reason is given for this in the church minutes. In 1922 the pastor resigned and a special church meeting was called on 3 April. At this meeting tributes were paid to Mr Wightman but reference was made to 'the persecution (of the pastor)... at the hands of his so-called friends'. In reply he spoke of friendships formed but also that 'the leaven of corruption had crept into the church'. This was obviously a sad state of affairs. In view of the difficulties the church had been through, one would have expected the members to be looking for a man of experience with a known track record to be the pastor to heal the wounds and restore unity in the church. It speaks volumes for Kevan that they recognized him as a man of outstanding gifts and grace, young though he was, and were willing to issue their call.

At the next meeting of the church, on 21 July 1924, a letter transferring him from the church worshipping at Meyrick Road was read, and Kevan, who was present, then took the chair, presumably commencing as pastor at this point. On 7 August an application was made from Church Hill Baptist Church to the Meyrick Road church for the transfer of F. W. Kevan, Mrs Kevan and Miss Ethel Kevan, 'now that they are living in Walthamstow'. By this time the second daughter, Hilda, was at work and the previous October had become engaged to be married, so it seems that she remained in the area where she had grown up.

No reason is given for the family's move but it enabled them to take a smaller house which would not have the same overheads, perhaps in a less expensive district. In spite of the way the church minute recorded their transfer from Meyrick Road, they did not actually move house until two days before their silver wedding anniversary in September. Frederick Kevan wrote the diary entry for that day: 'We can say without question that during the year we have experienced more of divine mercy than ever before. This Anniversary is spent at our new home in Walthamstow where God has given us the great joy of seeing our son a settled pastor of the church at Church Hill, Walthamstow. "Unto thee, O Lord, do we give thanks!"'

As will become apparent the Kevan family were still dependent, at least to some extent, on Ernest Kevan's earnings. Kevan was taking a great step of faith in answering this call, particularly in view of the financial condition of the church and also because there was no manse. However, he did not live with his parents, but in Rectory Road, not far from the church building.

The Recognition Services for Kevan as pastor took place on Tuesday 7 October, and began with a prayer meeting at 7 o'clock in the morning. The afternoon and evening services were reported by the *Walthamstow Guardian*. Usually referred to simply as the *Guardian*, reports of events in the church often found a way into its pages. Under the heading 'New Pastor', its coverage included:

> Afternoon: Pastor C. J. Welford of West Ham Tabernacle gave an address on 'A Gospel Church'. Mr Ernest F. Kevan gave an account of his conversion and call to the ministry. It was at the age of ten years that the Holy Spirit began a work in his heart, and when fourteen years old he was led to confess Christ as his Saviour by being baptized. Pastor John Hunt Lynn, of Bethnal Green, a minister bordering on eighty years of age then gave an address on 'The Joy of Service'.

> Evening: [Mr Kevan] laid emphasis on the Deity of Jesus Christ, the full inspiration and infallibility of the Bible, the free and sovereign grace of God in determining from all eternity to save a vast multitude who should be brought to believe in His Son for salvation, the redeeming work of Christ who had come, born of the Virgin Mary by the Holy Spirit, who lived a perfect life and died an atoning death as the substitute for all who trust in him, the effectual calling of the Holy Spirit whose invincible power brings every redeemed soul to Christ, and the necessity of proclaiming the Gospel everywhere. [Pastor Philip Reynolds preached on] 'Go, stand and speak... all the words of this life'... The choir, under the leadership of Frank Cudmore, with Miss Mary Morgan at the organ, gave a beautiful rendering of Sir John Goss's well-known anthem, 'O taste and see how gracious the Lord is'.[4]

[4] *Walthamstow Guardian*, 10 October 1924.

The *Gospel Herald* report in the November 1924 issue adds a few more details, though it omits all reference to the anthem. It repeats word for word Kevan's doctrinal statement which may have been made available at the service. It also says that in relating the circumstances leading to his acceptance of the pastorate Kevan was greatly confirmed by the promise: 'Call unto me, and I will answer thee, and show thee great and mighty things, which thou knowest not' (*Jer.* 33:3). It notes that he was the eighteenth pastor of the church. The evening service must have been a long one. Pastor Reynolds' sermon was only the charge to the Pastor; there was a charge to the church as well, plus two more short addresses.

An encouraging beginning

The months Kevan had spent preaching before becoming pastor seem to have laid a foundation for his ensuing ministry. A short column in the *Guardian* of the Anniversary meetings early in 1925, some four months after his recognition services, contains this paragraph:

> Mr J. Sharpe, the church secretary, gave a report which recorded the settlement during the year of the present pastor. There had been nine additions to the membership by baptism. Many activities were being pursued in Sunday School, Bible Classes, Young People's Society, Woman's Meeting, tract distribution, and in other ways. Foreign missionary work had also received keen interest and practical support.[5]

This was the 292nd anniversary and Kevan gave his children's address on the Sunday morning on the 292nd chapter, the 292nd verse and the 292nd word in the Bible! In the years to come he was to become well-known and loved for his

[5] *Guardian*, 13 February 1925 (or possibly 13 March 1925, the handwriting is indistinct).

children's addresses; what he made of these references can only be speculated. In addition to the Sunday services there were also meetings on the following Tuesday. In the evening three 'stirring addresses' were given by Strict Baptist pastors; and the *Guardian* does not fail to mention that the choir rendered two anthems, 'O taste and see' and 'I will lift up my eyes'. It seems an encouraging beginning.

In the summer of the same year Kevan attended the Keswick Convention in the Lake District in North-West England. This is only noteworthy because, in general, Strict Baptists were suspicious of the teaching which was given there and some churches would have warned their members against it. Whether this was his first visit is unknown, but thirty-three years later he quoted an illustration which he heard in one of the addresses,[6] so it made an impression upon him. Even in those days there was a variety of emphases at Keswick[7] and Kevan would probably have particularly appreciated the Bible Readings given by Dr Graham Scroggie that year.

Although there was consolidation and growth, the early years of his ministry must have proved difficult for Kevan, with considerably conflicting emotions. As his letter of acceptance indicates he continued to work at the Home and Colonial, but he got up at five in the morning and studied for two hours before he set out. Hard worker though he was, this was a pace which he would be unable to keep up.

In January 1926 he became engaged to Jane Basham, more generally known as Jennie, a member of the church. It is likely that he began to feel affection for her early on in his ministry as he got to know the congregation. Kirby comments: 'None of the church members had the least suspicion

[6] *The Keswick Week* (1958), p. 139.
[7] See Ian M. Randall, *Evangelical Experiences* (Milton Keynes: Paternoster Press, 1999), pp. 14ff.

of this budding romance, for, as always, the pastor had been the soul of discretion.' He also says that her parents were humble, but faithful Christians, and that her mother died within a few days of giving birth to her. Her father came from Suffolk; he remarried but his second wife died when Jennie was six. For some years after that an aunt, Miss Holly, brought up the family.[8]

Jennie was a very active worker in the church, teaching in the Sunday School, helping to run a missionary working party and leading a Young Women's Bible Class for a while. The church minutes for 1923/4 mention her name several times, mainly in connection with the Sunday School, but she was also chosen to visit women who had applied for baptism. It was the custom then – and still is in many Grace Baptist Churches – for those who ask to be baptized to be visited by two members who would bring a report and recommendation back to the church meeting. The fact that a young lady who was still in her twenties was chosen for this task shows the respect in which she was held by the church and its officers.

She was, however, not far off being seven and a half years older than Ernest, being born in September, 1895. She reached the age of nineteen at the beginning of the First World War and at its end there were nearly two million more women in Britain than men. Most of the men who had lost their lives were of her generation. It would not be surprising if she had begun to believe that marriage was unlikely to come her way. More than that, it was not so usual in those days for marriages to take place in which the woman was older than the man. Though he was twenty-four and she was thirty-one, age difference was obviously no bar in their case and they were married on 21 May 1927.

[8]Kirby, *Pastor and Principal*, p. 17.

Years later, after Kevan's death, Jennie was to say that when she was young she would hear Christian people talk of their experiences of the Lord and would long to be like them. It seems that she went through a similar experience to that of Ernest before she came to a living faith in Jesus Christ. She was not intellectual or academic but unassuming, centring her life on the home; she complemented Ernest and proved to be an enormous help to him. She was always rather amazed and thankful that he had chosen her to be his wife.

5

Enlarging the Work

NATURALLY, KEVAN'S PARENTS WERE delighted by his marriage in 1927, but it also created financial problems as they could not now expect him to provide for them. While Ernest and Jennie were still on their honeymoon, this entry was written in his mother's diary, its grammar highlighting the concern and confusion it reveals:

> Since our dear son has been married & we have needed more pupils for music and to let one room but it seems to get worse and worse – no-one comes for room and one by one my pupils are leaving through circumstances they cannot avoid. What it means we cannot tell. but we know that our heavenly Father is too wise to make a mistake and too good to be unkind. 'Hitherto has the Lord helped us.'

This illustrates the reduced circumstances of his parents. His mother clearly had been making some money by teaching music and they now also needed a lodger, a common way in those days of gaining a steady income. It is easy to understand their relief when, at the end of July that year, a lady took the room. 'One feels that she has been sent to us by God. We do thank him for hearing our prayers & sending a tenant for our room.'

Some time in the same year Kevan's overwork caught up with him. This must have been not long after his marriage. At a church meeting at the end of September he referred to a time of illness and reported that he had been told he must do all possible 'to avoid another serious nervous breakdown.' The term 'nervous breakdown' was common at the time and could include a number of symptoms that would be diagnosed differently today; nervous exhaustion may be the best way to describe what he had experienced.

As a result he told the church that he was resigning from business and would continue, if necessary, on his present salary. His mother wrote: 'He had to make a choice, he has chosen to work "the great work" of the Lord, thank God for the choice he has made.' It was agreed that a 'pastor's fund' should be set up, but the possibility of building a manse, which had been recently mooted, had to be set aside. The accounts for 1927 show that one hundred and thirty pounds, four shillings and nine-pence went to the pastor and supplies, the latter meaning the expenses of visiting preachers. Even allowing for the considerable difference in the value of money between then and today, that seems a very small amount. It is a measure of his dedication to the Lord and the church that he chose to continue in his calling.

Life in the church

In March, 1926 a monthly evening service for young people had been commenced. Kevan was following a trend which had already been set. Ian Randall, in his book, *The English Baptists of the 20th Century*, which focuses on churches in the Baptist Union, says: 'There were increasing concerns that Sunday Schools were not sufficiently connected with the worship life of the churches. Baptist and other churches began to set up 'Young Worshippers' Leagues'. He then goes on to speak of 'monthly services for "Worshipping Children"'.[1] Two years later the Young Worshippers' League at Church

[1]Randall, *English Baptists*, pp. 107ff, 144.

Hill had fifty-eight members with an average attendance of forty-six. No doubt the sermon would have been suitable for younger people and a young, enthusiastic pastor, gifted at speaking to children and young people, would encourage them to attend these monthly services. Kevan was clearly prepared to learn from what was happening outside of Strict Baptist circles and in certain respects to widen the practice of the church.

During the same year it was decided that 'all *baptized believers* would be welcome to communion with this church'. In the inter-war years several churches within the Metropolitan Association took the same step and this caused not a little controversy which continued for a number of years afterwards. The church became a member of the Free Churches Council in 1928, though this was long before the ecumenical movement as we know it; other Strict Baptist churches had also done the same. That year the *Guardian* reported that the Sunday School had one hundred and thirty-eight scholars, and the Women's Gospel Service one hundred and five members. There were nineteen tract distributors who also gave out 100 copies of the *Church Hill Baptist Monthly Messenger*. Open-air services were held constantly throughout the summer and monthly during the winter. 'All these activities were being carried on in a willing and harmonious manner by a band of earnest workers and all financial needs were being met.'[2]

At the heart of the services of worship would have been the preaching of the Word. In 1983 the oldest member of the church, Mrs Rhone, a member for sixty-eight years, wrote: 'I well remember the ministry of Pastor Kevan. He came to us in 1924 and was with us for 10 years. We all learned a great deal under his ministry; he was a very fine teacher and preacher.'[3]

[2]*Guardian*, 3 March 1928.
[3]*Grace* magazine (August 1983), p. 8.

The practice of regularly working through a portion of Scripture was unusual in those days and it is unlikely that he followed it. Later he recommended preaching on 'big texts'. His preaching was both expository and doctrinal with plenty of application. The doctrines of grace were at the heart of his ministry and he rejoiced to preach the gospel to the unconverted.

Not surprisingly the church had a busy weekly programme, as the printed notices reveal. There was a 10.30 a.m. prayer meeting on Sunday mornings, and as well as the usual services of worship, Sunday School and Bible Class, there was a Men's Meeting at 3 p.m. This was a meeting that Kevan himself would have been glad to lead as often as he could. In addition to a Children's Service on Thursday evenings there was a Girls' Missionary Working Party on Mondays and a Boys' Missionary Woodwork Party on Fridays. These were primarily craft evenings with the results being sold for missionary work but with the added advantage that they would have been very helpful for the children who came along. Walthamstow was basically a working class area and poor or otherwise disadvantaged children attended. To be introduced to creative and useful work which was of benefit to others would also be of benefit to them.

The weekly church programme was completed by a meeting for Prayer and Praise on Monday evenings, Christian Endeavour on Wednesday and a Devotional Service on Thursday. A 'Devotional Service' rather than a 'Bible Study' indicates that the aim was devotion to the Lord rather than simply understanding the Bible.

From time to time there were special meetings; for example, in September 1932, E. J. Poole-Connor gave a week of devotional meetings as well as preaching on the Sunday, speaking at the Men's Meeting and the Thursday afternoon Women's Gospel Service. In November, 1934, the *Guardian* published a group photograph of those attending this latter meeting, describing it as 'the largest gathering of its kind in the town'. There are some one hundred and fifty women in the picture, all wearing hats as custom dictated. This meeting must have attracted a number of ladies from outside the church as well as church members.

The printed notices of the church's programme of meetings had this footnote: 'The Pastor will be in the Vestry on Monday evenings from 7 to 8 p.m. Any friends who wish to see him on any matter are cordially invited to come at that time.' There is no doubt that Kevan was also assiduous in visitation, and always ready to listen to enquirers and those with problems. Years later he was to say that the minister who was doing his job properly would not have time for door-to-door visitation as he would always be in and out of the homes of members of the congregation, Sunday School scholars and those who needed help.

It was during this period that his mother, Kate Kevan, spoke to the women at Church Hill for the first time in 1926, commenting: 'May He make me a winner of souls for him.' The notes of one of her women's meeting addresses still survive. This is on the subject of 'the tongue', based on James 3. She opens with the Great Fire of London, one small fire in a baker's shop leading to a great conflagration. In speaking of the dangers of the tongue she mentions wives nagging their husbands and thus driving them out to the pub! But she ends with the positive use of the tongue. To help her in preparing Sunday School lessons and talks to women and to keep these relevant, she kept an exercise book in which she noted down, for example, 'Applications of Scripture to everyday life', 'Scripture references to nature' and 'Scripture references to common things'.

In 1928, Jennie Kevan was knocked down by a motor car

and badly hurt. No other details are known about this accident; she was always considered rather frail, but she recovered well and proved to have a greater resilience than had been anticipated. At some point Ernest and Jennie applied to go abroad as missionaries but they were turned down because of the state of her health. Almost certainly this must have been an application to go to India with the Strict Baptist Mission.[4] At what date the application was made, however, is uncertain, but the only time when this seems possible is in the first two years or so of their married life. Kevan was always concerned for mission, but it was in the purpose of God that his ministry should be in his own country.

At the end of January 1930, Ernest and Jennie moved and came to live with his parents. Kate wrote in her diary: 'May God reward & bless them for their thoughtfulness and grant us each to live to his praise.' Frederick's health was deteriorating and as Kate herself did not always enjoy good health she was finding it difficult to cope on her own. They were to live with their son and daughter in law until each passed into the presence of Christ. Ernest and Jennie must have recognised the needs of his parents as a reason for the Lord keeping them in the ministry at home.

Planting a new church

Though there was evidence of God's blessing upon the church at Church Hill the situation in the Metropolitan Association as a whole was very different. At the Annual Meeting of the Associated Churches in the same year, March 1928, a letter was adopted and directed to be sent to all the churches. It begins:

[4]Philip Grist, who was himself a missionary in India and has done some research into its history, is fairly sure that he has heard that this was the case.

> It is a matter of common knowledge that for some years past the Churches in the Association, with some exceptions, have made little or no increase in numbers. The membership of all the Associated Churches is only 18 more than it was 15 years ago. The number of baptisms in 1926 was 13 less than in 1912, and at least half the Associated Churches have had no baptisms during the past four years. This year (1927-28) the Churches are in a lower numerical condition than for many years past. What the SPIRITUAL condition of the Churches is can only be conjectured, but the lack of divine blessing is evident.

After calling for constant prayer about the situation the letter continues:

> Another fact also burdens our hearts, one which, we think, is closely connected with our present condition. For some years past no new districts have been opened up around London for the establishment of Strict Baptist Churches or Mission Stations. This is the primary object of the Association as expressed in paragraphs II. and VIII. of its Constitution and Rules, and it is felt that we ought to express our love of the Truth of God and our faith in His power by making every endeavour to extend the area of our ministry. With united prayer and effort this can be done, and we believe it would be the salvation of our Churches, so to speak, if we were whole-heartedly to engage in it for the glory of God.

This letter drew a reply from Kevan dated 9 June 1928, on behalf of the officers and church at Church Hill. It includes these words:

> This situation has already been the subject of our prayers and it is our purpose to continue to make this a matter for special prayer, beseeching the Lord to manifest His power

> and blessing upon the preached word, and that real spiritual revival may be realised. We at Church Hill are much concerned with the winning of souls and the reaching of those who do not attend a place of worship... The important and urgent need of the new housing areas round London has been a matter of concern to some of us even prior to the circular letter, and we hail with pleasure the fact that attention has been called to this. NORTH CHINGFORD, about 3 miles from Walthamstow, is one of these new housing areas. Hundreds of new houses have been erected and the need for the Gospel there is urgent. Consequent upon this the following unanimous resolution was passed at a recent Church Meeting: 'Resolved to endeavour by the help of God to establish a preaching station at North Chingford.' The ways and means are under serious and energetic consideration and good progress has been made.

Rather surprisingly it appears that the first concern of the Church Hill church was to raise money so that they could have a base from which to begin. Kevan described what was done in the April 1934 edition of the *Gospel Herald*:

> The Walthamstow friends decided to cast the matter upon the Lord, and if the Lord showed His favour by sending the necessary money they would take that as the token that they were to proceed. In many remarkable ways God did send all the money needed for the enterprise. Readers of this magazine and Strict Baptists all over London and up and down the country sent aid. The Metropolitan Association of Strict Baptist Churches warmly supported the project and rendered practical help. A prominent freehold site – the last remaining valuable corner in the centre of the town – was purchased, just before it was captured by a local publican. In September, 1929, the present property was opened free of debt, and the occasion was marked by memorable meetings.

It would be good to know how the church went about evangelizing the Chingford area, but all we have is a continuation of the article in the *Gospel Herald*:

> For the first two years the Church at Walthamstow deputed six of its members to attend regularly at Chingford to form a nucleus around which others could gather. Pastor Kevan preached one Sunday evening in every month, and willing servants of the Lord supplied the pulpit at other times. The early work was naturally not at all easy, but there was a gradual development of activity, and now, in addition to the Lord's Day Services, there are a flourishing Sunday School, a most encouraging Women's Meeting, a week-night service, and a children's meeting... The Holy Spirit has been pleased to bless the Gospel through His servants, and quite a number of friends from around the chapel found there the joyful sound which became a blessing to their souls. One and another applied for baptism; others, already baptised, joined the church by testimony.

The Held-Out-Hand

In 1932 the church commenced a venture which combined gospel and social work. The economic depression which began in 1929 was increasing in severity and as a result there were many men out of work with little money and nothing to do. The initial desire to bring the gospel to these men came from a man called Tommie Tye. Kevan, in an article in the *Gospel Herald*, wrote:

> He was a jewel indeed, and one which will adorn the Saviour's crown with rare beauty. 'Tommie Tye', as he loved to be called, was the man through whose vision and eagerness to win souls the meeting for unemployed men was commenced at Church Hill, Walthamstow.[5]

[5] *Gospel Herald* (October 1934).

Tye was converted from a gambling lifestyle in 1894, but he must have joined the church at this period, for Kevan wrote, 'His account of his conversion given at the Church Meeting stirred every heart.' A brief version of this account appeared in the *Gospel Herald* article in Tye's own words. He spoke of attending a Gospel meeting in which several verses of the Bible were obviously quoted:

> The Master was speaking to me. When I got home I had a bit of supper, changed myself and went to work. Between the hours of 2 o'clock and half past, while I was working, for I was working up above all the other men what they call the valve. I was among the dust and smoke and steam, attending to the valves, among all the noise banging of shovels and banging of retort's doors. In all of the noise I heard a voice saying 'Come to me, and I will give you rest,' and I went down on my knees in the dust and cried out, 'Lord, what must I do to be saved?' and the voice answered and said, 'Believe on the Lord Jesus and thou shalt be saved,' and I believed, and was saved, even unto this very day. Amen. Praise the Lord!

A committee of six men was formed, including Tye, to arrange the meetings for the unemployed, though neither Kevan nor his father were members of it. This committee decided on a Wednesday afternoon meeting which would be free of all formality, with refreshments to start with, and hearty singing, solos and short talks. They began in October 1932. Handbills were produced; Kevan, his father and the others, to quote Kirby, 'contacted men of all walks of life in the parks, recreation grounds, public libraries, as well as the streets' inviting them to the meeting.[6] There were fifteen men at the first meeting, but five weeks later the *Guardian* was reporting:

[6]Kirby, *Pastor and Principal*, p. 18.

> Some idea of the success achieved by the Church Hill Baptists in the short time that their organization has been in existence, may be gathered from the fact that the weekly attendance of the workless has reached an average of 150, and the committee anticipate further growth. They have adopted a system of keeping a record of those present in order that, where possible, they may make enquiries into the home circumstances of any absent person, for to quote the words of Pastor Kevan, in his talk with the men, 'If you are not here I shall be banging on your door knocker to find out if your wife is ill. I would not have a single member of our company away through home troubles and not know of it.'[7]

The meeting was given the name, 'The Held-out-Hand'; a hand held out both to welcome and to help. Men of all ages and all types attended, some 'of no fixed abode', who lived rough. Those who came regularly could become members and each received a badge which was worn in the lapel. When Kevan spoke of 'banging on the door knocker', it was members he had in mind, and his visit, as he indicates, was firstly to see if any help was needed. Kirby tells us that the men called Kevan 'The Sergeant-Major', and that they idolised him. He also explains why:

> [Kevan] and his helpers collected clothing, boots and food parcels for those in greatest need. The weekly meetings were packed almost to suffocation. Often one could see men, considerably advanced in years, completely broken down when something happened in the meeting that reminded them of their younger days... Mr Kevan also made a point of visiting them when they were sick. More than once, with jacket off, sleeves rolled up and an apron around his waist, he would get on his hands and knees and scrub a floor. At

[7] *Guardian*, 8 November 1932.

> other times he would change the bedding of a sick man. This sort of thing went on week after week.[8]

Kevan was very involved personally in this work, but it is worth noting that when he wrote of it he gave all the credit to Tye. In 1934 there were some one hundred and twenty men who were receiving some sort of practical help. In his next church Kevan would start up another 'H-o-H', and some other churches, including the church at Hainault Road, Leyton, followed suit. There was a combination here of practical help and support at a time of great social need, a gathering adapted to the persons who would be attending, and a presentation of the gospel. It is remarkable that Kevan was able to get on so well with these men; they must have sensed the genuineness of his concern and responded to the warmth of his manner. At only twenty-nine years of age they recognized in him a sense of authority and leadership combined with a real interest in their welfare, both material and spiritual. Doubtless what had happened to his father, and the effect that had had upon his own life, gave him a sympathetic bond with the men, and others in need that he would meet with in pastoral work. God had been preparing him through his own hardships.

At that time the death penalty was in force and remained so until 1965. In later years Kevan was to recall with great seriousness that on one occasion he was called to minister to a man in the condemned cell before he went to his execution. This must almost certainly be the same person who is referred to in his book *Let's Talk*:

> I have been at the great Law Courts of England and I have listened to the wise and learned judges as they have sat there in their impressive wigs and gowns. I was once present on a very solemn occasion when the judge put on the black cap

[8]Kirby, *Pastor and Principal*, pp. 18, 19.

> and sentenced a man to death. This was a terrible moment, but it was the proper working of the law against a man who had done such a wicked thing.[9]

The likelihood is that it was through the H-o-H that he came into contact with this man, either directly or perhaps through a relative or friend. In speaking with a condemned man on the edge of eternity, Kevan would certainly have seized the opportunity to urge repentance and faith in Christ.

[9]Kevan, *Let's Talk*, p. 66.

6

A Notable Anniversary

THE YEAR 1933 SAW the 300th anniversary of the church, which had been formed on 12 September 1633. Kevan decided to make a real occasion of this and the celebrations lasted over four days, Saturday 9 to Tuesday 12 September. There were twelve meetings, three teas (price 6d) and one luncheon (price 1s 6d), all of which must have been particularly exhausting for the church officers, members and the ladies who did the catering. Eleven different speakers gave addresses, apart from Kevan himself and those who took part in a Conference on the Tuesday.

The proceedings began on the Saturday with a Prayer Service for half an hour. After this Dr Whitley spoke on 'Baptist Beginnings, A.D. 1593-1687'. In the evening it was Kevan's turn: 'The Story of Three Hundred Years'. Kirby records: 'Ernest Kevan himself delivered a masterly address in which he spoke in glowing terms of those Puritan forbears who had originally come together to form the church. He argued strongly that Calvinistic doctrines were not incompatible with evangelistic enterprise, and concluded with these significant words:

> The times in which we live call upon us for our witness. Let it ring true to modern needs so that men of today may see that we care for them. Times have changed, customs and modes of thought have changed, but the deep spiritual longings of men and the grace of God remain the same. We

> do not need a new Gospel, but we must surely seek to present that old Gospel in words and pictures suitable to the present time. Obsolete phrases and methods are just as out of place as an Elizabethan costume would be in this congregation tonight. Let us seek to present the timeless Gospel in a way finely adapted to the ever-changing moods of men and women. Our message is the same as our fathers', but our mood of presenting that message, and our methods of evangelistic effort, must be those of the twentieth century.[1]

On the Sunday afternoon there was a demonstration by the Sunday School and Christian Endeavour entitled 'Three Centuries of Baptist Witness'. Over the months beforehand the various departments of the church saved pennies for a special Tercentenary Fund and at the end of the demonstration eight thousand pennies were handed over to the Treasurer – though who counted them and how he transported them to the bank are not revealed!

The Monday was called 'Free Church Day' and a note on the original brochure said: 'By the celebrations of this day it is intended to stress the importance of the Free Church principle, freedom of conscience, and religious liberty, and to associate with those whose ancestors shared in the same struggles as our forefathers.' Following a devotional service at which Rev. H. Tydeman Chilvers – by then pastor of the Metropolitan Tabernacle – preached, the evening meeting had speakers representing the Congregationalists, The London Baptist Association and the Presbyterians. Their subjects were respectively, 'What is a Free Church?', 'Why Baptists took their stand' and 'The long conflict for religious liberty.' Such a meeting was surely very unusual for a Strict Baptist Church; though the subjects were, and remain, of great importance. Kevan took advantage of the opportunity this anniversary gave to make

[1]Kirby, *Pastor and Principal*, pp. 17, 18.

his own members and many other believers, both local and from other Strict Baptist churches, aware first of all of the history of the early Baptists in this country, and then the truths and principles which they believed and for which many of them suffered imprisonment and loss.

The Walthamstow church itself had been formed originally by seventeen believers, seven of whom were in prison for a two year period at the time. These had been convicted as Nonconformists who had met to worship God according to conscience outside of the Church of England and they took the further step of becoming Baptists. Kevan wanted Baptists to know their heritage, to value it and live up to the high standards of dedication shown by those at the beginning.

The Tuesday was called 'Foundation Day' and was the busiest day of all. There were three services and a Luncheon Conference. At 12 noon there was a tercentenary sermon preached by Pastor R. Robinson, well-known in Metropolitan Association circles at that time. At 3.45 the service was called 'Thankful Commemoration', with two sermons, again by Strict Baptist pastors, on 'Christ – the Head of the Church' and 'Christ – the Theme of the Church'.

The 'Tercentenary Gathering' began at 6.45 p.m. with J. B. Collin in the chair; he was the man behind the Strict Baptist Bible Institute and the six students all came for the day's proceedings. There was a Statement of History by Kevan and three sermons: 'The Meaning of the Past', 'The Call of the Present' and 'The Hope of the Future', the last one preached by Pastor George Bird, a close friend. In addition to the meetings there was an Exhibition in the School Hall which was open during the intervals between meetings: 'Ancient Minute Books, Oil Paintings, Pictures, Manuscripts, Publications of former Pastors, Documents, Trust Deeds, and other objects of historical interest will be on view. Short Explanatory Talks will be given.'

The middle of the day had not brought any break in the proceedings as there was a Luncheon Conference which had as its subject 'The Church and Modern Social Problems'. Perhaps not surprisingly the *Guardian*,[2] which gave about eighty-four column inches (7 feet or 2.13 metres!) to the Tercentenary Celebrations, devoted by far the largest part of its report to this Conference, its subsidiary headline being 'The Duty of the Church in Social Reform'. Kevan introduced the subject by saying that the church could not live on its past, and they must not spend their time in happy contemplation as they looked back, but learn and understand what they were to do in the times in which they were living.

The opening speaker was the Bishop of Barking, Dr J. T. Inskip, a noted Evangelical, who reminded those present that the Church had just celebrated the centenary of the abolition of slavery throughout the British dominions. 'That had been brought about by the work of a few great Christian men, dating they might say, right back to the great evangelical revival affecting the great churches and the Church of England.'

The Walthamstow church had played its own part in the abolition of slavery as Kevan records in his book, *London's Oldest Baptist Church*: 'The Church remained very loyal to its long interest in the wider and more public affairs on which Christianity should let its voice be heard. It was at the request of the Church, in 1792, that Abraham Booth preached the famous sermon against the Slave Trade, and the Church, on that occasion, gave a collection on behalf of the Society for the Abolition of the Slave Trade. In 1830 the Church agreed to petition both Houses of Parliament against Negro Slavery. The Church very evidently had some strong thinkers on this

[2] *Guardian*, 15 September 1933.

question.'[3] Later Charles Stovel, when he was pastor, joined with William Knibb in fighting for the emancipation of slaves.

A number of Aldermen and Ministers took part in the Conference. It did not reach specific conclusions; rather it aired the subject and reminded everyone of the increasing social needs of London as depression gripped the country. There is one footnote that is worth adding. During the course of the proceedings the chairman referred to a minister who wore his clerical collar 'to let the people know his identity'. At some stage Kevan was to adopt a clerical collar, unlike almost all his Strict Baptist colleagues. It may have been that he too wanted people to recognise him as a minister, hoping that this would open up opportunities for conversation and spiritual advice.

Mrs Rhone, whose memories of Ernest Kevan were mentioned in the previous chapter, had this to say about the anniversary: 'The most outstanding event of Pastor Kevan's ministry was the celebration of the Tercentenary in 1933'. She said that these 'celebrations attracted many new people into the church', but she has to add: 'sadly many were to leave the following year when Pastor Kevan left us to go to New Cross.'[4]

'London's Oldest Baptist Church'

In preparation for this anniversary Kevan spent three years researching the history of the church, and the resulting book, with the above title, was published by The Kingsgate Press in time for the celebrations. It is extremely detailed, very thorough, and fascinating for those interested in Christian history. However, it is rather dated in places and although well-written, at times one senses Kevan's comparative youthfulness. The Introduction is by 'The Rev. W. T. Whitley, M.A.,

[3]Kevan, *London's Oldest Baptist Church*, p. 110.
[4]*Grace* magazine (August 1983), p. 8.

LL.D., F.R.Hist.Soc., Honorary Secretary of the Baptist Historical Society', to quote his title as given. In writing of British Free Churches he says: 'Of these Free Churches, the Baptists now at Walthamstow are the earliest important example... But even London has no longer any evangelical free church remaining earlier than the Baptists who met in 1633.'[5] It is striking to notice this use of the phrase 'evangelical free church'.

Kevan adds this note at the beginning:

> The author desires to express his gratitude to all who have assisted him in the production of this record. Especially he would gratefully acknowledge his indebtedness to the Rev. W. T. Whitley... for invaluable counsel and information, also for kindly reading through the manuscript; to the Rev. E. A. Payne, B.A., B.D., B.Litt., for making available his grandfather's manuscripts regarding Charles Stovel, and for many useful facts; and to his father, Mr. Frederick W. Kevan, for his practical help in many ways.[6]

Kevan obviously knew a number of local ministers from other denominations, but his research had also brought him in touch with two men of considerable scholarship. It would be interesting to know whether such contacts had any bearing on his decision to study for a Bachelor of Divinity degree which he must have started by this time. The reference to Rev. Ernest Payne's grandfather is to William Payne, who had been a deacon of the church, but was sent with another deacon to help in founding a new church in Clapton, the church in which his grandson would grow up. William Payne appears to have gathered a number of manuscripts from the past history of the church together and left some records of his own.

[5]Kevan, *London's Oldest Baptist Church*, p. 5.
[6]Kevan, *London's Oldest Baptist Church*, p. 7.

In his book Kevan sets out the history of each century and then a chapter follows with outstanding characters from that period. Some of the events and people that he records seem to cast light on his own views and outlook. He was obviously very moved by the sufferings of the early Baptists who founded the church:

> What courage is here! There is an old motto which surely moved and sustained these brave hearts – 'Rather Deathe than false of faythe.' Men and women in prison because of their desire to worship God according to their consciences, illegal even as Independents, in the eyes of the law with no right to exist, are here, during the very term of their imprisonment, daring to take a further step by repudiating the State Church in its practice of Infant Baptism! Imprisoned in the foulest of dungeons, they fear not to form their purpose of adherence to the Scripture, in defiance of cruel intolerance, and to place themselves one step farther away from conformity to the wishes of their most bitter persecutors![7]

Nor is he slow to draw the conclusion:

> These are the pioneers of Baptist privileges. Shall the sacrifice and suffering by which they won those privileges be despised? The freedom for which they fought, the principles they held, and the faith that possessed them are the precious heritage of Britishers to-day.[8]

Kevan's concern for a practical Christianity and, in particular, for those in special need is very evident. Over the centuries the church had been involved in many efforts to alleviate poverty, to petition Parliament, and not only to teach children the gospel but also how to read and write. Only twenty years

[7]Kevan, *London's Oldest Baptist Church*, p. 23.
[8]Kevan, *London's Oldest Baptist Church*, pp. 21-2.

after the church was founded we find that Samuel Richardson, who was a colleague of John Spilsbury the first pastor, wrote a book entitled *The Cause of the Poor Pleaded.*

Spilsbury and Richardson had also been involved in preparing, and both signed, the 1644 and 1646 Baptist Confessions of Faith, drawn up by seven London Particular Baptist churches. Kevan gives several quotations from the 1646 Confession drawing attention to its Calvinism and also what it says about the church. But there is one quotation, given without comment, which is on quite a different subject:

> The preaching of the gospel to the conversion of sinners, is absolutely free; no way requiring, as absolutely necessary, any qualifications, preparations, or terrors of the law, or preceding ministry of the law, but only and alone the naked soul, a sinner and ungodly, to receive Christ crucified, dead and buried, and risen again; who is made a prince and a saviour for such sinners as through the gospel shall be brought to believe on him.[9]

This article must have been framed against the tendency of some Presbyterians in the Puritan era to favour what was called 'Preparationism'; that is that there must be a 'law-work', a convicting, humbling work of the Spirit before anyone should be encouraged to believe in Christ for salvation. The early Baptists, who saw many conversions in this period, seem to have thought that at times this was taken too far, leaving people looking to themselves rather than looking away to Christ in faith. The fact that Kevan included it shows the emphasis he put on preaching the gospel freely to the lost, but may well also have been a reminder to some of his Strict Baptist contemporaries that they had departed rather a long way themselves from the practice of their forefathers.

[9]Kevan, *London's Oldest Baptist Church*, p. 31.

The book records that on 7 July 1700, the church minutes said: 'It was then agreed that our young Brethren should have the Liberty of the Little Roome to meete in on a Lord's Day in the morning from seven o'Clock to nine.'[10] We would like to know more about this meeting – was it perhaps for prayer? – but there is no more information. Kevan includes a number of incidents of church discipline, some of which achieved the result of restoring those who had offended. He comments:

> It will be good to tarry at this juncture to notice the important place given to church discipline in these days. Church membership was not a state into which one might float and out of which one could float with equal indifference. It was not a privilege to which were attached no obligations and vows. One of the weaknesses, surely, of the Church to-day is the hopelessly slack view that is taken of the responsibilities and obligations of church membership.[11]

'Hopelessly slack view'! He was probably justified in this stricture. Further on we read this:

> A pleasing fact is observed in 1831. Miss Mary Herriot, a teacher in the Sunday School, having been baptised ten years before, was sent out as a missionary to India. The Church may thus claim, in the person of Miss Herriot, to have been among the leaders in showing the place of women in modern foreign missionary work.[12]

Two of Kevan's predecessors started out with very little education: Charles Stovel, who was to write forty-eight books, and Abraham Booth, who wrote *The Reign of Grace* and became the leading Baptist theologian of his day. Kevan was surely inspired by their example to strive to follow in

[10]Kevan, *London's Oldest Baptist Church*, p. 49.
[11]Kevan, *London's Oldest Baptist Church*, p. 78.
[12]Kevan, *London's Oldest Baptist Church*, p. 110.

their footsteps. He wrote of Booth:

> The call to preach to a cultured London people in contrast to ministering to a country congregation made him almost insatiable in his thirst for information. He devoted himself to most serious studies. He put himself under stern discipline in the acquisition of Greek and Hebrew and Theology. His scholarship, learning and wide reading are apparent to all who read his works, yet he never allowed his studies to interfere with his pastoral duties. Although he aimed at thorough learning he was averse to all titles. An American University feared to offer him the degree of Doctor of Divinity, lest he should decline it.[13]

Kevan was deeply impressed with the character of those in whose shoes he was following. He quotes Dr Gill's account of Samuel Wilson's handling of church meetings:

> You will not easily forget his conduct at your Church Meetings, where he presided becoming his character and office... What lenity to offenders, what compassion to backsliders, what reluctance to pass the awful sentence on the incorrigible and with what tears in prayer he would weep over such unhappy professors![14]

And there is a further note about Abraham Booth:

> One of the members of his Church waited on him, and mentioned to him what he supposed were the defects of his preaching. 'You do not touch upon such and such articles, of which I am very fond; and I really find that I cannot profit by your ministry as I wish.' The good man, instead of yielding to resentment, or going into angry disputation, only paused awhile, and then meekly said, 'Ah, brother! so far am I from

[13]Kevan, *London's Oldest Baptist Church*, p. 120.
[14]Kevan, *London's Oldest Baptist Church*, p. 114.

> being astonished at your not profiting under my ministry, that I often feel amazed at God's making me useful to anybody at all.'[15]

Kevan also noted that Abraham Booth and others desired to set up an academy for the training of ministers. This did not materialise in Booth's day, but not long after his death the Stepney Academy was formed, which was to become Regents Park College.[16] Kevan was not only impressed by ministers. He mentions a number of deacons, the last of whom, Ezra Cudmore, he had known, as he died of a good old age in 1931. Here is part of what he had to say about him: 'They were exceedingly difficult days in which Mr. Cudmore was called to serve, but he fulfilled his task with such integrity and perseverance as places the Church under a perpetual obligation to him.'[17]

Members of the church were not simply concerned for Baptist causes, dear to their hearts though these were. Another deacon, William Fox, who was instrumental in setting up the first Sunday School in connection with the church, had a wider vision than that. '[T]he idea of a *plan of Universal Education* originated with Mr. Fox, and the honour of the project of uniting Episcopalian Christians with all sects of Protestant Dissenters to carry the design into effect belongs also to him.'[18] At this early period there is no doubting Kevan's commitment to the Strict Baptists, but he seems to have seen them as a denomination within a wider Baptist identity, which in its turn was part of the worldwide Church of Jesus Christ. Speaking of the long line of ministers and laymen who belonged to the church he says: '...all have rendered service to

[15] Kevan, *London's Oldest Baptist Church*, p. 128.
[16] Kevan, *London's Oldest Baptist Church*, p. 121ff.
[17] Kevan, *London's Oldest Baptist Church*, p. 185.
[18] Kevan, *London's Oldest Baptist Church*, p. 141.

the denomination and the whole Christian Church which it is impossible fully to estimate.'[19]

This recognition of what he called 'the whole Christian Church' is seen in the way he invited ministers from other denominations to take part in the anniversary celebrations. It is clear that from early on, while he greatly appreciated his own 'denomination', he was not as narrow in his sympathies as would have been the case with some other Strict Baptists. It may be that attending the Keswick Convention also helped to give him a wider vision. Moreover, his attitude to the Baptist Union might have been influenced by the fact that the church he pastored had been in the Union less than forty years previously.

The new church at Chingford

By March 1934, things had progressed so favourably with the church planting work at Chingford that the Church Hill church meeting was able to pass the following resolution:

> Recalling with gratitude the blessing God has given, both at the foundation and during the continuance of the work at our branch chapel, KINGS' ROAD, CHINGFORD, and feeling that the time is now appropriate for the formation there of a separate Church, WE, the Church worshipping at Commercial Street Memorial Baptist Chapel, Church Hill, Walthamstow, at a Church Meeting held 5th March 1934 hereby GRANT HONOURABLE DISMISSAL to our Brethren and Sisters... for the purpose of forming themselves into a separate and distinct Strict Baptist Church at Chingford. This dismissal to take effect as from 23rd April 1934. IN SO DOING, we wish them the enriching blessing of the FATHER, SON, and HOLY SPIRIT, in Whose Name and fear this step is taken.

[19]Kevan, *London's Oldest Baptist Church*, p. 187.

Seventeen members were thus dismissed to form the new church. On Tuesday 24 April, an afternoon and evening meeting were held, and at the latter the new church was formed and I. L. Jones recognised as the pastor, having recently completed his studies at the Strict Baptist Bible Institute. There were six speakers at the evening service, but it was a very special occasion, and there was doubtless a great spirit of thankfulness and praise to Almighty God.

Not everything, however, had been plain sailing. An appeal for help in the planting of the new church had also been placed in the *Christian's Pathway* magazine. This apparently led to some critical letters being sent to the editor and an article appeared in the January 1929 issue of the magazine:

> We wrote to the Pastor at Walthamstow [Mr Kevan], and after telling him that we had not been in the neighbourhood of Walthamstow for 30 years or more, we said, 'It is said that your Church is not Strict Baptist, and the assumption is that the *Church, if there is one formed*, will be an Open Communion Church, and that it is not right that such an appeal should appear in a Strict and Particular Baptist Magazine, which professes to stand for the old paths... It is also thought that the Appeal is being issued by those who will not preach the glorious truths of sovereign electing grace.' And then we asked him the following questions:
>
> 1. Is it true that you invite all baptized believers to sit down at the Lord's Table, irrespective of the character of the Church of which they stand as members?
>
> 2. Is it true that you do not preach the doctrines of Sovereign electing love? or in other words do you preach Freewill and Duty-faith?
>
> 3. Therefore is it true to say that you are not Strict and Particular Baptists?

Kevan's answer is then given:

> Let me say unhesitatingly and unreservedly that we stand for all the old truths for which the *Christian's Pathway* stands. When the work at North Chingford is sufficiently matured, a Church will, God willing, be formed. Since that Church will be on the same pattern as the Church here at Walthamstow, let me describe ourselves.

Here he gives the articles of faith of the church, which consisted of fourteen points. He then goes on:

> It is not true to say that we are not Strict and Particular Baptists. We are such. I, as minister, and we, as a Church, believe and preach the doctrines of sovereign electing love, and we do not believe in Free-will and Duty-faith. We stand firmly for the doctrines of the Eternal Sonship, Eternal and Personal Election, Particular Redemption, saving faith not a legal duty, but the gracious gift of God, Effectual Calling and the Final Perseverance of the Saints. We are not an Open Communion Church. We admit none but baptized believers. We have not added the further restriction that only those of Strict Baptist Churches may sit down, but we understand the point of view of those who do feel the necessity for that additional restriction, and we appreciate the motive. We do, however, exercise very careful discretion regarding those who as baptized believers seek to sit down with us.

In order to attend the Lord's Supper at Church Hill it was necessary to have a communion token. This might only have been a card, or something similar, to identify that a person could attend, and it was when visitors asked for this that 'careful discretion' would be applied.

The magazine article, presumably written by the editor, concluded by wishing that the Table was confined to Strict and Particular Baptists, but rather half-heartedly endorsed the opening of a place of worship which would declare 'all the blessed truths, for which we, as a denomination stand' rather than leave the field open for the General Baptists 'and all other "isms"'. It is a pity that the desire to plant a new church should arouse such questions, but this incident accurately reflects the attitudes that were then to be found amongst Strict Baptists. The answer enables us to understand Kevan's beliefs at that time and see that some alteration took place in the years to come. By the time the new church was established it was known that he would soon be leaving Church Hill, so its formation stands as a fitting culmination to his first pastorate.

The church at Church Hill prospered under the ministry of Ernest Kevan. The *Guardian*, summing up his ministry at the time when he left and commenting on the fact that he was only twenty-one when he began, said, 'He won instant popularity and the attendance at the church became three times as great.'[20] That may be a worldly way of expressing things but by the grace of God a work for God's glory was undoubtedly accomplished. In his resignation letter to the church secretary Kevan himself said this: 'As I look back over the 10 years of my pastorate here I am filled with wonder at the goodness of God which has preserved me and the grace that has used me. For the souls won to Christ and for all the work established let praise be given to God.' Our problem is that we can only look at the externals of his ministry and the work of the church. But looking from the outside everything seems to point to the fact that a deep and spiritual work was done; conversions took place, a new church was planted, the church itself was built up; God was surely glorified.

[20]*Guardian*, 27 April 1934.

7

'Zion', New Cross

AFTER TEN EVENTFUL YEARS at Church Hill, Kevan was called to the pastorate of Zion, New Cross, south of the river Thames in what was then the borough of Deptford. This was the largest church in the Metropolitan Association at the time. The pastor of Zion, Leonard Hills, died in 1933; his death appears to have been quite sudden and unexpected. The church had a membership of two hundred and forty-two and occupied, as it still does, a fine building which can seat many more than that. They set about looking for a replacement and it is not surprising that the young pastor of Church Hill caught their attention. In November of the same year his name was brought before the church as the next on a list which the deacons had drawn up. At the end of January 1934, the church voted by eighty-eight to six to issue a call to the pastorate, to which Kevan replied affirmatively. He also wrote a letter of resignation to the Church Hill secretary:

February 1st, 1934

My dear brother Sharpe,

It is with very mixed feelings that I am writing to you today to ask you to convey to the church my resignation of the Pastorate. The reason for this is that I am led to accept what has come to me as a very clear call to the Pastorate of the Church at New Cross. It is only in my consciousness of God's guidance in this very important step that I am able

> to bring myself to terminate the very sacred and happy fellowship I have enjoyed with my dear friends at Church Hill.

Throughout Kevan's life it is possible to see his assurance that God guided him in every new step which he took. There can be no doubt that he considered carefully all that moving to a new pastorate would mean for him and his wife, and also took into account the condition of the church that he would be leaving. But over and above prudential and providential reasons his language indicates that he felt personally and consciously guided by the Lord. In this he fitted into a pattern which was almost universal among evangelical believers in his day, but it is an emphasis which does not find so much favour in our times. His letter continues:

> The years have been made sacred by many memories of the loyalty and love of the church. The bonds of love forged between us will last into eternity, and my regard for the church I love so well shall suffer no diminishing. I can review the past ten years with deep joy and thankfulness to God for all that they have meant. They have been years of proving the faithfulness of His promise to guide and keep. They have been years in which many testings have come, but His grace had brought both Pastor and people through to the victory.
>
> Lest any friends should think in their hearts that it is an easy thing for the Pastor to leave his church, I want to say now what a very great wrench this step will mean to both Mrs Kevan and myself. We shall not be leaving you without sympathy and love that yearns for your richest blessing as a church. The Head of the church is still yours, even though He removes one of His servants. I commend you to God and to His protecting grace. My heartfelt prayer is that without undue delay the Lord in His wisdom and goodness may send you another Pastor, and that through

> such a God-sent man the work of God may grow and the church go on from victory to victory. 'The Lord of Hosts is with us; the God of Jacob is our refuge.'
>
> Undoubtedly I shall have many opportunities of saying personally what I say now, but I would like you to convey my love to all the members and to assure them individually of my prayers.

The welcome meetings at Zion took place on 5 June 1934. Unfortunately the report in the *Gospel Herald* noted: 'Considerations of space forbid a detailed description'. 'Friends from Walthamstow flocked over in great numbers to show their love for Pastor Kevan' is followed by the telling comment: 'the majority of them being Brothers of the H.O.H. (Held Out Hand), a Men's Meeting founded by Pastor Kevan.' There were three addresses in the afternoon meeting, one of which was given by George Bird, and between three and four hundred friends partook of tea. The evening meeting was chaired by J. B. Collin and some seven to eight hundred people were present. 'Stirring messages of exhortation and encouragement were delivered by Pastors W. S. Baker, R. Robinson, D. E. Westcott and E. F. Kevan.'[1]

Family matters

A manse was purchased for the Kevans at 95 Breakspears Road, Brockley, a mile or so from the church. This was a reasonably large house and it would also be used for young peoples' activities as well as the Kevan family which, of course, initially included Mr and Mrs Kevan senior. Kevan and his wife had now been married for seven years and she was nearing her thirty-ninth birthday; no children had been born and they must have begun to wonder whether they would

[1] *Gospel Herald* (August 1934).

have any of their own. This was undoubtedly a grievous disappointment to them both. They loved children and felt it very deeply that they never had a family. When Kevan comes to Genesis 4:1: 'I have gotten a man' in the commentary on Genesis which he wrote for the *New Bible Commentary*, he says: 'The birth of the first human baby must have been a wonderful experience, especially in the light of all the events connected with the sin of Adam and Eve.'[2] I have not found any other writer on Genesis who expresses anything like that.

In later years Jennie Kevan was present at a seminar for engaged couples; when the subject turned to children the student next to her was embarrassed to find her sitting there with tears in her eyes. The sorrow of Rachel and Hannah in the Bible can be reflected today and we generally know little of the inner experience of other people. Jennie gave herself unstintingly to support her husband in his work. The *Kentish Mercury* of 24 December 1943 said:

> No record would be complete without a reference to the whole-hearted co-operation of his wife, Mrs Kevan, who has loyally supported her husband in all his numerous activities and who has proved a gifted leader of all sections of Women's work in the Church.

Norman Trussler, who knew them in the New Cross days, commented:

> Dr Kevan was blessed in his marriage. In many ways Mrs Kevan made it possible for him to become what he was. Her love, loyalty, sacrifice and practical service were always in the background, but he depended on her more than most people knew. One day I called at their home in New Cross and found him busy preparing a Correspondence course for

[2] *The New Bible Commentary* (London: Inter-Varsity Fellowship, 1963), p. 81.

> the Strict Baptists, but it was Mrs Kevan who had the job of typing his work.'[3]

Another of her responsibilities was to keep his filing system in order; this became legendary and she called it 'his toy'. It was once described as 'almost as big as the man himself'.[4]

For the Kevans the lack of any children of their own was to some extent compensated for by their ministry to children; his love being particularly channelled into children's talks and enterprises for young people. Kirby says:

> Probably one of the greatest joys of Ernest Kevan's pastorate at New Cross was his work in the beginners' department of the Sunday school where he attracted as many as ninety youngsters between the ages of five and seven. He simply loved these children and was never happier than when he was with them.[5]

Years later when he had left the pastoral ministry he often used to say that what he missed most was his regular contact with boys and girls.

The Sunday School minutes and the centenary brochure of the Sunday School produced in 1949 indicate that when he arrived at Zion there was no Sunday School Superintendent and Kevan took this on for three years. This position was Superintendent of the Senior or Main School. It was some years later that the Primary Department needed rebuilding. In the time of the previous pastor, Leonard Hills, the Sunday School, in all its departments, had over five hundred children on its books.

One correspondent who attended the church in those days says this about Kevan:

[3]Norman Trussler in a review of Kirby's book in the *College Review*.
[4]William Porch in the memorial edition of the *College Review* (Autumn Term 1965), p. 9.
[5]Kirby, *Pastor and Principal*, p. 22.

> As a child I remember one thing about him; he was a conjurer. He used to entertain the children during Sunday School parties. I remember on one occasion that he stressed that there was no magic, just sleight of hand, and to prove it he showed how one of the tricks was done.

Kevan also introduced 'Campaigners' into the church, an evangelical uniformed movement for young people, even devising a younger group of Campaigners which was called 'Bairns' and had its own band.

There is a photograph of Kevan in his early days at New Cross. He still has quite a lot of hair, though it is clearly receding. His eyes are bright and penetrating and he has a smile which is in contrast to the more sober photographs of later years. He looks full of energy and enthusiasm, just the person to be full of ideas, ready to innovate and to motivate others and lead them in service. He was, of course, only thirty-one when he moved to Zion.

Beyond the local church

Kevan's interest in children's work and young people's work was not restricted to his own church. He was instrumental, with others, in forming the Strict Baptist National Sunday School Association. The Metropolitan Association, the Suffolk and Norfolk Association and the Cambridgeshire and East Midlands Union each had their own Sunday School work. However, the hymn book, Scripture Examination, *Seed Thoughts* and lessons lists were all produced by the Metropolitan Sunday School Committee. The purpose of the National Association was not to limit what each local group did independently, but to bring representatives of each Association together so that all were involved in what had previously been done by London alone. Together with Pastors Oliver Clark and Percy Crees, Kevan also helped compile a young people's hymnbook containing some six hundred hymns.[6] This was far from being a modern songbook, but it did try to help younger people by using simpler hymns while introducing them to the richness of British hymnody.

Kevan was also instrumental in the introduction of the 'Fellowship of Youth' (F.O.Y.), aimed at those in their late teens and early twenties, taking the chair at the inaugural meeting in 1934. At the beginning of the third annual rally, in 1937, he conducted the singing of hymns and choruses while the various groups from different churches were gathering. The programme seems to have been particularly crowded. One young lady received a prize for her essay on 'The Responsibilities of Youth in the Church' and Paul Brand, who became well-known for his work treating lepers in India, gave an address. The final speaker was Kevan who is reported to have given 'a most suitable and suggestive message... in spite of limitations of time'. 'He stressed especially the importance of our reading. When our thinking faculty is yielded to God, and we read that which is pleasing to Him, our baser thoughts will be crowded out.'[7] Kevan was realistic about the temptations that young people faced. Some years later he remarked that those who read detective stories gain by using their enquiring detective minds when reading the Bible. Perhaps, though, he would not have said that of today's detective stories.

Kevan was always careful to show appreciation. When speaking at one F.O.Y. meeting he referred to their secretary, a seventeen year old girl, commenting on her unusual efficiency. She had told him all he needed to know as a visiting speaker concerning the kind of people to whom he would be speaking, in addition to details of timing, venue and meeting

[6]Kirby, *Pastor and Principal*, p. 21.
[7]*Gospel Herald* (March 1937), p. 54.

agenda. It was by thoughtfulness like this that he was able to win his way into the hearts of people.

The same *Gospel Herald* that reported the F.O.Y. rally in 1937 also included this note under 'Holidays 1937':

> There really can be no question in the minds of the young people that visited Broadstairs and Swanage last year as to what they will do this year. They are quite certain that there cannot be a holiday to equal an F.O.Y. holiday. 'Hill Crest' school has again been taken from July 31 to August 28. Standing in its own extensive grounds, it offers scope for those who play tennis, podex, cricket and similar outdoor games. Everyone is free to make his or her own plans for spending each day. Bathing is pleasant and safe.

The host and hostess for the first fortnight that year were Mr and Mrs Kevan. Miss Betty Hughes was to write: 'When I look back on my holiday in Swanage, I can honestly say it was the happiest holiday I have ever spent.' She mentions some of the activities:

> ...hikes, tennis and table tennis tournaments, motor-coach and boat trips, concerts and pow-wows [!], the latter being times of prayer, praise, informal discussion and testimony', and adds: 'there was a wonderful spirit of *fellowship*... When you are with young people that love Jesus Christ as their Saviour and acknowledge him in everything, this is bound to make a holiday successful.

She had this to say about the Kevans: 'We owe a special debt to our Host and Hostess, who did everything in their power to make us happy. Particularly were we impressed by the love they showed us all, and by the way in which they glorified Jesus Christ in all they did.' Kevan himself said:

> There were some first-timers, who had feared to come lest

> it would be 'stiff and starchy' – those fears were removed in the first two hours. There were others who were just longing for a jolly holiday, yet one in which spiritual things were uppermost. These longings were satisfied; for the prayer times morning and evening, the quiet 'Heart-to-heart' talks in the pow-wows twice a week, the private conversations on the best things, all on the background of fun and friendship that filled the days, provided for that very desire.[8]

Faithful to the end

In 1936, Frederick Kevan passed to his eternal reward aged sixty-one. The appreciation in the *Gospel Herald* by Pastor R. Robinson, who knew him well and took the funeral service, said:

> Our brother had for many years been a sufferer, and only a bright, brave spirit enabled him to accomplish what he did. During his last illness he was confined to his bed for a month, and the Home-call came on Saturday, February 1st. At 11 am he said, 'God bless you all, and gather you into His eternal salvation through the merits of the blood and righteousness of the Lord Jesus Christ,' while half an hour afterwards, he spoke his last *connected* sentence, 'All the great things of the Gospel, I ever believed in, I still (a long pause for breath, about a minute)... believe in.' After this he grew weaker and at 5.15 he breathed his last. He had received his crown (2 *Tim.* 4:7,8).[9]

The words quoted above remained with his son and were very precious to him throughout his life.

His wife wrote in her diary that day: 'My precious darling husband entered into the rest and peace of the homeland at 5.30 p.m. "The Lord gave, the Lord hath taken away, blessed

[8] *Gospel Herald* (October 1937), pp. 211-12.
[9] *Gospel Herald* (March 1936), p. 56.

be the name of the Lord."' Frederick Kevan's contributions to *Seed Thoughts*, though often written in great weakness, were very thorough and Christ-centred and must have stretched both teachers and children. The obituary in the March *Seed Thoughts* has this conclusion:

> He did much when he was able to come face to face with scholars and teachers; but many will agree with the thought that has been expressed that Brother Kevan was mightier through *Seed Thoughts* than even in his physically active days.[10]

Bill Brown remembers

Bill Brown was brought up as a child to attend Zion. Later he became a Strict Baptist pastor himself. In 2008 he wrote down some memories of the days when Kevan was pastor. Only a few months later, Bill was called home so what follows here is probably one of the last things he ever wrote:

> At that time [that is, when Kevan became pastor] I was a boy of eleven or twelve years of age, but as my memory serves me, it was usually possible to find a seat most Sunday mornings, but unless you arrived by about 6.15 in the evening, the only seats available would be in the back of the gallery where the seats were rather small because that is where the Sunday School Primary used to meet on Sunday afternoons. That was the situation in the 1930s and it remained like that during the whole of Pastor Kevan's ministry until the war broke out in September, 1939. I became a Christian at the age of fourteen in 1935 and was baptized by Pastor Kevan on the 29th December of that year... A small group of us used to go to the Manse regularly to be taught the elements of Christian doctrine. When the first indication of war came in about 1938, Pastor Kevan was one of the main members

[10] *Seed Thoughts* (March 1936), p. 41.

of the Peace Pledge Union which was formed in order to persuade young men to become conscientious objectors and very many of the young men of Zion did so.

The Sunday School in the 1930s was very large indeed. There was a Sunday morning school at 10 a.m. when there were about 40 children present. In the afternoon, the Primary School met in the chapel and occupied the back of the gallery in small seats. There was a Junior School in the lower schoolroom and a Senior School in the upper schoolroom. There were two Bible Classes in the 2 vestries and another school in the Mission School in Baildon Street, less than half a mile from Zion. In all, the Sunday School was full to capacity and there was usually a waiting list of those wanting to join. For some years Pastor Kevan was the superintendent of the Senior School. [If there was a waiting list this means that numbers must have continued at about five hundred, as they had been during the time of the previous pastor.]

Pastor Kevan was a regular visitor and was careful to call upon anyone who was absent from Sunday worship times. I was too young to be involved in the Held Out Hand (H.O.H.) but knew that he encouraged men, usually unemployed, to meet in the chapel, I think on Thursday afternoons. I have to confess that sometimes I found it quite difficult to understand some of Pastor Kevan's sermons, but I am quite sure it was my ignorance and not Pastor Kevan's education which was the cause. Pastor Kevan had been a scholar at Dulwich College and sometimes he took some of the young men there on Saturday afternoons to see the college team play rugby. At that time there was a Zion Baptist Football team, and because there were not enough members of the church to make a team of eleven, there were some non-Christians who joined that club. However, the time came when the non-Christians became the majority and they joined a local Sunday Morning Football League.

> Pastor Kevan broke off relations with the team and tried to prevent them using the name of Zion.
>
> Pastor Kevan used to write a weekly column in the local newspaper, the *Kentish Mercury*, and in this he followed what Pastor Leonard Hills had done before him. I also remember that on Friday evenings we used to meet in the attic room of the manse to play table tennis and other games. Pastor Kevan then had a 'middlelogue' rather than an epilogue so as not to allow people to leave earlier in order to evade a time of worship.

The opening mention here of large congregations is confirmed by the church minutes. In June 1935, there is a note about 'seating difficulties caused by larger congregations' and in September of the same year: 'Friends were asked to cooperate with the stewards now that the congregations were so much larger.' The same minutes also note 'that Pastor's Bible Study Class took place in the Manse on Saturday evenings at 7.45 p.m.'

It is probable that now there are not so many evangelical Christians who are pacifists, but this was not the case between the two World Wars when there was widespread revulsion at the hideous slaughter of the First World War. The Peace Pledge Union was formed in 1936 and it is not particularly surprising to find Kevan taking a very clear line and encouraging young men not to join the Forces. After 1918 and on into the fifties and beyond, this was very much a live issue. Once National Service ceased it seems that the issue dropped into the background, with the 'Just War' theory and a biblical case for the defence of the realm making something of a comeback at the same time. It is an issue that deserves careful thought rather than mere acceptance of either position.

The account given of the Sunday School accords with what is known from elsewhere. The school began in 1849, some seven years after the beginning of the church and gradually rose to a prominent place in the life of the church. In 1949 its centenary was celebrated with a twelve page booklet outlining its history and including statistics and photographs. The centenary booklet of the church looks rather small by comparison, but as this was produced in 1942 allowance has to be made for the problems caused by wartime.

Sunday Schools were in their heyday in the inter-war period and there was a great emphasis on winning children and young people – 'the church of the future'. In September 1933 the church took part in the Deptford Churches 'Win the Children' Campaign. However, there is no evidence that in Kevan's day the Sunday School took precedence over other aspects of church life; the picture rather seems to have been one of spiritual blessing in all the ministries of the church. The *Kentish Mercury* was later to say of Kevan:

> Notwithstanding his special interest in all that appertains to the young life of the Church, Pastor Kevan has shown an equal regard for the middle-aged and aged: he has proved himself a model visitor, and during the past four years of war, has maintained a regular contact, by correspondence, with the evacuated members of the Church and congregation, including members of H. M. Forces at home and abroad.[11]

Other aspects of church life

Zion did not have all the problems that Church Hill had when Kevan took up the pastorate there, but it was not without its difficulties. Kirby records that a deacon at the time described his call as 'the first move towards unity in a very disunited church.' Kirby goes on: 'Although a young man he had the strength, grace and tact which the situation demanded, and

[11] *Kentish Mercury*, 24 December 1943.

under his able leadership the church members were encouraged to work together as a team.'[12] This is an important comment because so many churches contain factions and the ability to draw everyone together in the gospel and to work together harmoniously is one of the key qualities needed by a pastor. Kevan exemplified this to a considerable degree and it stood him in good stead for the future.

The church minutes for January 21, 1935 record: 'It was laid down that the interpretation of the Rule (9) as regards occasional communion with churches outside the denomination should be left to each individual member.' Rule (9) in 'The Articles of Faith and Rules for Church Order observed by the Members of the Baptized Church of Christ assembling at Zion Chapel, New Cross Road, Deptford', to give it its full title, states: 'That if any member of this church take the supper of the Lord with any other assembly that is not of the same faith and order, or is not *wholly* a baptized church, and after being reproved for so doing, shall declare his or her intention to persist in the same practice, then such member shall be withdrawn from.'

This muddled rule – 'or is not *wholly* a baptized church' nullifies 'that is not of the same faith and order' – and the conclusion of the church meeting, illustrate the sensitivity that there was over the issue of transient communion. It would have been simpler to have rewritten the rule, but that would probably have caused even more dissension. The decision, however, was a liberalising one rather than a strict interpretation of the rule.

Later in the same year at a church meeting in September: 'The secretary congratulated the Pastor on the unique distinction he had received in being awarded the Bachelor of Divinity degree at London University, the first ever achieved

[12]Kirby, *Pastor and Principal*, p.20.

in our denomination.' At this time Frederick Kevan was still alive and he wrote a letter to Dulwich College to inform them of his son's success. By the time of the graduation ceremony the following May he had died and Kate Kevan accompanied Ernest and Jennie on her own to the Albert Hall when Ernest received his certificate. She wrote in her diary: 'With our son we have the proof of the promise "Them that honour ME I will honour".'

There must, however, be some question over whether he was the first person to obtain a BD 'in our denomination'. Apparently there were some Strict Baptists who hoped that he might become a tutor in their Bible Institute. It is doubtful whether this was ever a serious possibility. The Report of the Institute at the end of 1937 says: 'To find a man with the necessary educational qualifications, with a gift for instructing others, faithful to the truths we are assured the Scriptures teach, would be no easy matter. After much prayer, and careful consideration, the Committee was led to an interview with Mr Ralph Woodfield BD.' He duly took over in 1938. So here was another Strict Baptist with a BD; though whether he got his degree before 1935 or afterwards is not known, nor even where he came from.

The man behind the Bible Institute[13] was J. B. Collin, a wealthy businessman who was very generous in his financial support of various Strict Baptist causes and was also the President of the Strict Baptist Mission. He lived in the same road as Kevan in Brockley. He believed firmly in the 'same faith and order' rule. The first principal of the Institute was James Willoughby, who had an MA from Trinity College, Dublin. He began his ministry in the Church of Ireland but

[13]Grist, 'Strict Baptist Bible Institute'. For Collin and Willoughby see also Wilfred Kuhrt, 'Strict Baptists between the Wars – Two Notable Men', in *Grace* magazine (August/September 1988), p. 18. Also Wilfred Kuhrt, 'Strict Baptists between the Wars', *Grace* magazine (July 1988), p. 15.

came to the English Strict Baptists via the Irish Baptists. He was a good scholar but somewhat eccentric; on one occasion he preached a sermon in which every word was of one syllable! The number of students at any one time seems to have been a maximum of six. The Annual Meeting of the Institute in 1939 was held in Zion and Kevan was one of the speakers. The Report for that year also says: 'On 3 May we were pleased to receive a visit from Pastor E. F. Kevan; his lecture on "Ministerial Life" was instructive and helpful.'

A later principal was Charles Breed, little known outside of Strict Baptist circles, but of whom Kevan said that he was one of the finest theologians of his generation. Nearly every Annual Report of the Institute from 1940 onwards contains a Special Resolution:

> The wearing of clerical attire became the subject of a conversation in Committee, and it was agreed that our students past and present should be informed that it was unanimously decided that this practice is against the best interests of the students and ministers themselves, and also injurious to the reputation of the Institute. The Committee appeals to all past and present students to respect its strong and settled conviction.

It is sad to see such an emphasis on a minor matter. By this time there is no doubt that Kevan had begun to wear a clerical collar. In the circumstances it is hardly likely that he would have been invited to become a tutor. The Institute closed in 1962.

In 1936, the church decided to change their hymnbook to the *Baptist Church Hymnal (Revised Edition)*, but added fifty hymns of their own choosing. The Centenary Brochure of 1942, probably written by Kevan and certainly having his approval, has a section called 'Sing Praises to God'. 'The

Church has always encouraged congregational singing, and has made a practice of keeping the various musical auxiliaries in the background. In the days when the singing was assisted by a choir, the latter, together with the American organ, were accommodated in the back gallery!' Out of sight, presumably! There is a reference to the present organ 'of a very pleasing tone, and it has given excellent service as the ideal leader and reverent accompaniment of simple, hearty, congregational singing.'

The brochure continues:

> 'Zion' has been altogether outstanding, as far as our own denomination is concerned, in the number of hymn-writers it has produced. Their verses have been great in quantity, and far from negligible in quality, especially as regards hymns suitable for children to sing.[14]

The *Baptist Hymnal* replaced *Steven's Selection of Hymns* and the implication was that a number of hymns written by those from the church would be included in the fifty added to that book. The practice of church members writing hymns for use in their worship is by no means the recent thing it is sometimes thought to be.

[14] *Constraining Love*, Centenary Brochure, August 1942, p. 11.

8

Doctrine and Development

IN 1936, KEVAN TOOK the Baptist Union examination which enabled his name to be put on the ministerial list of that Union. There are questions about this that have no ready answer. I will attempt a possible reason a little later. There were, of course, Strict Baptist ministers who joined the Baptist Union. Wilfred Kuhrt, who wrote about the Strict Baptist Institute, says that all four of his fellow-students at the Institute eventually went into Baptist Union churches. What is unusual here is that, as we shall see, Kevan was still committed to the Metropolitan Association which was generally looked upon as another denomination.

There is not much evidence of pastoral problems within the church from the material available; in this matter relatively modern church minutes differ rather considerably from the minutes of the early days of Baptist churches, which were often almost completely taken up with matters of discipline. There is, however, a record of one problem that arose in 1937. A member of the church wrote a letter to Kevan accusing him of 'modernism'. Kevan brought the letter and the matter to the next church meeting and the person who wrote the letter then protested that he had not been told that this was going to happen.

It is not clear what the statements were on which this accusation was grounded. It appears to have concerned the doctrine of the last things, but it is difficult to understand how this can be. In the Articles of Faith of the church the relevant one is entitled 'On the Resurrection' and reads as follows: 'That the dead will be raised, both the just and the unjust; that the righteous will rise first, will be wholly conformed to the likeness of the Lord Jesus, be gathered to him, and abide with him for all eternity; but that the wicked will be driven away in their wickedness into everlasting punishment.' At the church meeting Kevan affirmed his adherence to all the articles and his published writings bear witness to this. Eventually this man and a number of his family left the church. This event illustrates the sort of distressing trial that ministers sometimes experience.

The coronation

The year 1937 saw the coronation of King George VI and Kevan has this to say about it in his book of children's talks:

> I went to bed one night at about seven o'clock, because I wanted to get up at two o'clock the next morning. I can see the surprised look on your face and can almost hear you say, 'Whatever for?' I had planned to meet four of my friends, and we were going up to London, near Trafalgar Square, so as to get a good place among the crowds where we could see the king's coronation procession. I wasn't one of those fortunate people who had a ticket to Westminster Abbey, where the crowning took place, but I had made up my mind that I wanted to see the king with his crown on his head. I had often seen the king wearing either a bowler hat, or a peaked cap belonging to a uniform, but I wanted to see him wearing the crown. I waited and waited. The crowd sang and laughed. I changed from one foot to the other all through the long hours from about three o'clock in the morning till three o'clock in the afternoon. But I was rewarded. The long procession of sailors and soldiers

> and airmen, with men from all parts of the world, went swinging by. Then came a number of great people in fine-looking carriages – and now! Just listen to the shouting and cheering! Louder and louder it became and at last there they were – the King and Queen on their Coronation Day! In a high golden carriage drawn by magnificent horses there was the King – and His Majesty King George VI, wearing the wonderful crown that tells of the good government of our great country. Yes! And there was the Queen also. She was wearing the Queen's crown. It was ever such a wonderful moment. I couldn't shout: a mysterious kind of lump came up in my throat when I thought of all the deep meaning of the British crown. 'Fear God,' I thought, 'Honour the king' (*First Epistle of Peter*, chapter 2, verse 17). That's what the Bible says.[1]

This is such a vivid portrayal of that occasion and the effect it had on him is so marked that one feels that here there is an insight into some deep emotion. This is heightened by the fact that it was actually pouring with rain during the procession,[2] but he doesn't even mention that. Not every Christian would feel as he did about the British crown, but I think that many Londoners, and people from across Britain, would have felt very much the same emotion. In his case he would look back on our history since the Reformation and see the hand of God upon our country – not in the sense that this was a 'Christian country', but understanding that the providence of God had raised up the country and the Empire that they might fulfil a purpose for the furtherance of the gospel. Although he looked at this very much as a believer – 'Fear God', would always come first for him – yet there is something here of the spirit which British people took with them into the Second World

[1]Kevan, *Let's Talk*, pp. 76-7.
[2]William Shawcross, *Queen Elizabeth: The Queen Mother* (London: Macmillan, 2009), p. 404.

War, which was then less than two and a half years away.

The presidential address

On 8 March 1938, Kevan became President of the Metropolitan Association for the coming year and delivered his presidential address in 'Zion' Chapel. This was a powerful sermon delivered with conviction and obviously widely appreciated. It was printed in full in the *Gospel Herald* and also separately as a brochure. He gave it the title 'Doctrine and Development'. It gives an insight into his outlook and priorities at that time.

He began by asking, 'What is the reason for our denominational existence?' He said that every denomination must justify itself or it has no right to our tolerance. He continued: 'Whilst keeping to the fullness of the Gospel in all its aspects, and ever seeking the salvation of souls, our denomination exists for the purpose of bearing witness to distinctive and fundamental doctrines.' This led him into the first part of his address: 'Doctrine'. He had some important things to say as he opened up his subject:

> The uncertain thinking and vague teaching in the Church at large today make it imperative that a place of honour be given to the exposition of Christian Doctrine... A significant feature of the present time is that people are coming into our congregations, and joining our churches, who have been driven from their old connections by ritual or modernism. These believers appreciate our staunch adherence to evangelical truth and our emphasis on experimental Christianity. It is incumbent upon us to see that they are given a helpful and clear understanding of our doctrines, for these are the factors which have contributed to our stability... Further, the higher standard of public education demands the much clearer teaching of our distinctive doctrines.

He then linked behaviour to right doctrine:

> Only a true understanding can really make for steadfast service: it is clear thinking that makes clear acting... 'Your life cannot be good,' said Dr Parker, 'if your teaching is bad. Doctrine lies at the basis of life.' Truth is the foundation of conduct: doctrine is the foundation of life... It is doctrine which gives form to our thinking and strength to our service. Strong doctrine makes strong character.

Here we are getting to the heart of the man. He was a good exegete, and he knew that all doctrine must be based on proper exegesis of Scripture, but he believed that the purpose of exegesis was to discover the coherent truth that God has for his people in his Word. Supremely Ernest Kevan was a theologian; someone who desired to understand and then declare the teaching that he found in Scripture. He would have deprecated, I believe, the all-too-common present emphasis on exegesis at the expense of theology. For him, *sola scriptura* meant that Scripture, in the words of Gerald Bray:

> ...is a unity, and that its teaching can therefore be systemized in a coherent structure of belief. This offers a guide to the correct interpretation of difficult passages and provides the foundation of the Church's teaching ministry.[3]

He turned next to the particular truths which he believed the Strict Baptists stood for:

> Without the remotest appearance of arrogance, I think we must say that the distinctive mission of our denomination in regard to doctrine is the proclamation of THE SOVEREIGNTY OF GOD IN SALVATION. This involves the

[3]Gerald Bray, 'Whatever Happened to the Authority of Scripture?', in Melvyn Tinker (ed.), *The Anglican Evangelical Crisis* (Fearn: Christian Focus, 1995), p. 58.

doctrine of eternal election to salvation through predestinating grace. It means that God's purpose in the salvation of a sinner is not left to the chance of his circumstances, nor is it to be thwarted by human obstinacy. It proclaims that grace is triumphant within the human heart, and God's calling of those whom He has eternally chosen is effectual. It declares that the Holy Spirit stirs the dead soul to life, and every conversion is a wondrous miracle.

This is a grand conception of God's ways. The conviction of God's sovereignty removes all limitations in preaching the Gospel, and gives strong assurance in prayer. It vindicates the majesty of Christ in that He is revealed, not as feebly waiting for man to accept Him, but rather as enthroned in glory, and from that throne bestowing pardon on the humblest sinner who seeks His mercy. We do not present a Christ who amiably wants to save sinners 'if only they will let Him.' We proclaim a message in which 'The Lord God Omnipotent reigneth.' We proclaim Jesus as 'the mighty to save.' We preach a Gospel which God the Holy Spirit makes effective even while we proclaim it, so that hearts are melted and consciences awakened.

Now these doctrinal principles with all their inspiration are distinctive of our denomination: they constitute at once our right to existence and our call to action. Our mission is tenaciously to hold these truths and courageously to spread them... There are encouraging signs that... the theological pendulum outside our denomination is beginning to move in the direction of the distinctive truths which we hold. These theological signs seem to me to make the call to the fulfilment of our denominational mission more insistent than ever... By our faith and action let us cause men to know that the name 'Strict Baptist' stands for a man possessed of clear and vigorous convictions, convictions that make him 'steadfast, unmoveable, always abounding in the work of the Lord.'

From doctrine Kevan proceeded to the second part of his address, 'Development':

> Doctrine and development go together... Development – in the form of increasing evangelistic activity – is the only way to make ourselves consistent in our profession.

Here he maintained that this had been the main aim of the Association. He confessed that though there were evidences of forward movement on the whole they have been marking time, and addded:

> I think this is sometimes due to the fact that our Church members have too slender a hold upon our distinguishing doctrines. For the purposes of consolidation and advance, I appeal to every one who removes into another neighbourhood to settle within a Strict Baptist Church. I entreat those who come from bigger churches not to be contemptuous of joining a little struggling community. Go in and pull your weight. I add also an affectionate appeal to the members of the little Churches that they receive such friends cordially, and 'not to doubtful disputations'. May God take away the uncharitableness and suspicion that exist between some Churches, for these are among the things that arrest our advance.

He issued powerful pleas for action:

> How much can be accomplished if we have a mind to do it! Pastors! Deacons! Are there any of these new estates near your Churches? If so, let us together try and see what extension of our witness is possible. Denominational expansion... calls for the heroism of sacrificial giving and sacrificial living. Who has the vision? Who will eschew the comfort of their fireside chairs and be willing for the Lord to thrust them into the harvest field? I am appealing for

> whole-hearted men who, conscious that they are not called to preach, are nevertheless willing to use their out-of-business hours to the uttermost... Who will step forward?

And so he moved to his conclusion:

> I believe that the hour of our denominational destiny is near. Men and women are hungering for the 'strong meat' which we have to give to them. Believers everywhere are turning wistful eyes and longing hearts towards the bold certainties of Divine Sovereignty, which have ever been characteristic of our denominational witness.[4] Let us lift up our voice that it be heard! I have said much about the propagation of the great doctrines for which we stand, but lest any should be thinking in themselves that surely they are only secondary to the work of saving souls, I want to say that it is precisely through the truth of the Gospel in its fullness that men will be saved. Let us, then, as far as God has vouchsafed us light, stand for that truth in all its glorious wholeness.
>
> In concluding this message, I want solemnly to remind you that, when all has been said and done by us in fulfilment of our mission, it is power from on high that we need. 'O Lord, send the power just now.' Let us, on our knees, seek the experience of that power through prayer and consecration to our Saviour. One believer aflame for God may transform a cold and lifeless Church; that Church, in turn, may be used of God to the quickening of the whole denomination; we, as a denomination, may then be the means, through the Holy Spirit, for the revival of the whole Church of God.

This was a necessary and powerful message. The words of Kevan quoted in an earlier chapter occur in it: 'The standard

[4]For evidence of a resurgence of Calvinism in this period, see David Bebbington, 'Lloyd-Jones and the Interwar Calvinist Resurgence', in Andrew Atherstone & David Ceri Jones (eds.), *Engaging with Martyn Lloyd-Jones*, (Nottingham: Apollos, 2011), pp. 38ff.

of our denominational spiritual life is nothing to be proud of; and closer inspection reveals many things which fill us with sorrow of heart.' There is within this message, I think, an implicit appeal to put aside introspection and internal bickering, replacing these with a renewed commitment to the central, unifying doctrines of God's sovereignty and to reaching out to the lost. These positive notes would always remain central in his thinking.

The message was given to the Metropolitan Association. Why then had he joined the Baptist Union ministerial list two years earlier? It is at least possible that at times he wondered whether to leave the Strict Baptists, but more likely there may be a clue in his final words. He was not concerned for revival and quickening solely among Strict Baptists. He desired that such blessing would then overflow to what he calls 'the whole Church of God'. It is almost certain that by this time he was getting known beyond Strict Baptist circles, so it looks as if he thought that having his name on the Baptist Union list would open up wider avenues of opportunity for ministry. His position was a strange one, for he never belonged to any church affiliated to the Baptist Union, nor did he ever take any active part in its affairs. This issue will arise again later.

9

The Second World War

On 30 September 1938, Kate Kevan had written in her diary: '*God* has given us *peace*, when all the world expected war. "Oh, that men would praise the Lord".' This was the day after the Munich Conference from which Neville Chamberlain, the Prime Minister, returned declaring, 'Peace in our time'. Events, however, were to prove otherwise, and as 1939 opened the clouds of war were already gathering. It was Kevan's task as President of the Metropolitan Association, to write the New Year's Message in the January issue of the *Gospel Herald*. He based it on the words: 'Lo, he cometh with clouds.'

> The year that we have left behind has been one of grave anxieties. Everywhere men have shown signs of being over-wrought and highly strung; the clouds have indeed been about us. And when we look forward it seems that the horizon is a dark one... when Moses entered into the black cloud on Mount Sinai we are told that he entered the 'thick darkness where God was'. What a strength it is to know that God is there! We are, perhaps, likely to be over-occupied with national and international problems... I want you to concentrate your interest and energy upon the work of Christ's glorious kingdom... With the social order tumbling about us, with morality undermined beneath us, with political chaos and perfidy on so many sides, let us look right on, and say, with Paul, 'Woe is me if I preach not the gospel'. Presently the cloud shall rend and the shining

> of His coming will dawn on our longing vision. 'Oh, how glorious when we meet Him in the air!'

The war, of course, was to bring many new challenges and it is very difficult for anyone now to capture the atmosphere in London as the six years that it lasted went by. It is impossible to appreciate the conflicting emotions aroused by the fall of the Low Countries and France and the remarkable escape of so many troops at Dunkirk, or the fear of a near-certain invasion and the spirit of defiance that existed together. The bombing, with its destruction and death, left a city dingy and grey with craters and bomb-sites. In the beginning it was largely evacuated of children, young men were called up, young women summoned to fields or factories.

Life, and church life, was hugely dislocated. People and children came and went as bombing increased or decreased. Travel was restricted and difficult and the blackout made evening meetings problematic in the wintertime. Unsurprisingly more people turned to the churches; people in London were drawn together, differences became submerged for a while, and this was the case with the churches too. Denominational differences amongst evangelicals were lessened by days of prayer and the obvious importance of an evangelistic ministry amidst suffering and death. Amongst believers the emphasis was on assurance and hope, confidence and comfort for the bereaved and the frightened.

Bill Brown, whose memories were recorded in a previous chapter, gave a rather amusing account of the day on which war was declared:

> On the 3rd September, 1939, we were gathered as a congregation for morning worship and Pastor Kevan had just begun the service when Mr Chapman, the caretaker came up to the pulpit and informed the pastor that war had been

> declared. Almost immediately we heard the air raid sirens and Pastor Kevan instructed the congregation to leave the building and return to their homes. I was talking with George Leng, the Sunday School Superintendent, when we realised that Mr Martin, the organist, had not come down from his seat at the organ. Mr Martin was somewhat deaf (which was unusual for an organist) and he relied on a light signal from the pulpit to indicate to him when he was required to play the hymns. So Mr Leng and I returned to the chapel in order to explain to Mr Martin what had happened.

Why the sirens sounded so soon after the declaration of war when it was hardly possible for German bombers to have taken off is not known, unless it was a practice to make sure they all worked. The King and Queen in Buckingham Palace also heard the mournful sound and took refuge in the air raid shelter.[1]

There is a note in the *Gospel Herald* for October 1939 concerning Sunday Schools:

> These last few weeks have been very disappointing for many. Hopes which had been built up high have come crashing down, and many longings seem destined to be unfulfilled. This aptly describes the feelings of those who have been praying about, and working for, the special effort of November next for the recruitment of Sunday-school scholars. We had hoped for much, but now, as the result of the evacuation, many schools are worse off than ever, and some have no scholars at all.

The note went on to end positively but there was little realisation of what was to lie ahead for Sunday School work in London, indeed for gospel work and for London in general.

Kevan also has a letter in the same issue of the *Gospel*

[1]Shawcross, *The Queen Mother*, p. 488.

Herald. Firstly, there is an appeal for volunteers to undertake preaching appointments. Then he addresses church members scattered by the general evacuation from London to country areas and asks them to make it their first duty to find out where there is a Strict Baptist Chapel in or near the neighbourhood in which they have come. It was his hope that by the arrival of Strict Baptists into some of these outlying districts struggling Strict Baptist churches might be revived. Finally he adds:

> I have one further request to make which is felt very deeply by me. I wonder whether, in these times when our people are being scattered, I may appeal for a removal of those sectional barriers in regard to the Lord's Table which exist within the borders of the denomination. May I appeal that all Strict Baptist Churches everywhere be willing to admit to the Lord's Table all members of other Strict Baptist Churches? I feel that this constitutes a wonderful opportunity of welding us together and of eliminating all the barriers within the denomination.

How far such a plea was heeded is unknown, but it shows that Kevan was deeply concerned about the question of the Lord's Table and the differences that existed amongst Strict Baptists.

For a while the *Gospel Herald* published 'Topics for Bible Study' for the Fellowship of Youth. Kevan wrote the notes for January and February 1940. In the January issue these were on a missionary subject: 'Open Doors Today', based on Revelation 3:7-13. In the course of this he said:

> Doors seem to be fast closing. Germany, Russia, Spain, Rumania, Poland, Finland (as I write at the moment)... There is still an 'open door' in India, Africa, China, South Sea Islands, South America, and England.

Then he gives some statistics for China, Japan, Egypt and Turkey. Egypt had twenty-six missionaries per million, the largest number in this grouping; Turkey the lowest with five per million. Kevan had a continuing concern for overseas mission everywhere, although taking a particular interest in the Strict Baptist Mission in India. When much later the Evangelical Fellowship of India invited him to visit and minister there, he accepted on condition he could spend three weeks with 'my friends of the Strict Baptist Mission'.

It is interesting that he included Spain in his list of countries. As he knew, the door had already been closed there for some time. A member of Zion, Miss Alice Brown, was out in Spain with the Spanish Gospel Mission when he came to the church. In 1936 she was back in this country and in July a valedictory service was arranged for her in September before she returned to her work. However a minute for September 21 says: 'Postponement of the above meeting owing to the state of the country.' The Spanish Civil War had broken out by August and she was never to return to work in Spain. Zion also had several missionaries who served with the China Inland Mission, as it was then. After the war two of its members went out to India with the Strict Baptist Mission.

In the February 1940 issue of the *Gospel Herald* he also wrote some notes for a young peoples' discussion on the subject: 'Do miracles happen today?' In the course of this he said:

> Will you obtain and *study* a most challenging book? *The Faith that Rebels*, by Dr. D. S. Cairns (3/6). It is a rebellion against the modern pseudo-scientific rejection of miracles. (You will not agree with *all* that the writer of the book says: I do not agree either. So if you are unable to read any book except those with which you agree, do not read this one!)

He did not attempt to answer the question in his notes; what he wanted to do was to promote discussion that was thorough and considered all angles. The book he mentions is long out of date. He recognized that some people find it difficult to read anything that they do not agree with, but he evidently expected many Christian young people to be prepared to study challenging books. This was undoubtedly his own practice.

That same month in 1940, Kate Kevan passed away. The goodness of God may be seen in this. This was the period known as the 'Phoney War'. But on April 9, Germany invaded Denmark and Norway and by June 22, Holland, Belgium and France had also all fallen leaving Great Britain facing a hostile Europe alone. Soon after this came the Battle of Britain, fought in the air, and followed by 'the Blitz' on London. Blitz is a shortened form of the German word *blitzkrieg* meaning 'lightning war', an overpowering assault using all the means of war available. However, in this case it referred to the attempt to bomb Britain into submission. Mrs Kevan senior was to miss all this. She is particularly remembered for praying for Hitler in the Sunday morning prayer meeting. Her prayerfulness and grace lingered on in the church, and there are still (2009) one or two who can just recall her.

On 12 October 1940 there was a conference held at Chadwell Street on 'Bible Christianity and Its Counterfeits' and Kevan gave an address which served as an introduction to a discussion. He covered Modernism, Romanism and Spiritism. He began by saying that these seem very far apart from each other in their spirit, but they can be grouped together in the following way: 'Modernism we may regard as False Inspiration. Romanism we may regard as False Mediation. Spiritism we may regard as False Communication.'

He said that the main point of contention with Modernism resolves itself into the question: 'Is the Bible man's discovery of God, or is it God's revelation to man? Is it man's exploration of his own mind to find God, or is it the opening of God's mind to man? Is it a question or an answer?' He looks at Romanism in its practical aspects. 'Between the sinner and his God appear to be put:' the 'Mediation of Mary'; the 'Mediation of Church Authority'; the 'Mediation of Priestly Office' and the 'Mediation of Repeated Sacrifices'. 'Over against the false mediation of Romanism, the scriptural position is that "there is one God and one mediator between God and men, the man Christ Jesus".' On Spiritism, which was quite in vogue in those days, he is unequivocal:

> In so far as there is reality in the facts of Spiritism, its communications must be said to come from the Evil One himself. What is certain from the Scripture, and from the fact that Christ is Lord of the dead as well as the living, is that these communications purporting to come from the dead do not come from the departed ones at all, but from 'the father of lies'.[2]

Three days later, a Tuesday, there is a laconic minute in the church book: the pastor 'went to Torquay for an operation. On the same evening a bomb fell in the Manse garden, damaging the house, but causing no serious injury to the occupants.' We do not know what the operation was for, nor whether Mrs Kevan went with her husband to Torquay, or who 'the occupants' of the Manse might be. It is possible that some church members who had been bombed out were staying there temporarily; that sort of thing happened frequently in those days. As a result of the damage to the house the Kevans moved into a flat for the next three years.

The church building was also slightly damaged, but this was not serious. Later, in 1944, it was much more severely damaged and the congregation met in the school hall for

[2] *Gospel Herald* (January 1941), pp. 6-8.

two years. We have already noticed Kevan's commitment to the Peace Pledge Union. Once the war started he helped those who applied to be put on the Register of Conscientious Objectors. There was a form to be completed initially and then the applicant had to appear before a Tribunal consisting of a chairman and perhaps three others. It was possible to bring representatives and Kevan would go along with those who wished him to.

The war seriously affected the life of the church, particularly the Sunday School. The Sunday School Centenary brochure of 1949 says:

> On the outbreak of the Second World War, the School had a great set-back, and with the commencement of aerial warfare attendances were reduced to as few as twelve... During a break in enemy activity, and because of the continued evacuation of the scholars, Pastor Kevan felt that in order to rebuild the School, we should have to commence with the youngest. New furniture was purchased for the Primary department, and... The Primary was transferred to the Upper Schoolroom...[3]

It was with the ending of the Blitz that Kevan put so much effort into the work amongst young children and the primary section was built up to ninety children. This was put under the leadership of a Miss Cooper, but when bombing was renewed inevitably the Sunday School was again reduced in numbers.

In October 1942 the *Gospel Herald* contained the following advertisement: 'Light in the Blackout. Enjoy the light of God's Word in the Winter Evenings by studying with our correspondence courses'. There were six courses each with ten fortnightly lessons. Kevan wrote three of the courses: 'A General Introduction to the Bible'; 'The Four Gospels'; and

[3] *These Many Years*, Zion, New Cross; Sunday School Centenary, p. 3.

'The Minor Prophets'. Earlier in the year he had obtained the degree of Master of Theology from London University; so also had Principal Woodfield of the Strict Baptist Institute, who wrote the course on 'The Doctrines of the Bible'.

In 1942, the church at Zion celebrated its centenary. There were four days of meetings and a centenary booklet was published. This ends with these paragraphs:

> We can hardly close this little booklet without some reference to the terrible conflict which is raging all over the world, and which, as we write, has not yet reached its climax. London has experienced many terrible air raids and, as a result, two of our members have been killed. Our Manse has been rendered uninhabitable, but we rejoice that our Pastor and his wife were both uninjured, and our Chapel has remained intact, although the premises have suffered slight damage.
>
> As a result of the war, much of our work, especially among the children, has received a bad setback, but we have very good congregations in spite of evacuation of many of our members from London to safer areas.
>
> So we are able to conclude on a note of heartfelt praise to God for all His goodness to us. As we look back over the record of the last hundred years, we realise that the faith, hope, and love of God's servants have accomplished great things in 'Zion', and so we take courage and go forward, knowing that 'God holds the key to all unknown' and our chief desire is to do His will gladly.[4]

Some time in the early forties Kevan became a member of the Westminster Fellowship for ministers. This Fellowship was started in 1941 by Dr Martyn Lloyd-Jones who had come to Westminster Chapel in central London, close to Buckingham Palace, in 1938. Initially this was to assist G. Camp-

[4]Kevan, *Constraining Love*, p. 12.

bell Morgan but he continued to minister in the Chapel until 1968. In 1943 Kevan became a member of the Committee of the Evangelical Library and was to serve on it for the rest of his life. When the Library opened in London in 1945 after its removal from Surrey, Kevan co-wrote an article in the *Evangelical Quarterly*, drawing attention to its facilities.[5]

Kevan had also written in 1943 an article for the same periodical entitled 'The Re-emergence of Calvinism'. He clearly had the background of war in view:

'It is the heartsickness of men and women today that makes them turn away from the optimistic humanism on which they have been fed and long for the health-giving tonic that is found in Calvinism.' When speaking of Calvinism's concept of God he said:

> In what terms do men pray for revival? It is that God would 'break in' upon human life, that by His Spirit He would sweep through the world in mighty blessing, breaking down the hearts of men in penitence and faith. What is this but a longing for a God Who is above and beyond?[6]

Serving the local community

In spite of his work within the church and in connection with various Strict Baptist organizations, Kevan still found time to be involved in a number of activities in the community. He held many local offices including the following: Chairman of Lucas Vale London County Council School Care Committee, Chairman of the Deptford Council of Christian Churches, twice Chairman of the Deptford Ministers' Fraternal, composed of both Church of England clergy and free church ministers, and President of the New Cross and District Prayer

[5]D. M. Lloyd-Jones & E. F. Kevan, 'The Evangelical Library', in *The Evangelical Quarterly*, 17:3 (1945), pp. 221-5.

[6]Ernest Kevan, 'The Re-emergence of Calvinism', in *The Evangelical Quarterly*, 15:3 (1943), pp. 219, 220.

Fellowship for Ministers and Missionaries. This latter organisation arranged big united local Conventions in 1942 and 1943. He also served as a member of the After-Care Committee of Lucas Vale School, and was for nearly two years a member of Deptford Youth Committee.[7] Regarding the Deptford Council of Christian Churches, Bill Brown said, 'In those days that Council was not involved in the Ecumenical Movement.'

There can be no doubt that in the Council and the Fraternal there were ministers who were liberal in their theology; indeed from what Kevan said later at least part of his reason for attendance at the fraternal was to present the biblical and evangelical alternative. However, the situation was confused because in the first half of the twentieth century there was a great deal of what was known as 'liberal evangelicalism'. Those who were evangelistic and called people to faith in Jesus Christ were all known as 'Evangelicals', even if they held to critical views of the Bible.

This goes a long way to explain, for example, the leading article in the *Baptist Times* of 6 May 1943 which said of the Baptist Union: 'the denomination is evangelical through and through – but without the dogmatic intolerance which has sometimes marked evangelical emphasis.'[8] After the war the term 'conservative evangelical' came into vogue in order to try and make a distinction between the two sorts of 'evangelicalism', but they were not generally so distinguished in the pre-war period.

Kevan's involvement in local affairs was noted and appreciated. The *Kentish Mercury* in a report of the church's centenary celebrations said:

> The present minister, the Rev. E. F. Kevan, B.D., M.Th.,

[7] *Kentish Mercury*, 24 December 1943.
[8] Randall, *English Baptists*, p. 209.

> received the call to the pastorate in 1934, and under his able and vigorous leadership the church has prospered, and is still prospering, notwithstanding the difficulties of these war days. Mr. Kevan, as a young man, has a sympathetic understanding of the many problems confronting modern youth, and has applied himself with energy to the practical outworking of these problems. Nevertheless he stands uncompromisingly for the Gospel of Calvary. As a mark of recognition of the public value of the work accomplished, and in appreciation of the many local men and women who have spent their lives in the service of the church and Sunday School, the Mayor and Corporation of Deptford will attend a special centenary service on Sunday morning, September 6th, at 11 a.m., when Pastor George Bird, of Watford Tabernacle, will be the preacher.[9]

During his time at Zion, Ernest Kevan was increasingly becoming known well beyond the Strict Baptist constituency and his immediate locality, both as a preacher and for his scholarship. This was to mean a considerable change of course for him and his wife.

[9] *Kentish Mercury*, 28 August 1942.

10

Two Invitations

DURING THE YEARS THAT Kevan was at Zion, New Cross, important developments were taking place which would give a radical change of direction to his life and ministry and also have profound implications for evangelicalism in Britain and far beyond. As early as 1933, preliminary discussions began about establishing a new evangelical college or institute in London. The two men who promoted this most vigorously were A. J. Vereker, the secretary of the Crusaders Union, and Dr Douglas Johnson, the general secretary of the Inter-Varsity Fellowship.[1] By 1939 an exploratory sub-committee of Rev. W. H. Aldis, Rev. J. Russell Howden, Dr D. Martyn Lloyd-Jones, J. W. Laing and Dr Douglas Johnson had been set up. In that year a report produced by its secretary (Johnson) included the following points:

> 1. The Bible Institute to be a residential College adequately staffed by well-qualified teachers, and conducted in accordance with the best educational standards, for example, as if it were a fully-recognized college of a British University.
>
> 2. That the Institute should aim at qualifying the students for diplomas and certificates recognized by the London University and other authorities.
>
> 3. That there should be a Doctrinal Basis in the Constitution of the Institute which will declare its position in

[1]See Douglas Johnson, *Contending for the Faith* (Leicester: Inter-Varsity Press, 1979), p. 300.

relation to Evangelical Belief in unequivocal terms.

4. Points of theology and doctrine on which there is legitimate difference of opinion amongst Evangelical Christians, should not be taught in such a way that only one viewpoint is given, or stressed at the expense of others. (It is recognized that this consideration will need careful thought, when the Constitution is drawn up.)[2]

However, within three months of the report being drawn up the country was at war. This inevitably disrupted the plans that were being made, but those concerned seem to have shown remarkable tenacity. It is not necessary here to go over all the events that took place before the new London Bible College, as it was to be called, was brought into being. Unsurprisingly there were many knotty policy matters to discuss, and there were different groups who saw different priorities for the College. It was agreed, however, that the College should major on Bible teaching, and its name was deliberately chosen to emphasize that.[3] The teaching was to be at the highest educational level and the College would prepare men and women for the service of Christ both at home and abroad.[4]

It is important to see the desire to establish London Bible College in the context of developments in evangelicalism at that time. Douglas Johnson, in particular, was at the centre of efforts to restore a vigorous and intellectually adequate evangelicalism which also corrected some of the imbalances that were evident. These included fanciful interpretations of Scripture, an over-emphasis on experience at the expense of

[2]Harold Rowdon, *London Bible College: The First 25 Years* (London: Henry E. Walter, 1968), pp. 13-14.
[3]Taken from the Prospectus of Full-Time Courses (1959), p. 14.
[4]See Ian Randall, *Educating Evangelicalism, The Origin, Development and Impact of London Bible College* (Milton Keynes: Paternoster Press, 2000), pp. 12-37.

doctrine, a rather too simple gospel and an attitude to the world based on taboos rather than thought-out, biblical principles. What was needed, it was seen, was careful exposition of Scripture which put God at the centre of things, brought out the fundamental truths of the gospel and would be applied to the everyday life of Christians and their role in society. London Bible College fitted precisely into this ambition.

By 1942 a brief doctrinal basis was agreed committing the college to the 'Fundamental Truths of Christianity':

> 1. The unity of the Father, the Son, and the Holy Spirit in the Godhead.
>
> 2. The divine inspiration and supreme authority of the Holy Scriptures.
>
> 3. The guilt and depravity of human nature in consequence of the Fall.
>
> 4. The substitutionary death of our Lord Jesus Christ, and His resurrection, as the only way of salvation from sin through faith.
>
> 5. The necessity of the work of the Holy Spirit in the new birth, and His indwelling in the believer for sanctification.
>
> 6. The personal return of the Lord Jesus Christ.[5]

It was, however, one thing to plan a new college with high academic standards; it was another thing to find a principal and lecturers who would measure up to these intentions. Oliver Barclay, in his book *Evangelicalism in Britain, 1935-1995*, says: 'The outlook for evangelical Christianity in the late 1930s was not very encouraging, even to most sympathetic observers.'[6] He continues: 'In academic circles it was

[5]Rowdon, *The First 25 Years*, p. 18.
[6]Oliver Barclay, *Evangelicalism in Britain 1935-1995* (Leicester: Inter-Varsity Press, 1997), p. 15.

almost universally assumed that a Classical Evangelical view of the Bible was dead.'[7] The situation was underlined by the fact that when the IVF wished to publish a book of basic Christian doctrine 'to help students who had recently come to faith in Christ' they turned to T. C. Hammond in Dublin. He produced *In Understanding Be Men* in 1936, just at the time when he was on his way to become the Principal of Moore College in Sydney, Australia.[8]

Although it had always been hoped that Dr Lloyd-Jones, who was the obvious candidate, would become the Principal of the college, when he was invited in 1942 he indicated that he could not see his way to accepting the invitation. It was intended that the college would begin in a small way with correspondence courses and evening classes, as there was no prospect of commencing residential courses while the war continued. In the next year, 1943, Dr Graham Scroggie was appointed 'to become director of London Bible College'. The minister of the Metropolitan Tabernacle was already seventy-six years old, and he only continued in post for a matter of months. It was proving difficult to find a man with sufficient qualifications and during those wartime years it probably needed to be someone who was already in London. However, Kevan had gradually become more widely known and it was through the influence of Dr Lloyd-Jones that in that summer he was invited to join the College staff. He had time to think and pray over this proposal and also to speak with Dr Lloyd-Jones about it.

In 1943 Kevan was forty years old; he had good qualifications and was in the prime of life. The initial appointment with the College would be on a part-time basis, so it would still be

[7]Barclay, *Evangelicalism*, p. 16.
[8]Warren Nelson, *T. C. Hammond: His Life and Legacy in Ireland and Australia* (Edinburgh: Banner of Truth Trust, 1994), pp. 88ff., 131ff.

possible for him to continue as pastor of Zion, New Cross. But while he had begun to think over the implications of this invitation something else took place which he interpreted quite clearly as the providential direction of God to him. For this it is necessary to go back in time and change location.

Trinity Road Chapel, Upper Tooting

Trinity Road Baptist Church in Upper Tooting, or Trinity Road Chapel as it is more generally known, was formed in 1870, mainly through the exertions of Mr William Winsford, in an area of London that was just being developed.[9] He and his wife were members of the Metropolitan Tabernacle, and they were helped in the early days by the support of C. H. Spurgeon, who at that time lived nearby in Nightingale Lane, and preached at the opening of the chapel in 1877. The church described itself as 'a Particular or Calvinistic Baptist Church' and its minister had to be a Calvinistic Baptist but from the beginning it had an open table and also an open membership. That is, Christians who had not been baptized as believers were able to join in the Lord's Supper and also become members of the church. This practice was adopted partly because a number of those who formed the initial nucleus of believers were not themselves Baptists and also in order to meet the needs of a large number of Nonconformist Christians who were at that time beginning to come out to the rural suburb of Wandsworth Common.

The trust deed of the church says:

> Though it is expressly intended that the Society assembling

[9]Details of Trinity Road Chapel are taken out of *From the First Day Until Now 1870-1970*, subtitled 'Being a record of the Church worshipping at Trinity Road Chapel, Upper Tooting, London, S.W.17, from its foundation in 1870 to its Centenary'. This was compiled by H. Carey Oakley. I am grateful to Mr Reg Warner for allowing me to borrow his copy.

> in the said Meeting House shall always be confined in the choice of a minister or pastor to persons of the Denomination aforesaid yet the members of the society for the time being shall admit to Church Membership any person or persons professing repentance toward God and faith in and obedience to our Lord Jesus Christ although such person or persons shall not be of the denomination aforesaid.[10]

However, the church only practised believers' baptism. This rather unusual arrangement was perhaps particularly suitable for a Strict Baptist on a pilgrimage to an interdenominational college.

In 1895, the Rev. Henry Oakley became pastor at Trinity Road Chapel. He had trained at Regent's Park College during the period of the Downgrade Controversy.[11] He was a strong supporter of C. H. Spurgeon, who had drawn attention to an increasing liberalism within the Baptist Union and had been censured by its Council. He was present at the meeting of the Union in 1888 about which Mrs Spurgeon wrote:

> The compromise at the City Temple confirmed the position of the modern-thought men in the Union, and made 'the vote of censure' the act of the whole assembly with the exception of the noble seven who voted against it.[12]

In 1934 Oakley wrote an account of this meeting in *The Witness*, the church magazine he began in 1897. In 1931 the

[10]Quoted in Ernest Kevan, *The Faith and Practice of the Church Worshipping in Trinity Road Chapel Upper Tooting*, reprinted in *The Witness*, Nov-Dec 2004.

[11]The 'Downgrade Controversy' began in 1887 with articles in the magazine of the Metropolitan Tabernacle, *The Sword and the Trowel*, drawing attention to an increasing liberalism within Nonconformity which denied the divine inspiration of Scripture and major Christian doctrines.

[12]*C. H. Spurgeon's Autobiography compiled from his Diary, Letters and Records by his Wife and his Private Secretary* (London: Passmore and Alabaster, 1900), vol. 4, p. 255.

church left the Baptist Union, though he was careful not to bring the matter himself to the church meeting.

Under his ministry the church grew until it reached some 400 members by 1920. 1938 seems to have been a particularly prosperous year spiritually:

> The year before the outbreak of the second world war proved to be a year of advance. At the annual meeting of members held in February, 1939, the church secretary reported: 'Was there ever a year in which the church received more from its risen Lord?' Mr Oakley had prayed that in the year which marked the Jubilee of his service as a Baptist minister, fifty new members might be added to the church before the end of January, 1939, and in this he had been joined by many of the members. Their prayer was answered and fifty-two new members were added to the church in that year.[13]

Oakley ministered for forty-seven years at Trinity Road Chapel, eventually resigning through ill health in 1942. Not long after, his health failed rapidly and on 17 June 1943 he entered the presence of the Lord. The Resolution passed at the church meeting in the following month concluded: 'The church resolves by God's help to follow His servant's high example in prayerfulness, confidence in the Bible and missionary service at home and abroad'.[14]

The invitation to Kevan

It was this church which was to invite Kevan to succeed Oakley in the pastorate. Early in 1943, the church secretary at Trinity Road Chapel invited the Rev. R. J. Park to preach 'with a view' to becoming Minister. However, Mr Park replied that he had just accepted a call to Muswell Hill Baptist

[13]Carey Oakley, *From the First Day Until Now*, pp. 26-7.
[14]Carey Oakley, *From the First Day Until Now*, p. 29.

Church, but he included the names of four men whom he had recommended for consideration by his deacons as possible successors to himself at Forest Hill. Among these four was the name of Ernest Kevan. He was unknown personally to the deacons at Trinity Road, although they knew that he was a Strict Baptist.

The church secretary, Mr Long, conferred with one or two friends who knew Kevan and having received strong recommendations from them agreed with his fellow-deacons that he would go to hear Kevan speak at a nearby Baptist Church. Kevan spoke on 'The Faith'. Mr Long was so impressed with what he heard and gave such a glowing report to his fellow deacons that they unanimously agreed to him paying a visit to Kevan at his home to sound him out about the possibility of a call, which he did.

Kevan, however, showed little interest in the possibility of a call but he did agree to preach at Trinity Road Chapel six months later (September 1943). Meanwhile the conviction that Kevan was God's man for the church grew so strong that a letter was circulated to every member of Trinity Road Chapel, urging attendance on the day of his visit and at a special church meeting to follow four days later. The outcome of his visit was that the church members unanimously invited him to become their minister.[15] This invitation was qualified by a commitment to release him if he was called to full-time service with London Bible College.

Such an invitation was exceptional, but what must have seemed so remarkable to Kevan was that it should come just at the time when he was considering the invitation to London Bible College. He did not know, of course, when full-time lectures would start at the College, nor at that time could he know what his precise role would be in the College, though

[15]Kirby, *Pastor and Principal*, p. 24.

possibilities may have been discussed with Dr Lloyd-Jones. He must also have realised that it would be a large step straight from a Strict Baptist pastorate into an interdenominational college. But here was an invitation from a Calvinistic Baptist church, yet one which had an open membership and was therefore, to some extent, undenominational in ethos.

It is likely that Kevan's theological views had already undergone some modification. Earlier we saw him affirming his denial of 'duty-faith'. 'Duty-faith' was shorthand for saying that it is the duty of a sinner to believe in Christ. Many Strict Baptists denied this on the grounds that it could not be the duty of a dead sinner to perform a spiritual act of which he was incapable. In addition they believed that this turned faith into a meritorious act. In his book *Salvation*, published much later in 1963 but certainly reflecting a view held for many years, he answered the first point by saying that man is duty bound to obey whatever God says. He concluded:

> The real crux of the discussion about duty-faith, however, is the opinion that this would make faith into a 'work' of legal merit and inconsistent with grace, but since the ability to fulfil this duty is effected by the grace of the Holy Spirit, no idea of merit can be conceived of in the doing of the duty. The believer has done what he ought to do, but he has done it entirely by the enabling grace of God.[16]

Kevan's mother, in her diary, shows a reluctance to use the word 'offer' of the gospel. Whether Kevan ever shared this outlook, which was also common among Strict Baptists, is unknown. He certainly showed an early desire to spread and preach the gospel. *Salvation* also makes clear his commitment to the free offer of the gospel:

> The necessity of presenting the gospel as a 'free offer' to

[16]Kevan, *Salvation*, pp. 110-11.

> every man lies in the very nature of the gospel... God who decreed the end – the salvation of the elect – decreed also the means – the universal offer of the gospel... A universal offer does not imply a universal redemption.[17]

The invitation to London Bible College must also have forced Kevan to think through his commitment to restricted communion. He had always been a Strict Baptist, though not belonging to those who limited communion only to members of churches of the same faith and order. If he was to join the faculty of an interdenominational college he would have to be clear about what he would do if the College were to celebrate the Lord's Supper on any occasion. However, if that did not arise, or if he would be permitted to abstain on the grounds of conscience, the whole ethos of the College would be quite different from what he had known in the pastorate. He had been very happy to preach beyond his own denomination, but this was quite a different matter. He had to be prepared to make a number of adjustments if he was going to the College.

The evidence suggests that he had been distressed by the attitudes over the Lord's Supper and the controversy that he found within the Metropolitan Association. It must be concluded, I believe, that he had decided that while admitting only baptized believers to the Lord's Supper was a logical position to adopt from Scripture, it was not consistent with the undoubted Christian standing and spiritual usefulness of many who did not accept believers' baptism to refuse to sit down with them at the Lord's Table. Later, when he became Principal of the College, he would give Strict Baptist students the option of refraining from attendance at College communion services. He would also meet with those who were called to Strict Baptist churches but from a different

[17] Kevan, *Salvation,* pp. 113-15.

denominational background, in order to ensure that they were fully aware of what would be expected of them.

A further matter which would also have exercised him was his commitment to the sovereignty of God in salvation, with its corollaries of human inability, election by grace, particular redemption, and the effective call of God which issues in saving faith. The eighth point of the draft report quoted earlier stated: 'Points of theology and doctrine on which there is legitimate difference of opinion amongst Evangelical Christians, should not be taught in such a way that only one viewpoint is given, or stressed at the expense of others.' Such a position would have to be accepted in an interdenominational college. However, this statement did not mean that lecturers had to hide their convictions and the distinctive doctrines or practices of their denomination; only that they were fair in their treatment of the views of others. No-one who heard him regularly would have failed to realise his own personal commitment to believers' baptism and to Calvinism.

In the circumstances it must have seemed to him as if the call to Trinity Road Chapel was a direct God-given opportunity to prepare himself for the possibility of ministry in an interdenominational college; a transition into a new and very different form of service. And this is what it proved to be, for he accepted the invitation.

11

Trinity Road Chapel

It was a huge wrench for Kevan to leave Zion. The letter which he wrote to the Church Secretary as a formal notification to the church indicates as much; but it has a wider interest than that, so it is given in full:

September 28, 1943

My dear Bro. Smith,

I do not know how to begin to write this letter to you because of the deep surges of feeling within my heart. I am now writing to you to let you know that I have felt constrained to accept the unanimous invitation of the Baptist Church at Trinity Road, Wandsworth Common, to become their Pastor. As I intimated to you in my letter to the deacons the approach from the Trinity Road Church was totally unsought and came to me as a complete surprise. I had no idea how my name came to be thought of by them in connection with the Pastorate. There are, however, other factors of unusual leading in the whole matter which have compelled me to believe that this is the call of God.

Will you please be so kind as to bring this before the church members at their next meeting? I shall be perfectly willing to be present at that meeting if you and the brethren would like me to be there. But I would assure you that it will impose an emotional strain which will not be easy to bear.

If I were not sure that this is God's way for me I could not bear to write to you. It is only under the compulsion of

> this knowledge that I can bring myself to write. Whatever you do, please let the friends know that it is nothing in them that has occasioned this decision. I would not have anyone think for one moment that I am unhappy or dissatisfied. It is uniquely and solely 'the Lord's doing', and in that, and that alone, can I find my assurance. My ties of love to you all at 'Zion' are unspeakable, and my joy in serving God among you has been more than I can utter. I cannot say all that I feel about it, and it is no use attempting to do so. My greatest delight and comfort will be to know that you will ever love me and will invite me often into your midst. I commend you all into the loving care of the great head of the Church at whose call I came to you ten years ago, and at whose bidding I now must leave you.
>
> Your affectionate Pastor...

The sentence: 'There are, however, other factors of unusual leading in the whole matter which have compelled me to believe that this is the call of God', must surely refer to the possibilities that were opening up by the invitation to become a tutor at London Bible College. What is perhaps most striking is the way in which he asks the secretary to bring his decision to the church meeting rather than be there himself. In the event he was present at the church meeting and perhaps in the end the emotional strain was not as great as he feared, but this does reveal an aspect of his character which was not readily evident.

Kirby wrote about him:

> Ernest Kevan has been described as a fundamentally shy man. While he was greatly respected by very many people, he did not find it easy to make close friends. There was a certain diffidence about him, and he was by nature extremely sensitive and tender-hearted.[1]

[1]Kirby, *Pastor and Principal*, pp. 55-6.

This letter confirms his sensitivity; something that was hidden by his strength of character and his unwillingness to show his feelings to others. If he anticipated an emotional strain at a church meeting among those who loved him and whom he loved, then it must be concluded that he experienced such strain on other occasions.

As already seen with his two previous invitations there was a very strong sense of the call of God. But, of course, this time his sense of God's calling was not simply a matter of a call to another church. When he accepted the invitation from Trinity Road Chapel he knew that if he was called to full-time work with London Bible College the church would release him. According to Kirby he was already 'conscious of a growing "pull" in the direction of academic work',[2] though this may not be the most accurate description of what he felt. It was not so much a matter of academic work as the work of teaching biblical truth and preparing men and women for service in the church of Christ world-wide. He would never have thought of himself merely as an academic. He was supremely a preacher and a pastor and it was to reproduce himself and prepare others for Christian service in many spheres that he felt called. It was for this reason that he left those he loved and a flourishing situation in order to devote himself wholeheartedly to what he believed God was leading him to in the future.

On Saturday 1 January 1944, a farewell gathering took place in Zion. A report by one of the deacons, Mr Boorne, in the *Gospel Herald* says:

> It would be impossible to disguise the fact that there was keen sorrow in many hearts at the departure of one who, under God, has been so greatly used in building up and consolidating the Church, and who is held in such high esteem.

[2]Kirby, *Pastor and Principal*, p. 25.

Pastor O. F. Clarke, the President of the Metropolitan Association, and Pastor Robinson 'both voiced the general regret that was felt at the departure of one who, being possessed of so many gifts, had given of his best to the life and service of the Denomination.' Mr Boorne presented the Kevans with a beautifully bound copy of the Bible and a cheque, summing things up with 'a short address of sincere and heartfelt appreciation of all the loving service that that had been rendered to the Church by Pastor Kevan' also especially mentioning Mrs Kevan's contribution. The meeting concluded with a buffet tea enabling the Kevans 'to give a last handshake to the large number of friends who had gathered to wish them "God-speed".'[3]

The new pastorate

Kevan commenced his ministry at Trinity Road Chapel on 4 January 1944. In moving to Tooting at the southern end of Wandsworth Common, he was only a mile or so from where he had been brought up. This ministry was to be a short one of just under two years, and on 10 January 1946, a Service of Dedication and Prayer, conducted by Dr Lloyd-Jones, took place upon Kevan's departure to the College. In that short time strong ties of Christian love and fellowship had been forged and the Kevans were to remain in membership at Trinity Road until his death. In 1970, in order to celebrate the centenary of the church, a booklet was written entitled *From the First Day Until Now, 1870-1970*. This booklet sums up Kevan's ministry in a paragraph:

> The war was still in progress and the flying bombs were soon to follow but, in spite of all difficulties, the church prospered. The Word of God was preached and taught with

[3] *Gospel Herald* (April 1944), p. 64.

> power and Mr and Mrs Kevan endeared themselves to all. Mr Kevan became editor of *The Witness* and each month wrote three articles – About the Bible (its history and its authors), Within the Bible (an exposition of the Epistle to the Romans), and From the Bible (an introduction to the study of Christian Doctrine). A booklet entitled *The Faith and Practice of the Church Worshipping at Trinity Road Chapel* was issued for the instruction of members and friends of the Church. A team of fourteen members was appointed to assist in visitation of homes. In these and many other ways, Mr Kevan's short ministry strengthened the life of the church.[4]

The mention of flying bombs (V1s, or more colloquially, 'doodlebugs' – bombs with wings which fell out of the sky when the engine stopped, destroying whatever they fell on) recalls Sunday, 25 June 1944. On that day the Kevans' home and the homes of many other members were severely damaged. The Kevans were away on holiday at the time and 'a score or more members of the church worked in relays, clearing up the debris and fixing waterproof sheeting to the window frames.'[5] Although we cannot be sure that Mrs Kevan was with her husband in Torquay when their previous manse was bombed, it is remarkable that he should have been away from his manses on the occasions when both were bombed. 1944 proved to be another difficult year for Londoners, who experienced the 'Little Blitz' earlier in the year before the start of the German *Vergeltungswaffe* (Vengeance) attacks, by V1s beginning in June and V2s in October. Once again there was a lot of disruption with fresh evacuations of children to safer areas of the country. Looking back it is astonishing the way church life carried on and even flourished in those days.

[4]Carey Oakley, *From the First Day Until Now*, p. 29.
[5]Kirby, *Pastor and Principal*, pp. 25-26.

Kevan excelled in his talks to the children at the morning service. For a time he had a miniature letter box standing on the table before the pulpit, into which the children were invited to place their 'letters to the Minister' as well as their answers to the questions he set following his addresses. He prized the letters he received very highly. His children's addresses were models of simplicity and clarity and were of topical interest, combined with wholesome humour and obvious spiritual lessons. At times he also took the young men out for cycle rides and they greatly enjoyed these excursions. He began a weekly Bible School on Sunday mornings which was enthusiastically attended by people of all ages.

As the war ended there was a new impetus to the work. Door-to-door visitation took place and a literature stall was set up at the church. When a fair was held on Wandsworth Common, a service was arranged for the caravan dwellers at which the choir sang and Kevan gave a simple message and an invitation to attend the Chapel.[6] During his pastorate thirty-nine new members were welcomed into the church. Kirby comments: 'Rarely has a pastorate of such brief duration had such a profound and lasting effect upon a church.'[7]

Kevan wrote a small booklet entitled *The Faith and Practice of the Church Worshipping in Trinity Road Chapel.* This did not attempt to set out a complete statement of the faith and practice of the church; it was an explanation of the church's position on membership and communion. The title is careful to speak of 'the Church Worshipping in Trinity Road Chapel', distinguishing the church, that is the people, from the building. More than a third of the booklet is taken up with a historical review from the beginnings of Baptist churches in Britain up to the time of Spurgeon and the founding of the

[6]Kirby, *Pastor and Principal*, p. 26.
[7]Kirby, *Pastor and Principal*, pp. 27-8.

Trinity Road Church itself.

The church also calls itself a 'Congregational Baptist Church'. It is not quite clear whether originally this was to indicate its inclusive nature, or simply, as with Baptist churches in general, to indicate the gathered church or congregational principle, though the evidence seems to show the latter. Certainly that is where Kevan began in his booklet: '...the Church consists only of born again believers in the Lord Jesus and... it comes into existence through the voluntary association of individuals who have avowed their faith in Christ.'

He noted that the 1689 Assembly of Particular Baptist churches left the question of restricted or open communion a matter for the individual churches, pointing out that in spite of this concession a very large number actually practised strict communion. About 1829 the Strict Baptists separated from the main stream of Particular Baptists and around 1842 open membership began to be practised by some of the latter. He had gone into the matter thoroughly. He said of Spurgeon: 'He threw all his weight into the encouragement of churches which, while closed in membership, nevertheless practised open communion.'

Kirby maintains that when Kevan went to Trinity Road the Strict Baptists expressed 'no bitterness' and added, 'it would be true to say that to the end he remained *persona grata* in Strict Baptist circles.'[8] This may be going a little far. Undoubtedly some were disappointed at the step he had taken, but he certainly maintained an interest in the Strict Baptists and frequently preached in their chapels and later sent College students to preach in them too. There were probably some who were afraid that he would draw students to London Bible College who might otherwise have gone to the Strict Baptist Bible

[8]Kirby, *Pastor and Principal*, p. 25.

Institute. However, it is likely that things actually worked out for the benefit of Strict Baptist churches, for a number of students who trained at London Bible College from other church backgrounds went into Strict Baptist churches as pastors.

It has already been mentioned that the Kevans remained as members of Trinity Road. The centenary booklet referred to earlier elaborates on this:

> The years that had passed since 1946 had seen the London Bible College growing in influence at home and abroad, as it attained the highest standards of evangelical scholarship, and as a steady stream of students flowed into the ministry, into the mission field and into schools and colleges. Under God, the directing hand was Dr Kevan's. We felt very close to all this at Trinity Road for, apart from Dr Kevan and his wife, we had members and close friends on the tutorial and clerical staff as well as among the students. Though the College, of course, had first call upon his time and energy, Dr Kevan's interest in and affection for his own church grew with the passing years. During the interregnum following the ministry of Mr Price-Lewis, he gave of his energy and counsel when approached with great generosity and with great benefit to the church.[9]

The Kevans were thoroughly at home in the church and they loved the fellowship they found there. When, some years later, the Rev. Ken Paterson moved to take up the pastorate, the Kevans came round for a meal with him and his wife before the induction. When it was finished Kevan talked through the whole membership with them, showing great insight in his understanding of every one of them.

Several members of the congregation at Trinity Road were to serve on the College staff and Henry Oakley was

[9]Carey Oakley, *From the First Day Until Now*, pp. 35-6. The Rev. Price-Lewis resigned in July 1963 to go into teaching.

commemorated by the *Henry Oakley Greek Prize*; one of six prizes that could be won. H. Carey Oakley, the son of Henry Oakley, who also wrote the centenary booklet, was the first to serve. Senior Classics master at the City of London School as well as a deacon at Trinity Road, he taught Greek at London Bible College for twenty years, beginning in 1945 with evening classes. In 1952 he joined the Faculty, and gave two days a week on his retirement from teaching in 1957. He is remembered as much for his gracious character as for excellence in Greek.

Joyce Williamson served as Kevan's private secretary from 1947 up to the time of his death. Timothy and Doreen Buckley also came from Trinity Road. Tim was appointed Extension Secretary in 1950 and, additionally, in 1957 became Director of Evangelism, retiring in 1990 after forty years' service. When the Lord called Kevan to Trinity Road it was not only a time of transition and preparation for him; he found there those who would serve with him faithfully in the work of preparing men and women for the service of Christ.

12

The Beginning of London Bible College

THE WAR MEANT THAT London Bible College had to start in a small way and the work gradually gained momentum. In October 1943, evening classes commenced and these ran through to the middle of December. Graham Scroggie lectured on 'From Genesis to Revelation'; Kevan on 'The Resurrection of Christ'; Dr Lloyd-Jones on 'The Task of the Christian Church'; E. J. Poole-Connor on 'The Second Advent of Christ', and J. W. Ewing lectured on 'The Inspiration of the Bible'. There was also a parallel course of missionary lectures, though this was not repeated as the response was not great – perhaps not altogether surprising in 1943.

In January 1944, Kevan was appointed to the first faculty of the College with two Anglicans, Rev. Frank Colquhoun and Rev. L. F. E. Wilkinson. Wilkinson was later to become Principal of Oak Hill College and was known by irreverent students as Elfie, a name derived from his initials. Harold Rowdon says:

> The work of the faculty which had been constituted in 1944 was not primarily that of teaching. Its brief was 'to organize and plan' the teaching of the college, though this by no means precluded its members from playing their part in the actual teaching.[1]

Colquhoun recalled:

[1]Rowdon, *The First 25 Years*, p. 48.

> I shall always regard it as one of the great privileges of my life to have been associated with the beginnings of the London Bible College, and so to have enjoyed for many years the close friendship of Ernest Kevan. In the very early days, during the war, when the College was far more of a dream than a reality – when in fact there was no 'college' as such, and certainly no principal – he and I were members of a small group known rather grandiosely as the Teaching Faculty, presided over by the late L. F. E. Wilkinson. This body was responsible for planning the work of the future college on its academic side, and we were the very first lecturers when evening classes began in 1944.
>
> It was at this time, as we met and made our plans together, that Ernest Kevan's far-seeing wisdom so clearly revealed itself. He, perhaps more than any of us, recognised the necessity of maintaining a high standard of evangelical scholarship and insisted that the new college must offer its students facilities for obtaining the requisite degrees and diplomas of London University. And it was he who was largely responsible for working out the details of the curriculum and determining the courses of study to be pursued.[2]

In the autumn of 1944, a three year course of evening classes was introduced comprising 'thirty-six subjects which were to be covered, four per term, two per night, on two nights of the week.' This syllabus was to remain substantially the same for many years and, with examinations, enabled students to gain a College Diploma. In 1946 evening classes also began for the Certificate of Proficiency in Religious Knowledge of the University of London.

One student who commenced in 1944 wrote of her experiences:

> I eagerly awaited the day of the first lecture. The room

[2]*College Review*, Memorial Issue (Autumn Term 1965), p. 4.

> where it was to be held... was in the Court House of St Andrews Church, Holborn. The church itself had been badly bombed. On the first Friday I arrived in good time to find the stairs blocked by eager Bible students queuing up to register. Perforce the lecture started late, as people kept coming in and the room could hardly have held any more. We sat at tables facing each other and at right angles to the lecturer... The atmosphere of the Court House is reminiscent of a College. Through the leaded windows could be seen the gently moving leaves of the plane trees, and in the evening the traffic of the day lessened to a murmur. One thing disturbed the tranquillity. We were not allowed to forget the war was still on. In 1945 we would hear the fly bombs, but did not allow them to interfere with the lecture. Usually the speaker did not appear to hear them, and mercifully none fell near... During the six courses on Doctrine by the Rev. E. F. Kevan, I could almost feel my brain expanding to grasp the expounding of the wonderful Divine Plan.[3]

Another early evening class student was P. G. Eyers. Kevan noticed that he consistently gained very high marks. On enquiring further it was discovered that he was an experienced teacher with good qualifications, belonging to the Brethren. He became a tutor at the College for five years until his early death at the age of forty-seven.

Correspondence courses began in 1944, the first prospectus stating:

> The courses are available to all students, irrespective of age, occupation or education; but it should be pointed out that the Lessons will aim at a high standard of general efficiency and will involve real work and effort on the part of the student.[4]

[3]Rowdon, *The First 25 Years*, pp. 95-6.
[4]Rowdon, *The First 25 Years*, pp. 98-9.

The first course was 'An Introduction to the Bible' prepared by Kevan, and other courses followed at intervals. Kevan started his series on Christian doctrine with 'The Doctrine of the Work of Christ' and went on to cover the full range of doctrine, also preparing the course on 'Homiletics'.

1,200 students had already enrolled for correspondence courses by December 1945. Many of those who attended evening classes or who took correspondence courses in the early days were Sunday school or Bible class teachers; from the beginning it had been intended to give help to these. While the evening classes were taking place, the correspondence courses being written and sent out, and the full-time syllabus was being prepared, Kevan was still a pastor, serving large and busy churches, and that in a time of war. His workload was enormous and his energy seems to have been almost inexhaustible.

Post-war problems

In October 1945, just a few months after the war had finished, Kevan was appointed to be the first, and at that stage, only resident tutor of London Bible College. The full-time college was to commence in January 1946, when he would have completed his pastorate at Trinity Road Chapel. This was a great change in his life, and though the basic syllabus had already been agreed there must still have been a great deal of preparation that was necessary as he continued his work in his last two months of pastoral ministry.

The immediate post-war conditions need to be appreciated, for this was very far from being a promising time to be starting a new college. By the end of the war, thousands of houses, churches and other public buildings in London had been bombed beyond repair. Gaunt ruins rose from brambles and thorns covering the rubble of a myriad bomb sites. The grime of war and London smogs – smoky fogs – had tarnished everything in sight. A recent book describing conditions at the end of the war concludes a long and depressing paragraph like this; 'Meat rationed, butter rationed, lard rationed, margarine rationed, sugar rationed, tea rationed, cheese rationed, jam rationed, eggs rationed, sweets rationed, soap rationed, clothes rationed. Make do and mend.'[5]

Austerity could only get more severe, as indeed it did. The same book quotes a clear-sighted realist:

> The Government will have to face up to the job of convincing the country that controls and hardships are as necessarily part of a bankrupt peace as they were of a desperate war. Every inch of useable English soil will still have to be made to grow food. People are suddenly realising that in the enormous economic blitz that has just begun, their problems may be as serious as the blitz they so recently scraped through.[6]

Christmas Day 1944 had been the coldest Christmas Day for sixty years and in January 1947 there began the longest and coldest spell of the twentieth century. To make matters worse there was a lack of coal and in London, the Midlands and North West, householders had to do without electricity every day for three hours from 9 a.m. and two hours from 2 p.m. Rationing and austerity measures continued on into the early fifties.

In spite of all this the full-time college opened in January 1946, with seven students, though others from several missionary societies joined them for lectures. It began in premises in Highbury New Park, north London, rented for a nominal sum from the China Inland Mission, as the Overseas

[5]David Kynaston, *Austerity Britain 1945-48: A World to Build*, (London: Bloomsbury, 2008), p. 19.
[6]Kynaston, *Austerity*, p. 103.

Missionary Fellowship was then known. This was 'a house of four storeys, a sub-basement and rooms suitable for use as classrooms as well as for bedroom accommodation'.[7] One of those first students was Murdo Gordon. He wrote:

> My first meeting with Mr Kevan took place when I was interviewed about my application to enter the London Bible College. About that meeting I remember very little. The second meeting was more memorable. A few days before the time came to join the College, then at Highbury New Park, I called round to leave some possessions in my room. The door was opened by no less a person than the Principal, but how unlike the carefully groomed person we usually knew, he appeared on this occasion! He had obviously been white-washing a room![8]

Murdo Gordon originally came from the Isle of Skye. He was brought to saving faith in London during the war. He took a BD degree at the College, and after two pastorates in England became Principal of the Bible Institute of South Africa, one of a succession of students from the College who were principals there. A fine scholar as well as pastor, he contributed to the first edition of the *New Bible Dictionary*, published by Inter-Varsity Press. Another of that first group, William Oram, said:

> Mr Kevan himself conducted most of the studies, though one or two additional lecturers also came in for certain subjects. The smallness of the College in no sense detracted from its high aims academically, morally or spiritually.[9]

Only a few months after the College began Kevan was unanimously appointed Principal.

[7]Kirby, *Pastor and Principal*, p. 29.
[8]*College Review*, Memorial Issue, pp. 6-7.
[9]*College Review*, Memorial Issue, p. 7.

Kevan was invited to join the College staff in 1943 but was only appointed Principal in 1946. He had, of course, no college training and all his experience up to that time had been in the pastorate. The likelihood is that it was anticipated that he would become Principal, but that both the committee and he considered it best to take things step by step. Kevan was doubtless grateful that he was given time to demonstrate that he could adapt himself to this new role and those behind the College were clearly appreciative of the way in which he proved himself.

A personal insight

Kirby explains that Kevan 'did not keep a full diary throughout his life.' He does, however, provide some diary jottings that Kevan made at this period. Presumably these were passed to him by Mrs Kevan, but no other diary records appear to have survived:

> Friday, 26th April 1946 – Up at 6.30 a.m. Prayer 7-7.30 a.m. Gal.3:27 – I have 'put on Christ' and therefore He should be seen when I am seen. God reminded me again that the College work is His, and I have but to do His bidding. O God, keep me in this trustful place.
>
> Monday, 29th April 1946 – Up at 6.0 a.m. Prayer at 7-7.30 a.m. It was hard to pray. Summer term begins.
>
> Tuesday, 30th April 1946 – Up at 5.30 a.m. Prayer 6-6.30 a.m. I told the Lord I trusted Him for grace and strength and wisdom. I told the Lord I trusted Him with the lectures as I now put myself into the work... Lord, make me one who is wholly devoted to Thee.
>
> Wednesday, 1st May 1946 – Up at 5.30 a.m. Prayer 6-6.30 a.m. Read in II Kings, chapter 9, of the unexpected divine call to Jehu. Wondered what the message was for me. O

> Lord, keep me humble, but ready enough to do Thy will wherever it takes me. Lord, make me just a CHANNEL. Help me to lead my students closer to Thee; give me the grace as I preside at the meals. O give my mind Thy light for the lectures, and power of clear expression.[10]

This gives a rare insight into his inner life. I remember I once went to see him and we talked about prayer, which I must have found difficult at the time.[11] He said something along these lines to me: 'I often find that when I come to pray it is helpful to remind myself that "he that cometh to God must believe that he is, and that he is a rewarder of them that diligently seek him"'. His words, and his whole manner, seem to fit exactly with these diary entries. Kirby comments: 'It is clear that Ernest Kevan was deeply conscious of his need of divine guidance for each step of the way in these formative weeks and months of the College's life.'[12]

Continuing development

Another early concern was finance. In 1943, six foundation gifts had been received amounting to £1,500 and there was £120 towards a building fund. By January 1946 this had been used up and the board of directors unanimously agreed on the following policy: 'To prepare each year a budget estimate of the cost of providing tuition, board and lodging for the ensuing twelve months and deduct from this amount the gifts of the Christian friends of the College for the preceding year and base the fees per student on this net cost. In this way each student would be expected to look to the Lord for the supply of money which the College needed to make

[10]Kirby, *Pastor and Principal*, pp. 30-31.
[11]I studied at London Bible College from 1957 to 1960.
[12]Kirby, *Pastor and Principal*, p. 31.

expenditure and income balance.'[13] This policy meant that many churches began to help students with support and led to an ongoing interest in the work of the College. At a later stage local authorities were able to give grants to students, though I have not been able to discover when this began.

Not long after the College had begun in Highbury New Park, John Laing (later Sir John Laing) offered some premises in Marylebone Road rent-free for a period of three to five years. This was a site in the centre of London, close to Baker Street underground station and the Evangelical Library. But the move meant more work. An article in *Crusade* magazine says:

> The move-in presented more trials and difficulties; seven or eight people had to move in while there was only one tap in the establishment. The Principal and his staff again lent a hand with painting and decorating; retiring, after their day's work, to the beneficent provisions made by the Borough Council for a bath.[14]

Permits were needed to buy furniture, so the College relied on gifts and second-hand shops to obtain a motley variety of chairs, beds and chests of drawers.

Autumn 1946, the beginning of the first full academic year, saw the College with twenty-three full-time students, four of them women. Unfortunately we do not know all the domestic arrangements at this time. In 1947 there were sixty full-time students of whom thirty-four were in residence and the rest attended each day from their homes or lodgings. In addition another twenty-four came in for many of the lectures: missionaries on furlough, ministers taking a refresher course and fourteen from the China Inland Mission.

[13] Rowdon, *The First 25 Years*, p. 84.
[14] 'The London Bible College, Today and Tomorrow', in *Crusade* (February 1957), pp. 10-12.

Whether Mrs Kevan, who had passed her fiftieth birthday when she and her husband took up residence in the College, had any specific responsibilities or not she was doubtless very much involved, and living on the premises would mean that she must have felt a concern that all student needs were met. There was a matron and two cooks to care for the most obvious material needs in 1947. Perhaps we can read between the lines a little in considering these comments from early students.

Raymond Ash, who later became a tutor, wrote:

> My student days were in the early years of the College, when, although there were many things it did not have, it did have a front garden! The rain not infrequently came through the ceiling, and the pipes on the walls of the old basement used to wander about going nowhere in particular! Mr and Mrs Kevan lived in the College in those days, and I remember how I missed him when he was not around. We really did not know how much he and his wife concerned themselves with our welfare.

And Bill Oram adds:

> In those early days there was a sense of domestic family life which cannot possibly be experienced in the tremendous expansion and development which has come to the College over the past seventeen years.[15]

Within eighteen months the accommodation was already proving inadequate and sleeping facilities for forty men students were provided in the Victoria area. The Kevans moved out in 1949, thus creating more space for classrooms, but it became clear that either another building had to be found or else the Marylebone building would need to be demolished

[15] *College Review*, Memorial Issue (Autumn Term 1965), pp. 6-7.

and a new purpose-built college erected in its place. In the end this latter alternative became the only realistic possibility. After difficult negotiations, and some setbacks, a new building was completed covering the whole site, with the Times Furnishing Company occupying the top three floors. The College, with the basement, ground and first floors, moved in at the beginning of 1958, and the official opening took place in the May of that year.

Prior to this there was a 'Babylonian exile' of over three years while lectures took place in the Chiltern Hall[16] a few streets away and in Aldis House, just around the corner from the College site. This had been bought as a hostel and reverted back once the new building was in use. The whole period proved a testing time, but 'a strong spirit of faith and prayer among students and staff' was recorded, and 'a deep assurance had settled in the hearts of many that the Lord might be purposing to enable us to raise the whole sum required in gifts from the Lord's people.'[17] In the event the bulk of the money came through the intervention of the Times Furnishing Company, but there is little doubt that Kevan would have seen this as the direct provision of the Lord.

[16]It was in this building, 78b Chiltern Street, that The Banner of Truth Trust began its publication ministry at the beginning of 1958.
[17]Rowdon, *The First 25 Years*, p. 79.

13

The College Principal

THIS IS A BOOK about Ernest Kevan, not about London Bible College. But something must be said about members of the faculty, although there is no attempt to mention all those who served. First, it is right to remember that at the beginning of 1946, Kevan had been a pastor for nearly twenty-two years. Kirby was to write:

> Although the name of Ernest Kevan will no doubt be remembered primarily as being that of a college principal, first and foremost he was a pastor. He was never more successful as a pastor than when he occupied the Principal's chair.[1]

This is undoubtedly correct, and it moulded his attitude to the College and its students. At the end of the first full year of the College, in the Annual Report for 1947, he wrote:

> Spiritual blessing in the individual and corporate life of the College has been most marked. The Principal's study has been the scene not only of discussions about various aspects of study, but of many heart-searching spiritual conversations and times of prayer. The privilege of these moments is indescribable. There is a prayerful earnestness which characterises the whole life of the College. God's blessing on our learning has been manifested in our living, and by means of a walk with God our ability to learn has been increased likewise.

[1]Kirby, *Pastor and Principal*, p. 5.

At the same time it must be stated that while he was a pastor to his students as well as a Principal, the discipline in which he lectured was primarily Christian doctrine, or, to give it its academic names, Systematic Theology or Dogmatic Theology. This is a theology which seeks to bring together all that the whole Bible has to say on the great themes of God, Jesus Christ, salvation and so on. If Randall, looking back over fifty years of the College's life, is correct when he says: 'Certainly LBC has contributed more to biblical scholarship than to systematic theology'[2], then I think Kevan would be a little disappointed. While he recognized the absolute necessity of sound biblical scholarship, he believed that this should lead on to an enhanced understanding of the greatness and glory of God and the magnificence of the gospel of grace. His pastoring was theological and his theology was pastoral.

The Faculty

It is not surprising that most of the early tutors had themselves served in the pastoral ministry and this, too, was beneficial to the atmosphere of the College. Kevan tried to keep a denominational mix in the Faculty, but generally it was Baptists who predominated. Among those who served for long periods of time were Rev. J. C. Connell, Dr H. D. MacDonald, Rev. Owen Thomas, Dr Guthrie and Dr Rowdon. Mr Connell served as Director of Studies and Dr MacDonald as Vice-Principal. Mr Thomas, an Anglican, the College Chaplain, had an arts degree in which music had been a component. So he took the course on 'The Music of the Church' and in the timetable for the autumn term of 1957 he is listed as lecturing on 'Dueteronomy'!

Dr Guthrie, one of the first students of the College, became a well-known scholar with many books to his credit. He

[2]Randall, *Educating Evangelicalism*, p. 276.

suffered from a painful stammer which he manfully conquered. He was a very gentle and humble man, his manner belying his considerable intellect. Dr Rowdon, a member of the Brethren, specialised in Church History. It ought to be mentioned that from 1955 there was a lady tutor; firstly Miss Rosina Parker and some years later Miss Margaret Manton, who had been a student at the College.

The real question is how they worked together as a team and how they related to Kevan, and he to them. Dr Rowdon said recently,

> I think I can truthfully say that we all respected Kevan so much that relationships were very positive and we were prepared to respect his views even when we were not in full agreement with them – not that this was often.[3]

That was said with the benefit of looking back over the years. When Kevan died, Rev. Harry Stringer, a Methodist minister and one of the early tutors who served for seven years, paid this tribute:

> It is impossible to imagine a man more fitted to be the first principal of the London Bible College. Intellectually, theologically, spiritually and as a leader, he was eminently suited to the task. It was amazing, seeing he had had no college training himself. He never was overbearing, or obtruded his own personality, but he was a real leader of men, and those who have been on his team which he gathered round him will endorse this. He was one of the truly great men I have known.[4]

Ian Randall in his book on the College refers to two events in the 1950s and 60s which need at least some comment. Mr

[3]Personal communication between Dr Rowdon and the author.
[4]*College Review*, Memorial Issue (Autumn Term 1965), p. 5.

H. L. Ellison, who had given evening classes for the College, became tutor in Old Testament in 1949. He wrote several books that were widely used at the time including, *Men Spake from God*,[5] on the Old Testament prophets and an exposition of *Ezekiel*.[6] The original Doctrinal Basis of the College had as its second point: 'The Divine inspiration and supreme authority of the Holy Scriptures', but in January 1953, this was enlarged to read:

> The Divine inspiration and supreme authority of the Holy Scriptures. For this purpose the Divine inspiration of the Holy Scriptures is to be taken to mean that the Scriptures are God-breathed, and that while no attempt is made to define the method of inspiration, such inspiration results in language which is the Word of God, and that the Scriptures are thus the Word of God by virtue of their inspiration and do not merely become so in the context of human experience.

According to Randall, the decision to make this addition was taken at a faculty meeting. In view of this, it is extraordinary that Ellison, a member of the faculty, should write in an article in *The Evangelical Quarterly* in October 1954, sentiments like this:

> To call the Bible the Word of God without some such qualifications, spoken or understood, suggests that the work of inspiration ended with the finishing of the record, and that the Bible now functions by virtue of some inherent power, so that anything that man may infer from it is necessarily legitimate. We do well to widen our conception of inspiration. The writing of the Scriptures was only the half-way house in the process of inspiration; it only reaches its goal and conclusion as God is revealed through them to the reader or hearer...

[5] H. L. Ellison, *Men Spake from God* (London: Paternoster Press, 1952).
[6] H. L. Ellison, *Ezekiel* (London: Paternoster Press, 1956).

> Possibly the strongest divisive influence has been that of dogmatic theology... God could have made Himself known in a series of theological propositions, but He used instead the experiences of men... Any effort to formulate men's living experience of God into a formal and self-consistent system is bound to be inadequate and to omit factors which for others are of vital importance.[7]

The following minute records Kevan's words to the directors:

> The Principal reported that his attention had been drawn to an article written by Mr Ellison and which had appeared in *The Evangelical Quarterly*. It presented views contrary to those held by the College, and it was felt by *the members of the tutorial staff* [my italics] and by a number of friends, including Dr Martyn Lloyd-Jones, that the article was undermining the position of the College. In the circumstances the matter had been brought to the attention of the Board. The position had been explained to Mr Ellison who felt that it would be wise for him to resign and a letter to this effect had now been received.[8]

The directors accepted the resignation, but Ellison was permitted to continue for the rest of the academic year, that is, for another two and a half terms. Randall comments that this episode was very painful for Ellison; it was surely painful for Kevan, too. Very regrettably Ellison gave a highly personal farewell address in which he spoke of 'the criticisms of the past-bound orthodox, the fears of the upholders of some dogmatic system that see their structure threatened and the frowns of those who would confine the truth to one

[7]H. L. Ellison, 'Some Thoughts on Inspiration', in *The Evangelical Quarterly*, 26:4 (1954), pp. 210-17. Available at http://www.biblicalstudies.org.uk/articles_evangelical_quarterly.php (accessed 9 February 2012).
[8]Randall, *Educating Evangelicalism*, p. 86.

tradition.' Randall adds: 'For Ellison, the "free" man was a cause of "offence to those who hug their chains and call them ornaments."'[9] Kevan's response was simply to read some Scripture verses including some of Paul's outspoken criticisms of the motives of those who questioned his own integrity.[10]

The fact is that the academic honesty and integrity of Kevan and the rest of the faculty were impugned before the whole student body. Randall says that Ellison revelled in being provocative and Rowdon described him to me as something of a maverick. There were students who appreciated his lectures on the Old Testament, and some felt sympathy with him. However, in order to uphold the integrity of the faculty and the College's commitment to its doctrinal basis, as well as for the spiritual good of the students, his resignation was inevitable.

For all his real insights into the Old Testament, and the value of being made to think, Ellison was not a safe guide for students. Not long afterwards he wrote a commentary on the book of Job, referring in the Preface to 'a period of suffering and distress, which profoundly affected my understanding.'[11] It is sad to read later of:

> ...a constant danger in any church, where the theological manual threatens to displace the Bible as the text-book for the young. It is always easier to teach the adolescent theology than the Bible. The danger is that he will become as orthodox but as empty as Elihu shows himself in this chapter.[12]

[9]Randall, *Educating Evangelicalism,* p. 87.
[10]I am grateful for some comments from John Eyers who was present on this occasion.
[11]H. L. Ellison, *From Tragedy to Triumph: The Message of the Book of Job*, (London: Paternoster Press, 1958), p. 9.
[12]Ellison, *Tragedy*, p. 110.

Mr Ellison was succeeded by the Rev. J. C. J. Waite, an old student of the College. Some of his lectures, as for example on Jeremiah, were outstanding and it is a pity he never put anything into print. In time he became dissatisfied with the BD syllabus and the need to consider so much liberal interpretation of the Old Testament. He left in 1961 to become the Principal of the South Wales Bible College (now the Wales Evangelical School of Theology).

Randall secondly mentions tensions which were raised by some of the articles written by Dr Ralph Martin in 1964. He writes: 'Kevan, when asked to comment, stated that "Dr Martin's reviews had attracted attention in that they were over-generous to the liberal position."'[13] At this point it is valuable to realise that all members of the teaching staff including the principal, and the secretary, had not only to agree in writing to the doctrinal basis of the College prior to their appointment, but they were required to do so 'at least once in every calendar year'. Also it was the governors who had 'the power to appoint, control and dismiss, and to define the duties of, the principal, the teaching staff, the secretary, and other employees and may make such regulations in the exercise of this as they think fit.'[14]

Kevan made it plain that Ralph Martin's 'evangelical views coincided exactly with his fellow members of the Faculty', but he considered that Martin, as a young scholar, tended 'to confuse the line between conservative and liberal views'.[15] Here the picture is different in that Kevan was clearly supportive of Martin. Martin, perhaps, tended to adopt the more detached method of academics in his reviews, but the difficulty of this for an institution like London Bible College is that members

[13] Randall, *Educating Evangelicalism*, p. 128.
[14] Memorandum and Articles of Association of London Bible College, 1959.
[15] Randall, *Educating Evangelicalism*, p. 128.

of the Christian public may judge that it is beginning to be open to liberal sentiments. Martin, who had joined the College in 1959, left in 1965 to become an assistant lecturer at Manchester University.

Martin himself was understandably reluctant to comment when I spoke with him recently. I believe he felt the governors had too much power; they, however, doubtless recognised their responsibilities as guardians of the commitment of the College to evangelicalism. In these instances Kevan found that it was no easy responsibility being principal of a College committed to the Bible. Difficulties with members arise from time to time in a church, but in a College which was under scrutiny by the evangelical Christian public on which it depended for its support the situation was far more difficult, requiring great wisdom, fair-mindedness and faithfulness. Moreover, Kevan was answerable to the governors who kept a fairly firm grip on what took place in the College.

Student problems

If there were problems with some members of the Faculty with which Kevan had to grapple, what about students? I am myself only aware of one incident that might be described as disciplinary, and this will be referred to in the next paragraph. There must have been times when students were rebuked in private by Kevan, but these remained private and unknown. Most students were rather over-awed by him, though gradually this altered as they got to know him better. He made a point of talking personally to each student in his or her first term. Many of them were glad to see him about aspects of their Christian life and the problems that they experienced and, while he could be direct in what he said if he believed that that was necessary, in general he was very sympathetic and helpful.

Randall mentions that 'in 1958 there was discussion of the stance to be adopted over "participation of students in professional acting." It was agreed that this was inconsistent with membership of LBC.'[16] This must have arisen because one student was acting on the West End stage in a production of 'Cat on a Hot Tin Roof' and a photograph of him appeared in a national newspaper – though there was no mention of his attendance at London Bible College. He only appeared at College for a short time. It is possible that he was given the choice of continuing at College if he gave up his acting, but if so he chose the latter. Randall, who does not mention the actual incident at all, notes that at the time the attitude was that 'the theatre was emphatically "worldly"'. This is true; but Kevan would not have believed that someone who was playing every night at the theatre could be devoting himself to his studies as he should. 'Professional acting' is not exactly a part-time leisure activity consistent with a college course.

Inevitably students tended to group together according to their beliefs or practices. It would be true to say that in the late fifties there was 'a Reformed group', though there was nothing formal about this and it had no definite boundary. Randall also mentions 'the hostility of a small group of students towards the view of the Bible held by LBC.' He also adds that no action was taken as they were all in their final year.[17] It may be that some of these came from a rather wider evangelical background in any case, but it is not surprising that a few struggled with liberal views of the Bible which were widespread in many churches. I remember hearing one student, probably on the fringe of this group, saying something

[16]Randall, *Educating Evangelicalism*, p. 98.
[17]Randall, *Educating Evangelicalism*, p. 101.

like this: 'I sometimes feel like going to Mr Kevan and saying, "Make me into an evangelical."'

Student days, whether in theological college or elsewhere, are days of finding out, of hearing new opinions, of re-examining what you were brought up to believe. It is disconcerting to be confronted with all sorts of new ideas, some of which appear to undermine beliefs you took for granted. Christian students and students at evangelical colleges are not immune from doubts, nor can they be simply protected from views which challenge their own. There is little doubt that the vast majority of students were very thankful for the teaching, and the attitude of Kevan and the Faculty, especially at the personal level, when it came to liberal and anti-Christian attacks on the evangelical faith. The great majority of those who were at London Bible College in the time of Kevan's principalship continued in their evangelicalism. Of those who have become liberal, it is likely that more did so after leaving college than during their student days. Sadly one or two subsequently gave up the faith altogether.

Randall also says that Pentecostalism and charismatic renewal began to affect London Bible College in the sixties,[18] but this is not quite accurate. There was a sizeable group of students in the late fifties who were very influenced by Pentecostal teaching and practice. This did not apparently affect their denominational commitment and was therefore similar to the later charismatic movement. In February 1959 one of the students, Colin White, was seriously injured playing rugby for the College team. As he lay in a coma in hospital frequent prayer meetings for his recovery took place. I was present at one of these when, half way through the meeting, one student who was involved with this group rose to say, 'I'm not praying that Colin will be healed, I'm praising God

[18] Randall, *Educating Evangelicalism*, p. 139.

that he is going to be healed', and others had the same assurance. But he died.

Dr Kevan wrote in *The College Review*:

> The College deeply sorrows over the death of Colin White on Thursday, 26th February, one of the most lovable men the College has known. The mysteries of life and death are beyond our present power to solve, but we believe in the love and wisdom of our Heavenly Father. A life of such usefulness to God seemed to be before Colin, and this is now cut off; but eternity alone will reveal whether God did not work more by Colin's death than even by his life.[19]

Kevan was a great help to those who had been so sure that he was going to be healed. They did not necessarily give up their Pentecostal views, but these were tempered by the experience of disappointment and mistaken certainty.

Another student incident may be mentioned. In one issue of *The College Review* an article appeared on the World Council of Churches, written by a student. It acknowledged the criticisms that evangelicals had but was also obviously quite favourably disposed to the WCC. When Kevan saw the article, which must have slipped through whatever editorial net there was, he had the article withdrawn and the whole issue reprinted (though not before some students had received a copy). He was clearly not only displeased with the article itself, but also felt that many Christians who supported the College would be distressed by it and wonder why it had been published and whether this meant the College endorsed its sentiments. After this the students had their own internal magazine, *Areopagus*, and *The College Review* continued as a student magazine available to the public.

Kevan was always gracious in his manner but he could also

[19]*College Review* (Spring Term 1959), p. 22.

be clear-cut and outspoken when he believed it to be necessary. In a book review he wrote:

> The real battle today is with the fifth columnist, who wears our own uniform, but is in the camp of the enemy. In other words, the great terms which for centuries have served to enshrine the great and precious truths of the gospel are now used to represent alien ideas. There is scarcely a word of the gospel vocabulary which has not been stolen away in this manner.[20]

Lecturer and preacher

At the beginning Kevan did most of the lecturing, but as the College grew and other members of the Faculty were appointed so his own lecturing workload diminished; most of the Faculty specialising in some particular discipline. The pattern that emerged was that each Faculty member lectured on four days out of the five-day College week. In the fifties Kevan followed this pattern, except for the summer term, when he only lectured on three days.

Because of his administrative work he did not lecture as much as the other tutors, and after being diagnosed with angina in the summer of 1958 his lecturing reduced even more. By this time Mr Connell was taking some of the Dogmatics – that is, Christian Doctrine – lectures and when Ralph Martin came in the autumn of 1959 he took on other Dogmatic subjects. He was, however, much more a New Testament scholar and he preferred the exegesis of New Testament books to lecturing in theology. Kevan was in India for the Spring term of 1960 and in the Summer term he only lectured twice a week. Ill health and the pressure of other responsibilities were reducing his contribution to lecturing, though it must be remembered that he also lectured at evening classes, as did the other tutors.

[20]Quoted in Carey Oakley, *From the First Day Until Now*, pp. 44-5.

We can divide Kevan's lecture subjects into three groups. First, came lectures on the Bible: Bible – Inspiration; Bible – Interpretation; and Prophetic Principles and Apocalypse. Second, were theological subjects: Theological Prolegomena (or Introduction), followed by God; Man and Sin; Person of Christ; Work of Christ; Grace; Church; and Eschatology. Thirdly, there were his lectures on Pastoral Theology, and then Homiletics, plus Practical Homiletics, in which men had to preach to the class and assess each other's sermons.

It was this last group of subjects that he was most concerned to keep for himself and it is probably these lectures for which he is most remembered. The subjects have been grouped in this way because I believe we have here in outline his whole approach to the work of ministry: proper exegesis and interpretation of a God-given Bible leading to an understanding of truth, which is then to be ministered in preaching and pastoral work.

There were, of course, set books for each subject and students were expected to have prepared for the lectures by reading. There was some debate early on about what books should be recommended and what not mentioned, but there were always a number of books not written by evangelicals that appeared on the book list, particularly for the university courses. This was partly because at that time there was a paucity of scholarly books written by evangelicals. Most students greatly appreciated Kevan's lectures, though perhaps not all. Some probably found them unnecessarily dogmatic, to others they were too Calvinistic and to others again, not Calvinistic enough! This latter arose because Kevan was always mindful that London Bible College was an interdenominational college, and it was necessary not to stress one viewpoint at the expense of others.

In dealing with election and predestination he said: 'the doctrine of unconditional election is that view which from apostolic times can claim to be in very large measure the historic doctrine of the Church.' Consequently, most of one lecture was spent on that subject, including answering the objections raised against it. Here is his final paragraph:

> According to the view represented by the doctrine of unconditional election it is God and not man who determines who are to be saved. This question may truly be said to be the turning point or watershed of the two great systems of theology into which the thinking of the Church has been divided throughout the ages. This point of conditional or unconditional election to salvation involves all other matters of difference, namely, the nature of original sin, the motive of God in providing redemption, the nature and design of the work of Christ, and the nature of Divine grace, or the work of the Holy Spirit. 'Thus', says Dr Hodge, 'in a great measure, the whole system of theology, and of necessity the character of our religion, depend upon the view taken of this particular question, it is, therefore, a question of the highest practical importance, and not a matter of idle speculation' (*Systematic Theology*, Vol. II, pp. 330, 331).[21]

His pastoral theology lectures were especially appreciated because they came out of a wealth of experience and he did not hesitate to give examples and illustrations from his own life. Men who anticipated entering the pastoral ministry themselves were required to attend these lectures, and so also were the women students – in case they married ministers (as not a few did)! It may be that others were at liberty to attend if they wished. Certainly there were always a large number of students present.

In some respects Kevan, inevitably, was a child of his times, and in some things he was unnecessarily prescriptive. He

[21]This is taken from duplicated lecture notes on the Doctrine of Grace. It is the conclusion of four lectures on Election and Predestination.

believed that ministers should always be treated with respect – no first names for him – for the ministry's sake, not out of personal pride. He taught that ministers should treat everyone alike in the congregation and have no special friends within it. His perspective on this came out in a sermon at the end of an academic year when, addressing particularly the leaving students, he said, 'I commend you to a life of loneliness.'

There was one occasion which will always be remembered by those who were there. Kevan was always immaculately dressed, and in one of his lectures he was stressing the need to be neat and tidy in appearance. As he was speaking Margaret Manton, then a student, noticed that there was a thread of white cotton hanging from the hem of his jacket. Greatly daring, she pointed this out to him, provoking a great deal of laughter in which he joined heartily. A little later she felt rather conscience-stricken at what she had done. The next morning just before College prayers she came up to him in the entrance hall, intending to apologise. However, before she could open her mouth he came towards her, and said, 'Miss Manton, just look me over before I go into Chapel, will you, please?'[22]

When it came to preaching he was concerned that there should be nothing about the minister's dress which could draw the attention of listeners away from the message. So no check suits or loud ties; pocket flaps either all in or all out, no row of pens in the top pocket or colourful handkerchief. And, of course, beware of gestures or mannerisms that are inappropriate, or would distract or cause people to laugh. What he would have thought of preachers with no jacket or no tie is not hard to guess, and as for wearing shorts! In the main his homiletic lectures contained good, sound sense, but some students later found parts of them unsuitable for their

[22]Kirby, *Pastor and Principal*, p. 51.

congregations. It might have been helpful if he had also told us the sort of message that was given at the Held-Out-Hand, but he did not envisage that sort of congregation at Sunday services.

Generally speaking he was a good preacher himself, but one would not compare him with Dr Lloyd-Jones, for their styles were totally different. He was not the greatest of orators, but his sermons were well-thought out and structured and he presented solid truth in a way that could be understood. One sermon he preached at College was based on 'Be ye therefore perfect, even as your Father which is in heaven is perfect' (*Matt.* 5:48). Frequently through that sermon he said: 'I am a perfectionist'; not with a capital 'P', but in the usual sense of the word. And he was; he aspired to perfection for himself, for his heavenly Father's sake, and he wanted his students to aspire to the same high end.

Another sermon at the end of a College year was based on Jeremiah 12:5: 'If thou hast run with the footmen, and they have wearied thee, then how canst thou contend with horses? and if in the land of peace, wherein thou trustedst, they wearied thee, then how wilt thou do in the swelling of Jordan?' In other words, 'If you find it tough in college, what will it be like on the mission field or in the pastorate or teaching?' While he wanted to prepare his students for what lay ahead, he would also remind them of where their resources would be found.

Kevan's preaching, of course, was not confined to College. In common with the other tutors, and men students after their first year, he was often out preaching on Sundays. On one occasion a student was due to preach at West Hill Strict Baptist Chapel in Wandsworth, but to their great surprise Dr Kevan turned up instead! The student had been taken ill at the last minute and as Kevan was free he took his place.

Selected quotations from Kevan's lectures on homiletics:

Read Christ out of a passage, not into it.

After the first flush of enthusiasm with a theme we often find ourselves empty. The answer is to stick at it. Never give in!

Allow a text a 'period of incubation' in your mind and heart.

Come to a text by the route that the writer came to it.

We must not only know Hebrew or Greek but have a doctrinal theology of the Bible. Check any teaching of a verse with the teaching of the whole Bible.

An effective sermon must be focussed around one formative idea.

First capture the outposts of the mind then you can storm the citadel of the heart.

Never be afraid to be simple.

Dr Black likens headings to fences in a public park. Each fence leads into a new area, but they do not obscure the view of the whole.

Luther: 'A preacher ought so to preach that when the sermon has ended the congregation should disperse saying, "The preacher said – that".'

The introduction must never overtop the sermon; this is like a large porch on a small house.

Clear away obstructions – assume nothing – never be afraid of being too simple; people understand very little.

Prepare the introduction last – Pascal: 'The last thing a man finds out when writing a book is how to begin.'

Stop when you come to the end!

Conclusion – beware of cheerful news that the sermon is coming to an end!

Never assume people apply the sermon to their lives.

Never represent Christ as weak and dependent on the sinner to patronise him.

Never let application be long, tedious or labouring. Often an abrupt conclusion which rings in people's ears after they have left is most successful.

Never have to explain an illustration.

An illustration is not a plaything but a weapon.

Beware of coarse or cheap illustrations; never below the dignity of the theme or the level of the congregation.

Beware of unbearably long stories.

The pruning knife makes sermons more fruitful.

Don't preach above people's heads. The man who shoots above the target does not prove he has superior ammunition, only that he cannot shoot.

A well-dressed person is one whose dress does not occasion remark.

Preach your message into your own soul and then preach it out of it.

Don't finish sermon preparation so early in the week that it is cold by Sunday; bring it to the pulpit hot.

The poorest man can be neat and tidy.

The preacher must be his true self in the pulpit, but avoid all oddities and eccentricities.

Poise affects speech.

Move about but don't run about.

The faces of the congregation will be your guide as to how you are doing.

In gesture use the arms carefully; you are not a windmill, or doing semaphore or the breast-stroke.

Gesture is the result of acting how you think, not thinking how you will act.

A radio is not made clearer by increasing the volume!

Avoid sarcasm and scolding.

Don't imitate – preach in your own style. Never wish you were someone else. Be yourself.

Forget homiletics when you are preaching, but not when you are preparing.

Don't be afraid; trust in the Lord.

14

'Uncle Ernie'

ERNEST KEVAN WAS KNOWN as the 'Sergeant-Major' by the men of the Held-out-Hand, but from very early days he was known as 'Uncle Ernie' by the students of London Bible College. Ray Ash said in relation to this: 'With typical student effrontery we called him "Uncle Ernie", which in some curious way represented our regard for him.'[1] After his death a number of students would compare him to a 'father', and in many respects he was fatherly in his interest and care for students. However, 'uncle', while having a close relational quality, suggests just that degree of distance that most students felt. Bob Campen said of him: 'Being admonished by him was painful, because he was loved, feared and esteemed all at once.'[2] This also is true; his rebukes were always measured, but they came with a special force simply because he was so respected and had such an evident love and care for all his students.

Upright and well-built, he was a formidable figure: dignified and austere in appearance, exacting in his standards, both for himself and his students, yet there was a quality that drew them to him. Hard working as he was, he also knew how to relax and to enter into the spirit of lighter moments of humour that a College of mainly younger people would provide. There was an effigy or mascot called 'Uncle Ernie', which I hesitate to describe as a doll-like figure, but can think

[1] *College Review*, Memorial Issue (Autumn Term 1965), p. 6.
[2] Personal communication between Bob Campen and the author.

of no other suitable description. At the College Christmas party in 1959, with his visit to India in the New Year in view, this figure, adapted with turban and appropriate dress, descended on a 'magic' carpet to be presented to him and graciously received.

In the *College Review* for the Summer Term 1958, there is a delightful page with two photographs. The bottom photo shows a number of students in the library and is entitled, 'Students at work'. The photo above, entitled, 'Staff at play', shows the staff wheelbarrow race on sports day and Kevan with a broad smile on his face steering J. C. Connell into second place. Another unpublished photo shows mayhem at the end of the race, as most of the competitors had collapsed leaving Kevan triumphant!

One event from the very early days in the old building at 19, Marylebone Road, when the Kevans lived on the premises, was long remembered. The Principal was having a bath, and one of the students who also wished to have a bath found the bathroom occupied for rather a long time. Other students told him that it was Kevan in the bathroom, but thinking they were pulling his leg he went and knocked loudly on the bathroom door, calling out, 'How long are you going to be, Ernie?' After a slight pause a very dignified voice answered from the bathroom, 'I shall not be long, Mr B.'[3] His horror can easily be imagined!

On the whole Kevan was remarkably tolerant of student extra-curricular activities and humour. However, someone who got on well with children and young people, and was not afraid of showing a sense of humour in his talks to them, would not have changed completely when charged with the care of students. His whole life shows that, in a remarkable way, he was able to emulate the apostle Paul and 'become

[3]Kirby, *Pastor and Principal*, p. 51.

all things to all people' and all for the gospel's sake. It would be a mistake to imagine that there was any conflict between Kevan's overall seriousness and his sense of humour and understanding of his students.

His sense of humour was rather dry. On one occasion a nervous student was asked to say grace at a meal, and came out with: 'Thank you, Lord, for this food. May it be used for the extension of your kingdom.' In recounting this, Kevan commented, 'As several of us were on a diet to lose weight it was rather an unfortunate remark.' And speaking of meals, once on the high table Dr MacDonald ventured the opinion that John Wesley was a good theologian, but Kevan disagreed. Dr MacDonald replied, 'But you must remember he did all his theology on horseback', and Kevan immediately responded, 'Oh well, he was a good theologian for one who did his theology on horseback!'

As a Christian man and a pastor there was nothing artificial or put on about him, he lived an all-round Christian life, but he did so with complete dedication to his Lord and his calling. He worked extraordinarily hard and he was always dignified but there was no gloominess or unnaturalness about him. He was engaged in a serious work, that of preparing students for – as he put it himself – 'the high services of the Lord Jesus Christ', and he gave himself to fulfilling his calling. But he did not tolerate slovenliness or unpunctuality, and he could be rather unreasonable and pernickety at times. He had little sympathy with students who arrived late for College when there was a transport strike that virtually paralysed London![4]

It is true that by nature he was reserved, but this meant he did not readily reveal his own feelings or open himself to close friendship easily, not that he was aloof or unapproachable to anyone who asked for his help. Quite the reverse; he

[4]Kirby, *Pastor and Principal*, p. 51.

was always more than ready to receive people. If you went to see him, you never felt you were interrupting his work; your concerns became his work. He gave you his complete attention; he never appeared in a hurry though he was so busy, and in general his advice was wise and given with courtesy and humility. Complete strangers would write to him and found him a willing correspondent. As well as natural reserve, he intentionally set himself, as a minister, to be the same to everyone. No-one was to feel that he had special friends from which they were excluded.

Similarly he sought to set an example before his students, not simply to teach them,[5] following in the footsteps of the apostle Paul who wrote: 'Be imitators of me, as I am of Christ' (*1 Cor.* 11:1). The first question in the Pastoral Theology examination in the summer term of 1960 (see Appendix 3) is this: 'Why should a minister seek to live in accordance with higher standards than his people?' There is no doubt he set himself to do this in his own pastoral ministry, and continued to do so in his role as Principal. He did this not only because he believed it to be right, but also so that those to whom he ministered would have a worthy example set before them. He knew that he failed to live up to his own expectations – and especially to the law of God – and he did not expect his students to try to emulate his own temperament or gifts. But he also knew that students would inevitably follow him, perhaps unconsciously, in many different ways and he wanted them to be able to do so safely. It is greatly to his credit, or rather, the grace of God in him, that in so many ways that example still challenges and inspires those who knew him.

Preparing for training

When the College was in the process of formation, Kevan

[5] I owe this insight to Andrew Anderson.

wrote a short piece entitled, 'Am I Ready for Training?'. Kirby included this as an Epilogue to his book.[6] Not only are the things he said about training for Christian service and a college course important and valuable in themselves, some of them cast a light on his own character and attitudes. He lists six areas of preparation.

The first is *spiritual preparation.* He lays an emphasis on people knowing that full-time training is God's will for them. 'No college exists just to give "luxury cruises in learning" to men and women who think they can afford it... Before you think of applying for admission to a Bible or missionary college, be sure you know something of God's will for you. You may not know just where He wants you to serve Him; but you must have the Holy Spirit's conviction wrought within you that, like Paul of old, you have been "separated unto the gospel" (*Rom.* 1:1).' He adds, somewhat wryly, but perceptively: 'It is important, however, to remember that having failed in business life does not constitute a qualification for entering the ministry! There are some who, because they have made a bad job of everything else, feel that the Lord is calling them into the ministry. You may take it as a fairly safe rule that if you are no good at your present employment you will be no good in the ministry'! He suggests reading Spurgeon's lecture on 'The Call to the Ministry'.

Secondly, there is *mental preparation.* He points out that if it is some time since a person has left school he or she may find a course of study demanding – so the best thing is to prepare beforehand. He says: 'Some colleges have an entrance examination for which you must work. This is useful in giving guidance to the college, but it is even more valuable for your own mind. You should have enough respect for learning, and for the college, to compel you to make yourself as worthy as

[6]Kirby, *Pastor and Principal*, pp. 58-62.

possible for the trouble that the principal and tutors will take over you.'

In the early days of London Bible College it was possible to gain Matriculation, and later GCEs, within the College. In 1959 the College entry qualification was reduced from five GCE O-levels to four, but potential students were assessed individually and exceptions were made. Universities demanded two A-levels in order to take a degree and in 1962 only students who already had these were admitted to take the degree; qualifying courses within the College were dropped. In those days far fewer pupils left school with A-levels than is the case today.

Thirdly he turns to *theological preparation*. Here his greatest concern is for balance: 'the mind established in the foundational things, but... nicely poised with regard to those aspects of doctrine upon which legitimate difference of judgment exists. Your theological preparation should therefore be of the sort that *inquires*. You will need to acquire the open mind for truth, even if it happens to be different from the ideas that you may have previously conceived. Theological bigotry is the greatest handicap from which you can possibly suffer. Your theological preparation for entry into a Bible college is not that of fixed or immovable opinions or prejudices, but that of general familiarity with the field of theological thought.' He suggests reading *In Understanding Be Men* by T. C. Hammond; first published in 1935 by Inter-Varsity Press, it was a standard introduction in the post-war period.

Fourthly he writes about *practical preparation*. He tells the potential student that one of the first questions he or she will be asked in an interview is, 'What Christian service are you now rendering?' He goes on:

> Colleges have no use for ornaments: and it is the men and women who by consistent and continued service can show

> that they mean business who are most likely to gain admission. If you have never done any Sunday school teaching, or open-air preaching, or some other similar form of gospel service you are not properly 'prepared' for entry into a training institution. Do all that you can, but be careful not to attempt forms of service for which you are obviously not fitted... If you find you do not 'get on' at all in either preaching or teaching then you will be well-advised to stop and think again before you enter a Bible or missionary college.

He also adds:

> Remember, too, in this respect, that the consensus of opinion among the people of God is one of the best forms of guidance concerning your practical fitness for special training. Seek the counsel of your minister in this matter: he will very largely be able to present to you the mind of the church concerning your practical abilities.

Next, there comes a brief word on *financial preparation*. 'While it is true that God calls upon us to live a life of faith, He has also given us sound judgment, and we must exercise this... if you really feel called to full-time training you will save up for it.'

The final section is on *devotional preparation*: 'the maintenance of your own spiritual glow. Even in a preparatory period it is so easy to become absorbed in theology or in practical service that you leave the soil of your own soul untilled and unwatered. The wise preparation for entry into a Bible or missionary college is to foster your own spiritual life.' Then follow some sentences worth inscribing on one's heart for all Christian learning and serving: 'Those learn most who love most: and the more we love God and His Truth the more apt we shall become in studying it, and the more sensitive we shall be to what the Spirit is teaching us in Holy Scripture. Remember that intellectual insight depends very largely upon spiritual perception.'

'Guided self-discipline'

This was the somewhat paradoxical way in which Kevan described the structure and rules for the students' College life, in particular for those who were resident. By the end of the fifties there were three student hostels in Nottingham Place, the street adjacent to the college building. Two, Aldis House and Laing House, were for men, with Mitchell House, across the road, for women. In understanding 'guided self-discipline' it is necessary to take several factors into account. First there is the culture of the times, then Kevan's belief that courtesy and formality belong together, and finally the practicalities of communal living. Students could be in rooms with as many as five beds in them and this required restraint and mutual understanding.

Kevan was very disciplined himself, and he believed this should be the same for all servants of the Lord, so he intended a regime that developed and encouraged the students themselves to become disciplined. In principle this was undoubtedly right, but two caveats could be mentioned. The first is that temperamentally we are not all the same and so there is a danger of not allowing adequately for individuality. The second is that some aspects of the way we think and act are culture-bound and when the culture changes corresponding changes have to be made in structures and rules.

With some two hundred and thirty students by about 1958, those who were not resident in the College constituted the larger number. In these days there are many schemes for theological and ministerial training that are part-time and may only involve a small number of nights spent away from home, if any. This has its value, but a full-time residential course has even greater benefits. Not only are there fewer diversions, library facilities and more opportunity for concentrated study, but there is also the inter-play of discussion and debate among students which is invigorating and expands horizons. The discipline of living together, especially when there are several in one room, helps to knock off rough edges and makes one conscious of the needs of others. It develops understanding and companionship and breaks down self-centeredness and individualism. In the case of London Bible College there were always students from other countries present, and this was particularly valuable; even more of these would have been better.

Kevan expressed things in this way in *The Handbook of the London Bible College*, a duplicated booklet of twenty pages which every student received[7]:

> The preparation offered by the College depends, not only on the Faculty and the lectures, but also on the atmosphere. This is affected by the contribution of each student. It is a group experience in which students live, work and associate together, with a self-control and a capacity for co-operation.

He went on to explain:

> ...the College endeavours to provide for the development of the personal character through corporate discipline. The College has very few rules [a statement about which some students might have had reservations], but the Faculty takes a high view of the fidelity of students in observing these and expects them to be kept with honour and with grace. The College does not employ a system of checking on a student's behaviour, but if rules are wilfully or continuously broken the Faculty does not hesitate to take strong measures.

[7]This copy is dated April 1959.

His next paragraph is important, and particularly so in the twenty-first century when the culture of individualism has become even more entrenched in our society:

> The world in which we live today is a particularly 'lawless' world, and the motto is 'every man for himself'. This philosophy of life tends to mould the outlook of even those who are dedicated to the Lord: it has been inherited by them from the unperceived influences of the standards of modern life. The Christian is to be 'not of the world', but you may find that there are some standards of behaviour which you have unconsciously imbibed from the world about you that you will need to 'unlearn'. This may especially be so in the realm of personal discipline and your attitude to the necessary rules of the College. I want to remind you that 'no man liveth unto himself', and therefore your own inclinations and wishes should not be the final factor in determining what you do.

One cannot help smiling at the final paragraph:

> Occasionally students become perplexed about what looks like a clash between the requirements of the College and what they feel to be 'the Lord's will'. In anticipation of any problems of this kind in your time at College I want to say straightaway, of course, that there can be no challenging the fact that the believer is to do only the Lord's will. At the same time, however, you must remember that if you believe that it is the Lord's will that you should join the College, then this carries with it the corollary that it is the Lord's will that you should honour the rules of the College[!].

The College day for resident students began at 6.30 a.m. (except on Sundays), and finished at 11 p.m. with 'lights out'. A note beneath the time-table says, 'Punctuality is a primary courtesy and is to be observed at all points of the time-table.' Weekdays began with Morning Chapel and for those in residence there was Evening Chapel also, and Morning Chapel at weekends. Each week there was a Devotional Service, and also a period of Bible Study in groups with one of the faculty as an Advisor. Every term there was a Quiet Day for devotion and prayer.

A time-table, of course, was inevitable, and was probably fairly well adhered to, but other matters caused some grumbling at times. For example, 'Students must always be fully dressed for formal meals, lectures and prayers. They will also wear gowns at such times and whenever they have occasion to see any member of the Faculty.' 'Fully dressed' would mean jacket and tie for men, and black gowns, which presumably were to encourage an atmosphere of learning, could be hot in summer. On one occasion Kevan visited the student House Committee while they were in session, wearing his gown 'out of respect for the committee', only to discover that they had discarded theirs! He was not amused.

All students, apart from those medically unfit or over 25 years of age, had to take part in sports in their first two years, except for any term in which there were university examinations, following the dictum 'A healthy mind in a healthy body'. Sports took place on Wednesday afternoons and there were a large number of options, from swimming to table-tennis. Apart from graduates or teachers and those who had done more than two years at College, everyone had to study on each weekday evening and it was not permissible to go to any meetings outside of the College; those who were not resident were put on their honour to keep to this. The reason for this rule is obvious, but it is possible a more flexible arrangement could have been made.

All students were addressed as Mr, Miss or Mrs and, of course, tutors were to be addressed in the same way.

However, as soon as a student left the College Kevan generally used his or her Christian name, particularly in letters, very often beginning, 'My dear...' whoever it was. Letters sent to students still at the College, however, were formal in their address, but could be very warm in their content, as in these cases:

> I would like to take this opportunity of assuring you, as I did in my earlier letter, of the prayers and affection and understanding of all the members of the staff. If ever you feel there is any time when we can be of help to you, please do avail yourself of us. I trust that you may find the fellowship of the college to be an increasingly blessed thing in your own experience.

And on a different subject:

> How very kind of you to write to me with your good news. I am sending you this letter to congratulate you on your engagement... I shall be very pleased to meet [with you both] at some convenient time and to join with you in prayer that God may bless you together and guide you in the knowledge and in the doing of His will.

1. *Frederick Kevan as a younger man.*

2. *Frederick and Kate Kevan in 1935.*

3. *Ernest Kevan in 1917, whilst at Dulwich College (aged 14).*

4. *Kevan aged 30.*

5. Church Hill Baptist Chapel, Walthamstow, where Kevan ministered from 1924 to 1934. It was here that he met his future wife, Jane (Jennie) Basham.

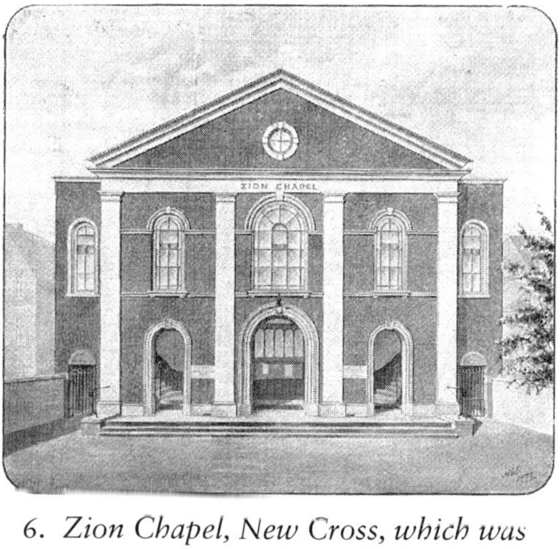

6. Zion Chapel, New Cross, which was erected in 1847. Kevan ministered here from 1934 to 1943.

7. *Interior of Zion Chapel.*

8. *One of the very few photographs of Mrs Kevan. She is at the front on the left, at an unknown occasion.*

9. The beginning of the full-time College in January 1946. Rev. Frank Colquhoun and Kevan can be seen on the back row. The seven students were Percy Nuttall, Bill Oram, Harry Thomas, Murdo Gordon, John Potter, Stanley Blunden and Michael Kelsey. Mrs Kevan can be seen on the left, standing behind the housekeeper, Rosemary Smith.

10. The premises owned by John Laing on Marylebone Road, which became London Bible College, until a new building was completed on the same site in 1958.

11. *London Bible College students pictured in 1948, with the Principal and his wife.*

12. *The new London Bible College building at 19 Marylebone Road, constructed on the site of the previous building. Dr Martyn Lloyd-Jones spoke at the official dedication of the new building in May 1958.*

13. *Kevan pictured at the field conference of the Strict Baptist Mission during his visit to India in 1960.*

14. *Above: The faculty take part in a wheelbarrow race at the LBC sports day in 1958.*

15. *Left: A victorious, and still immaculately dressed Principal, taking first place after other staff members collapse.*

16. *Kevan during his time as Principal of London Bible College.*

15

Prepared for Service

THE *Handbook* NATURALLY GAVE attention to both the spiritual life and academic work of a student. Kevan advises:

> Take care of your heart... Be on your guard against the deadening effect of an unprayerful familiarity with holy things. Seek God's face alone every day and remember that no amount of corporate worship can ever take the place of your solitary communion with God... a period is set aside each day in order that we may all learn to discipline ourselves to the value of a regular time of private prayer... the wise Christian will use it to develop deeply rooted habits of personal Bible study and prayer. Preparation must involve, among other things, daily repetition of certain essential spiritual exercises until they become part of your character.

The residential hostels had to be kept quiet between 7 and 7.30 a.m. so that students could engage in personal devotions.

If that was private and personal, the *Handbook* also says: 'All students are expected to be engaged in some form of Gospel work on Sundays.' This had to be undertaken under the direction of the Supervisor of Evangelistic Activities. Students were generally engaged in a fairly wide range of evangelistic activities, including Sunday School teaching, services in hospitals and old peoples' homes, open-air preaching, and squashes – informal gatherings which included a testimony or gospel talk. During the vacation there were evangelistic treks and campaigns (of various sorts). From their second year male students were sent out to preach in a wide range of churches throughout the London area; and some had student pastorates which might involve preaching once on a Sunday and a weekday afternoon visiting followed by the evening Bible Study and Prayer Meeting. Women students were sent out to take Women's meetings.

When it came to study, Kevan wrote: 'I think I can promise you plenty of work to do. There is no royal road to learning and achievement in the realm of study and scholarship is attained only by hard toil.' He warns those not familiar with the demands of study that they might find themselves depressed, but not to be alarmed by this. He reminds them of the all-sufficiency of God but also adds, 'It is possible to destroy your powers of study by overwork and thus bring discouragement to yourself. An older student will be only too glad to be a guide to you in the arrangement of study periods.' We might note also this section in the *Handbook*:

> Vacations are primarily for periods of uninterrupted reading and private study. Vacation employment is, therefore, discouraged, and only in exceptional circumstances and *with the approval of his adviser* may a student undertake such employment.

John Madsen, who came from Denmark, one of the early students, wrote:

> I remember from my first term how the Principal once told us that there was one thing absolutely necessary in order to become a good minister; and then he took a piece of chalk in his hand and wrote with capital letters on the blackboard: WORK. Last term our Principal lectured to us on Genesis and showed us how God put Adam to keep and guard the Garden of Eden which proved that man was made for work

> and cannot be happy without work. He added that he wanted us to be very happy![1]

There is one other note in the *Handbook* which is important because of the light it casts on Kevan's character and care: 'Any student may see the Principal at any time.' Through the years many students came to ask for help and advice in the privacy of his study. However, a note in a student's pigeon hole asking him or her to see the Principal usually caused a flutter of concern which generally proved to be quite unnecessary.

Although Mrs Kevan always took an interest in the College, once she and Dr Kevan ceased to be resident, she was not often seen there except on special occasions. However, at least from about the middle 1950s, a group of lady students was invited each week to afternoon tea with her. My wife recalls going with three others to the flat at Hampstead where the Kevans were then living. They talked together with Mrs Kevan, but to their disappointment she did not show them Dr Kevan's filing system which they had hoped to see. Moira Anderson, who later became Head of the Extension Studies Department of London Bible College, described her own visit in a tribute in the *College Review*: 'We were warmly welcomed by this shy but gracious, friendly lady who took a great interest in each of us as individuals'.[2] These visits may have been interesting to the lady students, but they were probably a real encouragement to Mrs Kevan, who was often on her own for long periods of the day.

Leaving students

What happened to the students when they left? It is not possible to give an overall picture, but it is possible to give a rough

[1]Annual Report, 1947, p. 11.
[2]From an undated tribute, almost certainly from the *College Review*.

and ready snapshot of those who left in 1957, 1958 and 1959. In total 131 students left in those three years, seventy-four men and fifty-seven women, though this should not necessarily be taken as indicating the usual proportion of men to women. Of these, fifty-two went into missionary work, twenty-four went into the pastorate or intended to do so, eighteen into teaching, another twelve went on to do further study, and twenty-five engaged in some other work, in some cases temporarily while they were seeking guidance about the future.

From the beginning it was always intended that the College should prepare men and women for the mission field. Sometimes missionaries on furlough would come for a year's study. In other cases graduates, doctors, and nurses would come for a year before going out to their field of service. Bearing this in mind, and the fact that 'missionaries' included women, in some cases wives, it is not surprising that more than twice as many went to the mission field as went into the pastorate; in those days it was extremely unlikely that any woman who went to the College would do so desiring to enter the pastorate, though some were involved in other forms of church work in this country.

Moreover, at the beginning, London Bible College did not intend to prepare men directly for the pastorate. This was probably because any who wished to go into one of the main denominations would usually be required to do a further course of study; and the College did not wish to appear to be in direct competition with other ministerial colleges. The only possible exception to the need for further study might have been in the case of the Baptist Union and from the beginning there were difficulties between the College and the Baptist Union which will be considered in another chapter. Of the twenty-four students mentioned above as going into the pastorate it is probable that only nine of these were going into Baptist Union churches. In 1949, the Fellowship of Independent Evangelical Churches asked if the College might prepare men from affiliated churches for the pastoral ministry and this was agreed, though it is not clear what difference, if any, this made to the syllabus. It was always envisaged that nearly all students would later be involved in some form of speaking ministry, and many in giving spiritual counsel and some form of pastoral care.

It is, of course, possible that some leaving students who went on to do further study went into the pastorate later on. The College always intended, if possible, to train those who would themselves become leaders and it is interesting to note that among the 131 who left there were a number of men and women who became well-known for their missionary and pastoral service.

The continuing contact

It is remarkable to see how much continuing contact there was between Kevan and so many students after they had left. Doubtless there was a closer contact with the earlier students and in the earlier days; as the College expanded it would have been impossible for everyone to keep in touch regularly, yet the ongoing relationship between him and many past students was quite exceptional. Edmund Heddle, one of the early students, said that Kevan told him in a letter, 'Once a member of the College, always a member of the College', and that was undoubtedly how he viewed things. Heddle goes on:

> He always had time for us, both in College and afterwards. As we went to his room his 'Come in' was full of genuine pleasure and though in the midst of a busy schedule of College life there was no sense of rush about the interview; rather you felt that he was just waiting to see you. His knowledge of each member of the College family was outstanding. When he stayed in our homes or dropped in

> at our Manses in the course of a journey, his conversation would reveal that he remembered us all. He was closely in touch with events in the Church and the members of the family. His letters were ever welcome and ours to him were always answered by return. His correspondence must have been phenomenal. His prayers continued long after we had left College... My last letter from him told of his great joy that our adopted daughter whom he had dedicated fourteen years ago had accepted the Saviour. He writes, 'Mrs Kevan and I would like you to know how much it means to us as we have prayed so often for you and the children God has permitted you to receive into your hearts'. None of us old students knows how much we owe to his prayers.[3]

Kevan always wrote personally to every student who passed a university examination, and also to those who received the 'Associate of the London Bible College' (A.L.B.C.) diploma. One such letter goes like this:

> My dear ——, I cannot tell you how pleased I am to see your name in the B.D. Pass List this year. This is a wonderful result, and a great reward to you on your untiring efforts and hard work. I congratulate you most warmly, and join with you in thankfulness to God for His enabling help.

He was frequently invited to take wedding services for old students, or at least to preach on such occasions. This was especially the case when it was the wedding of two students. It was his invariable custom, which he began in the pastorate, to give a copy of *Daily Light* suitably inscribed in such cases, and he must have given a considerable number of these over the years. His letters were also warm and appropriate; for example: 'I am writing to express to you the love and good wishes of Mrs Kevan and myself. Would you please be so kind

[3]Annual Report of the Governors, 1965, p. 10.

as to accept the enclosed little gift for your Wedding Day. I am so sorry I cannot be with you, as you so *generously* asked... May the Lord's presence be especially manifest to you both and His loving guidance be with you for all the coming years.'

He was also often invited to take part in an induction service to a pastorate and he was delighted to preach on these occasions if he was able to do so. On one occasion at least he revealed an uncharacteristic human frailty. Alan Gibson writes:

> He was due to preach at my Ordination service on a Saturday afternoon at Kentish Town in 1958. He had been gardening in the morning in Tooting and went into his study after lunch to prepare for what he thought was an evening meeting – only to find he had forgotten it was an afternoon meeting. When he did not arrive we waited a while, then phoned and Mrs Kevan explained he was on his way by car. We began the service and he was with us in time to preach. He confessed to me later that 'I did not keep to the speed limits across London at every stage of the journey!'[4]

Three more extracts from letters will show his continuing interest and prayerfulness for those who had left College and also show why so many loved him.

> I am delighted to have your letter which was awaiting me on my return to College today. I rejoice with you in both of the good things that you share with me... I am delighted to know of this guidance that you have received from God. I have a very warm regard for the Strict Baptists, and especially for so many of the churches... that I know so well. Do I understand by your acceptance of this invitation that you do feel quite happy about the strict communion which is practised there? You will perhaps remember we talked

[4]Personal communication between Alan Gibson and the author.

> over this when you kindly shared your thoughts with me some months ago. Will you please convey to the friends... my own very warm regards and prayerful good wishes for the coming years of your ministry among them. I shall be very interested to know any details of your settlement, and if there is anything I can do to help please rely on me for it.

Here is a letter in answer to one reporting the news of a birth:

> I am delighted to have your letter with its good news of the arrival of —— . I am sorry to know of the anxiety attaching to his arrival, but I rejoice with you in the gladness that now has followed. You may be interested to know that the birth of —— means triplets for the London Bible College family, for two other babies were born on the same day. May I take this opportunity of assuring you of the affectionate prayers of Mrs Kevan and myself that our great heavenly Father may give you all the parental wisdom and grace that you will need for training this little one in His ways. You will need courage as well as tenderness, and I trust that all needful wisdom and help may be bestowed upon you. I am glad to know of the Lord's help in your ministry, and assure you again of my deep interest in all that God has called you to.

Finally, a note after a preaching Sunday:

> Just a little note, but a grateful one to thank you for all your kindness to me yesterday and this morning. It was so lovely to be with you. I had a good journey back. God bless you in heart, in home and in church. I am sending *Salvation* with my love, under separate cover.
>
> Yours affectionately,
>
> Ernest F. Kevan

16

BD or not BD

At the College Christmas party in December 1959, a group of lady students performed a humorous sketch. This came at the end of a term in which the rising influence of Calvinism had been hotly debated; perhaps to some extent acrimoniously. In the course of the sketch a character appeared on stage soliloquizing: 'BD or not BD? That is the question.' The question arose because of the sermon preached by Dr Lloyd-Jones on the occasion of the official dedication of the new college building in May 1958. Dr Lloyd-Jones was, of course, known for his Calvinistic views, but in that sermon he also raised the question of the usefulness of the London University Bachelor of Divinity course for the work of the Christian ministry.

The sermon was based on 2 Timothy chapter two, especially verses fifteen and sixteen, and was, without any doubt, a very fine address. The reaction of Professor E. J. Young, of Westminster Theological Seminary in Philadelphia, who had come to give a series of lectures on the Old Testament as part of the College's celebrations, can be well understood:

> ...the highlight came in the address by Dr Martyn Lloyd-Jones. To hear Dr Lloyd-Jones preach is a memorable experience. Like few others he has the ability to expound the Scriptures in such a manner that what he says stays with one. His words were very appropriate for the occasion.[1]

[1]Iain H. Murray, *D. Martyn Lloyd-Jones: The Fight of Faith, 1939-1981* (Edinburgh: The Banner of Truth Trust, 1990), p. 311.

The transcript of the sermon that will be quoted is not necessarily word for word accurate, but it is close; accurate to the spirit if not actually inerrant.

Dr Lloyd-Jones began by pointing out that history shows that many theological colleges and seminaries for pastors that started out sound in the faith have changed completely over time: 'There are such seminaries today where we can say quite honestly that the only thing that remains of the original idea is but the name that is still given to the college.' He then proceeded to justify colleges but pointed out that Paul, in the chapter in question, makes plain the type and character of men that should be produced – 'faithful men', 'able to teach others', 'approved unto God', 'workmen that need not be ashamed, rightly dividing the word of truth'.

From this he proceeded to warning:

> ...it is a terrible thing when learning and scholarship and academic learning become the first thing and best thing. It is good to satisfy the demands of the Senate of London University but you can do that and not be approved unto God. So we have to be careful. We are always, as it were, walking on this knife-edge.

Because of the days in which we are living:

> ...it may very well come to a time when this very college will have to take a serious decision: is it going to have as its first and chiefest objective to satisfy the curriculum of the London University, or is it going to make certain that it is approved unto God. I am persuaded and confident and sure that if ever it should come to that, this College, this Faculty, this Governing Body will not hesitate but will be concerned ever and always to be approved unto God.

He went on to verse sixteen with its warning to 'shun

profane and vain babblings: for they will increase unto more ungodliness' and then moved back to the positive teaching of the passage. So he came to his peroration and the heart of his concern:

> Are the men and women more certain of the truth at the end of their studies than at the beginning? Are they more steadfast? Do they know God better and desire to serve God better than when they came in? What is the purpose of knowledge? What is the end of theology, of doctrine? Is it not to bring us to know God and as we know God we will see men, the lost under his wrath. It will kindle a great feeling of compassion within us… These are the things. It is not our head knowledge; our academic qualifications. Do we want more BDs than any other college in the country? Only on the condition that if at the same time the students know God better and love him more fully and have a yet greater zeal for his glory and the salvation of perishing souls… having been taught to defend the Gospel against the enemy, and to proclaim it to the lost and perishing. It seems to me that is the purpose of this college.

The sermon ended on a note of great encouragement:

> Remember this: the Lord knoweth them that are his… We must go on steadfast and confident in this assurance that when our work is done, we can be certain that 'henceforth there is laid up for us a crown of righteousness… at that day'.[2]

Murray comments: 'Professor Young, and no doubt others, had not seen the implications for the College which lay behind the preacher's theme. The Faculty certainly saw them and

[2]For a thorough discussion of Dr Lloyd-Jones' views on preparation for the ministry see Philip Eveson, 'Lloyd-Jones and Ministerial Education', in Atherstone & Jones (eds.), *Engaging with Martyn Lloyd-Jones*, p.176ff.

received the sermon coolly.'[3] Many of the students saw them also, with varying reactions. Randall says: 'From the point of view of the college the sermon seemed to raise questions about LBC's core commitment to evangelical scholarship.'[4] That puts it too strongly. Lloyd-Jones's concern was not about scholarship itself; he wanted an evangelical scholarship that prepared students to serve Christ and he questioned whether the BD was the best way to achieve that.

A College perspective

Iain Murray's account of this occasion and events leading up to it is the fullest that is available, but it is naturally written from the viewpoint of Dr Lloyd-Jones. I will attempt to set out the policy of the College, and its outworking, as I believe Dr Kevan and the faculty understood this to be. Ian Randall has shown convincingly that right from the very beginning it was always the intention that London Bible College was to prepare students for examinations with London University, including the BD;[5] this was the case even before Kevan came on the scene and while Lloyd-Jones was fully involved. At the end of the first academic year of the full-time College's existence, three students had passed the BD Intermediate Examination and seven the first part of the Certificate of Proficiency in Religious Knowledge.[6]

From the beginning most students took a London University course; the exceptions being those who did a one-year course, generally either missionaries on furlough or those with some qualification or skill who wished to have Bible training before going abroad. In the fifties students could take

[3]Murray, *The Fight of Faith*, p. 311.
[4]Randall, *Educating Evangelicalism*, p. 105.
[5]Randall, *Educating Evangelicalism*, pp.50,51.
[6]The London Bible College Fourth Annual Report, 1947, presented by Rev. J. Russell Howden and Mr Montague Goodman.

the Certificate of Proficiency in Religious Knowledge, a BA, the Diploma in Theology (DipTh) or the BD, but the first two had been dropped by the early sixties. While, understandably, Dr Lloyd-Jones referred to the BD, the other university courses were similar in content, though at different academic levels. Those studying for a DipTh attended the same lectures as those studying for a BD in a number of subjects.

Alongside the university course there ran the college course which included Dogmatics, Biblical Studies, Homiletics and Pastoral Theology, and Church History; this aimed to be as thorough and demanding as a university course. Or more demanding; one Oxford graduate complained that she now had to attend every lecture. After three years a student could obtain the College Theological Diploma which involved examinations in some thirty subjects. Those who also passed the BD or DipTh would gain the A.L.B.C. – Associate of the London Bible College – and if a certain level of marks was reached it was possible to gain distinctions in Dogmatics, Biblical Studies, Greek and Hebrew.

In general it appears that there were slightly more weekly lectures belonging to the college course than a university course, though it is difficult to be certain because of the variety of combinations of courses which were possible. This would not be the case, however, in the final BD year. It would not be appropriate to make too great a distinction between the courses; a university course was one component of a college spiritual training regime which included much more than just lectures and studying. It would be a mistake for those unfamiliar with theological training to imagine that London Bible College or Kevan thought that a BD by itself was adequate for training in Christian ministry; in fact it is doubtful if any theological college would have thought so.

In this connection it is valuable to note what Rev. J. C. Connell wrote in a brochure entitled 'Training for Ministers of the Gospel', one of a series on training for different aspects of Christian service, produced probably in 1962:

> The essential features of the course are instruction in the careful exposition of the Scriptures; in the great doctrines of the Christian faith; in the method and practice of preaching, evangelism, and pastoral work. In addition, the candidate will study for the Bachelor of Divinity degree, or the Diploma in Theology of the University of London. This more advanced study involved in the University courses develops the powers of mind, which fit a man to grapple with the many problems which face a minister in his pastorate. Some men may fear to embark upon such studies because they include a certain number of books which conflict with our own faith in the truth of the Bible: but there need be no fear, for the student is guided through the difficulties by tutors who are themselves assured of the absolute truth of the Scriptures, and he therefore finishes his course all the better fitted to help those who are troubled by the errors which they may read.

The figures of those who took the BD course in the period up to 1968 are somewhat different in the books by Rowdon and Randall.[7] We can reckon that it was somewhere between forty and forty-five per cent of all full-time students, though neither author gives any indication of the pass rate. All the university courses involved considering liberal views and reading liberal books, but if there had been no university courses this would still have been necessary if students were to be prepared to understand what was being widely taught, and if they were to defend a biblical evangelicalism.

[7]Rowdon, *The First 25 Years*, pp. 108, 110; Randall, *Educating Evangelicalism*, p. 172.

The DipTh examination papers for 1959/60 and BD papers for 1963 do not give much evidence of a liberal bias and virtually all the questions are of the sort that one would expect theological students to have been asked, whoever set them. The regulations of the Senate of London University at that time included these sentences:

> No question shall be so put as to require an expression of religious belief on the part of the candidate. No answer or translation given by any candidate shall be objected to on the grounds of its expressing any peculiarity of doctrinal views.[8]

The London BD syllabus introduced the student to the central ideas then current in theological and biblical studies. If it is valuable for some entering Christian ministry to have a reasonably broad understanding of current theological and biblical thought, to demonstrate a competent knowledge in a standard university course seems the best option. It must also be better for that to be taken in a college committed to Scripture, and in the context of a wider, orthodox, course of study. Dr Rowdon has said, 'over the years, "casualties" were kept to a very few, and were probably a tiny proportion of the casualties which would have resulted if all LBC students had studied theology at secular universities.'[9]

There can be no doubt that Kevan was in full agreement with taking university examinations. We cannot be sure why he took a BD and MTh himself, but he clearly believed that in a busy pastoral ministry it was valuable for him to do so. As it is possible that he had anticipated going to university himself, the idea of a degree would not be strange to him, but his primary reason may well have been in order to understand the main views that were being taught at university level, so

[8]Prospectus, 1959, p. 24.
[9]Personal communication between Harold Rowdon and the author.

that where necessary he could refute them and help those who were troubled at teaching that seemed to contradict or undermine the Bible. He had met liberal emphases in the ministers' fraternals that he attended and from the way he spoke in Pastoral Theology he seems to have given a good account of evangelicalism in them, when that was necessary.

He may have thought also that possession of a degree indicated to Christians that here was an evangelical who had studied alternatives and knew what he believed. A degree gave a certain standing, especially in those days, and it is easy for those who have degrees in other disciplines to overlook this. A degree commended a person as someone to be taken seriously. This may have been regrettable, but it was a reality, and the only way to gain a degree was to take a university course. It is likely, too, that Kevan had in mind the example of the Puritans. In *The Grace of Law*, he quotes from Miller and Johnson's book on *The Puritans*: 'The leaders of the Puritan movement were trained at the universities, they were men of learning and scholars.'[10] It would not be wrong for him to want his students to be recognized as 'men (and women) of learning and scholars'.

A broad range of Christian ministry

There were, however, other reasons for the College being committed to taking London University examinations at that time. In his Presidential Address to the Metropolitan Association, Kevan had included the words: 'the higher standard of public education demands the much clearer teaching of our distinctive doctrines.'[11] His concern over education must have increased with the passing of the 1944 Education Act which brought many church schools into the state education system

[10]Kevan, *The Grace of Law*, p. 41.
[11]Kevan, *Doctrine and Development*, p. 2.

and which required a daily act of worship and compulsory Religious Education.

The result of this was that a new breed of Scripture specialist arose trained, either at University or Teacher Training College, in a liberal approach to the Bible. Young teenagers were being taught things that sometimes their pastors had never heard of and had no real answer to.[12] The response was sometimes to contrast head and heart: if you feel it in your heart, then you don't really need to bother about answering it with your mind. Preachers would sometimes adopt this line, often with some punchy illustration in which an intellectual is put to flight by simple faith.

In 1946, Russell Howden, chairman of the College Board, declared: 'it must be apparent to all of us today that there is urgent need for a steady flow of convinced conservative and evangelical Christians into the ranks of the teaching profession.'[13] Kevan was very keen to train Religious Education (RE) teachers at London Bible College and great efforts were made to enable it to have a recognized Teacher Training Department, but these were all unsuccessful, nor could the College gain a place on the Ministry of Education's list of colleges approved for Teachers' Supplementary Courses. However, in 1961 the College was recognized by the Ministry of Education as 'an efficient establishment of further education'.[14] When I was at Grammar School I was taught RE for a year or two by a teacher trained at London Bible College and afterwards by one who was not, so I know something of the difference; though the latter was not particularly liberal, nor was she dogmatic or strident.

To mention RE teachers is a reminder that London Bible

[12]Cf. Barclay, *Evangelicalism in Britain*, pp. 56, 64. Also Johnson, *Contending for the Faith*, pp. 226, 252-3.
[13]Rowdon, *The First 25 Years*, p. 52.
[14]Rowdon, *The First 25 Years*, p.62.

College was not primarily a college for training pastors; and the statistics in the last chapter clearly bear that out. Dr Lloyd-Jones' address gives the distinct impression that he had the specific training of men for the ministry much more in mind than the wider role that the College aspired to. The College also hoped to prepare a significant number of men and women to teach in colleges overseas, as indeed it did. These needed to have approved qualifications, as did some of those who went on to the mission field. Certainly it is not essential for pastors to have taken any university course, and other Bible colleges did not require this; but London Bible College was set up with the intention of doing so.

According to Harold Rowdon it was Kevan's deep conviction that at a time when evangelicals were almost universally dismissed as obscurantists they needed to have recognized qualifications if they were to be listened to. The London Bible College Prospectus issued in 1959 says: 'The academic standards to which the College works are those of the foremost educational institutions in the country. Students are entered for the public examinations of the University of London, and their successes thus afford credentials that cannot be challenged.' It also adds: 'Year by year the Pass List of the University of London shows that the London Bible College has more B.D. successes than those of any other external college submitting candidates.'

It was possible, as Murray points out, for those who listened to Lloyd-Jones's sermon simply to understand it in terms of a general, and very necessary, warning against scholasticism and the pursuit of degrees for their own sake. But the Faculty and Kevan himself realised that he was calling into question the policy that the College had adopted. That it is better for a Bible college not to be involved in university degrees at all is a point of view that must be taken seriously, but it is not the only one that those committed to the Bible as the Word of God can take. Such an important milestone in the life of the College, with two thousand people gathered, would not seem to have been the most appropriate occasion for an address that appeared to question its policy – even if not everyone realised this. Kevan, as Principal and committed to the policy, must have felt it had a direct application to himself. Later that year the same issue arose again at the Puritan Conference in December, when there was a warm discussion between Dr Lloyd-Jones and Dr Packer on the one side and Kevan on the other.[15]

From 1958 onwards, Dr Lloyd-Jones had less involvement with London Bible College, and he and Kevan also drew apart, though this may have begun earlier and partly because they were both very busy men. However, Kevan did preach at Westminster Chapel in the summer of 1960 when Lloyd-Jones was away and possibly on some other occasions. In the course of time the College dropped taking the BD and for a while its own degree was accredited by the short-lived Council for National Academic Awards (CNAA). As with other theological colleges the London School of Theology (as the college is now called) has its own degrees validated by a university, in this case Middlesex University. There does, however, seem to be a considerable difference in principle between an evangelical college preparing students to take an external degree set by the theological faculty of a secular university, and having its own degrees validated by such a body.

The debate about the value of taking degrees as part of training for the pastoral ministry and Christian service continues, of course. However, this is surely a matter on which there can be a legitimate difference of opinion among evangelicals, and on which different colleges can take different stances. Any Christian college preparing men and women for

[15] *A Goodly Heritage*, The Puritan Conference 1958, pp. 6-7.

service is bound to deal to some extent at least with the obstacles that people raise to faith, with the arguments of the atheists, the major tenets of other religions and the past and current heresies that bedevil Christianity and confuse Christian people. It is not desirable, and scarcely possible, for anyone to understand properly and be able to answer effectively alternative viewpoints simply by reading books written by evangelical Christians. And in any case, some evangelical Christians have to write such books in the first place – and among other aims which London Bible College had was to produce those who would be able to do this.

So far as London Bible College is concerned we should take note of what Mr Connell said:

> The London Bible College is essentially a *training* college [my italics]. It is not an institution merely for instruction in theology, but the students are a body of men and women who have dedicated themselves to the Lord's service, and whose characters are being developed to fit them for the special ministry for which God is preparing them.

There is one footnote to this. The original motto of the College had been taken from 2 Timothy 2:15: 'Study to show thyself approved unto God', but in 1948 or 1949 this had been changed to Colossians 3:2. It is always timely to be reminded that God's approval is the most important thing.

17

An Interdenominational College

IN HIS DISCUSSION OF the BD degree, Iain Murray also says that though Kevan came from a Strict Baptist background 'he saw a better future for his students in such larger bodies as the Baptist Union churches. Initially the Baptist Union would not accept London Bible College men for its ministry...' and so Murray indicates that part of Kevan's strategy for changing that was to put as many men as possible through the BD course.[1] However, I believe that this was only true insofar as the policy of the College from the beginning included university courses; generally speaking, men and women with two A-levels or more would have taken degrees, others a different university course.

It must be remembered that the initiators and early leaders of London Bible College came from a variety of denominations. Ian Randall has an important sentence when he writes:

> It was recognized at this stage, in the 1940s, that the college could not expect to gain recognition as a place for ordination training (although some evangelicals were far from happy about the dismissive attitude to evangelical theology found in some denominational training colleges).[2]

He later adds: 'In the 1940s the concept of "ministry" was not strictly defined by LBC, since the college had indicated

[1]Murray, *The Fight of Faith*, p. 309.
[2]Randall, *Educating Evangelicalism*, p. 24.

that it did not see itself as providing full-orbed training for ministry in the denominations.'[3]

Though this is true, there can be little doubt that evangelicals from 'mixed denominations'[4] who were involved in various ways in the formation and work of the College, nevertheless hoped that students from it would later find their way into the ministry of their denomination. It would be strange if they did not. Kevan must have realized this from the very beginning; after all, the first faculty consisted of himself and two Anglicans. However, the Baptist Union was different from other denominations because in Baptist ecclesiology the local church is independent and therefore free to call its own minister. The same was true for churches in the then Congregational Union, but Congregationalism was more affected by liberalism. So if men from the College were to go into ministry in the main denominations, the Baptist ministry was the one they were most likely to enter.

London Bible College and the Baptist Union

The whole question of relations between the College and the Baptist Union is a difficult one. From the very beginning men from the College did go into the ministry of Union churches and later became accredited. They would have taken the Baptist Union examination and been probationers for three years before being fully accredited. As it turned out, the Baptist denomination had the highest percentage of students at the College, so it is not surprising that it also had the highest percentage of those who went into the pastorate; some figures are given a little later.

Even before the College began, questions were raised

[3]Randall, *Educating Evangelicalism*, p. 48

[4]By 'mixed denominations', it is meant those denominations in which there are both evangelicals and liberals.

within the Baptist Union about what its opening might mean for the Union.[5] The first reason for this was a concern that London Bible College might take students that would otherwise have gone to existing Baptist colleges, possibly threatening the viability of some. It seems very likely that this was part of the concern of Percy Evans, who was the Principal of Spurgeon's College in London (incidentally Spurgeon's College itself only joined the Union in 1938). Moreover the Baptist Union thought that Baptist colleges had all the places needed for those who wished to go into its ministry. This is understandable and was part of the reason why London Bible College originally did not set out directly to prepare men for the pastoral ministry.

Another reason is given by Randall: 'Indeed, the leadership of the BU regarded LBC students with some suspicion, afraid that they might lead churches out of the union.' This, he indicates, was the reason for Kevan's words quoted by Murray: 'When our men settle in Baptist pastorates they never cause trouble.'[6] Kevan doubtless had in mind that men from the College would strengthen the ranks of evangelicals within the Union, but he would not intend them to go into the Union in order to lead their churches out. Some years later some did leave the Union with their churches, but this was over specific issues that arose within the Union, when numbers of evangelicals left. There is a possibility of a third reason. Kevan was an accredited minister of the Baptist Union himself, but he never belonged to a Baptist Union church nor took any active part in the affairs of the Union. It would not be surprising if some thought his position rather anomalous and that he was only on the Baptist Union list in order to help his students into Union churches.

[5]Randall, *Educating Evangelicalism*, pp. 49-50, 82; Randall, *English Baptists*, pp. 226-8, 352-3.
[6]Murray, *The Fight of Faith*, p. 309.

The College prospectus offered 'Baptist History' and 'Baptist Principles' as subjects taught by Kevan, but it does not occur on the regular syllabus and it thus seems to have been an optional course for Baptist students. There were also two correspondence courses written by Kevan on the same subjects directly linked to the Baptist Union examination. The Correspondence Course Prospectus (1961) says: 'The London Bible College Certificate in these two subjects is accepted by the Lay Preachers' Federation of the Baptist Denomination.' In 1960, 'the Union agreed that those securing a BD at LBC could become probationers after two years in ministry.'[7] Even this seems strange given that London Bible College students had already been entering the Baptist Union ministry; perhaps it means that these no longer had to take the Union's examination.

In private Kevan was critical of the Baptist Union, suggesting that it was not acting in accordance with the Baptist principle of the independence of the local church. The fact that Randall can say of the Union Ministerial Recognition Committee that it '...consulted with Methodists, Congregationalists and Presbyterians. These denominations utilized only their own colleges for ministerial training'[8] suggest that there is some truth in this. During the period under consideration there is evidence of some tightening of the Union ministerial list.[9] Churches that were receiving help from the Homework Fund were encouraged to call someone on the Union list as minister and Area Superintendents could exercise considerable influence among the churches.

[7]Randall, *English Baptists*, p. 353.

[8]Randall, *English Baptists*, p. 228.

[9]A number of missionaries who were on the Baptist Union accredited list but served with interdenominational missions rather than with the Baptist Missionary Society had their names removed. If the same logic had been applied in this country presumably Kevan would have been a casualty also.

It was probably in order to try and build bridges with the Baptist Union that Kevan invited Rev. Ernest Payne, its General Secretary, to preach at a College Devotional Service on one occasion. Kevan had had contact with Payne many years before (see chapter 6), so this might also have influenced him. Payne was a noted liberal in his theology and this caused considerable disquiet among many of the students and representations were made to Kevan.

Interdenominationalism

Kevan was always very much aware of the interdenominational nature of the College; his concern was for all his students from whatever their background. In the Student Handbook he wrote:

> You will find among your fellow-students those whose Church and spiritual background will possibly be very different from that which you have known, and I want to encourage you to meet such with an open heart. Do not allow yourself to become suspicious of others whose ways or gifts may perhaps be different from your own… Let me encourage you, however, to seek to receive all the inspiration, and enrichment and help that you can from other evangelical believers and from all the new contributions they can make to your own knowledge of the Lord. You will endeavour, I am sure, to give to others whatever God in His mercy has entrusted to you, but in so doing you will beware of imposing on others either your own particular views or practices or standards

This seems also to express his own attitude to his inter-denominational role. At an early stage in the life of the College he drew up a statement which was agreed by the directors:

> In order to prevent the interdenominational position of the College being compromised in any way, students shall be advised verbally when entering the College that it is undesirable that any change in their denominational affiliation shall be made during their period of training.[10]

Although Kevan never hid the fact that he was a Baptist and a Calvinist, at times he seems almost to have bent over backwards in his concern to make all students feel accepted and to be fair to all viewpoints. This was partly because of criticisms of the College that were made, at one time that it was 'a nest-bed of hyper-Calvinism'.[11] When pressed in a lecture as to whether his Calvinistic position meant the doctrine of particular redemption he would not answer, but referred to Mr Connell who taught the course on the Work of Christ; he would not appear to be treading on ground which would be covered by another tutor.

As he taught the Doctrine of the Church he necessarily covered Baptism and had to explain the paedobaptist position and he did so with such cogency that one student, from his old church, Zion, New Cross, was persuaded to change his mind on the subject. After this man left college he entered into the ministry of the Church of England.

Rowdon has given figures of a survey done in 1968 of some thousand full-time students, which must represent nearly all such students up to that time.[12] Of those who went into pastoral ministry, ninety-three were in Baptist churches (out of 340 Baptist students), thirty-three were in FIEC churches (out

[10]Kirby, *Pastor and Principal*, p. 32.

[11]Quoted in Michael Fleming, 'London Bible College', in *Crusade* (August 1965), p. 16. Incidentally the article begins with Kevan saying: 'We have no place here for people who want to come just to carry off a degree.' The article appeared in the month that Kevan died.

[12]Rowdon, *The First 25 Years*, pp. 108ff.

of 107) and fourteen in the Church of England (out of 192). There were also thirty foreign nationals serving as ministers in their own countries, as well as smaller numbers in other British denominations and groupings. The figures would suggest that overall not many more than twenty per cent of all students went into pastoral ministry, and of these, those who went into the Baptist Union comprised just under half. Kevan's concern and sympathies embraced all who came to the College and the College policy was not driven by any one element in its work.

As a sidelight it is interesting to notice a letter that he wrote to the *Gospel Herald* in 1961 on the closing of the Strict Baptist Bible Institute, though by then it was known as the Calvinistic Theological College.

> Dear Mr Editor,
>
> Seeing your paragraph in the current issue of *The Gospel Herald* about the Calvinistic Theological College, I am writing to express my affectionate sympathy in the necessity of the closing down of this work so nobly conceived in the early days.
>
> Because of the last sentence in your paragraph expressing the hope that 'somebody will do something', I wonder whether I may – on the basis of my long and much-prized spiritual experience within the Strict Baptist Denomination – respectfully offer any help that the Churches might feel that the London Bible College could give to their young men. It has been a privilege during this past year to be the channel for sending two of our former students into the Strict Baptist pastorates in Suffolk, and it would be a great joy to me personally to be permitted to do this again and again. Your readers will know just where we stand here in relation to the great truths of free grace and to the inspiration of the Bible. With warm regards,
>
> Yours most sincerely,
>
> Ernest F. Kevan, Principal

At around that time at least four students went into pastorates with the Strict Baptists, none of whom came from a Strict Baptist background.

Nevertheless, Kevan was naturally concerned for and interested in those who did go into the ministry of Baptist Union churches. There was a London Bible College Baptist Ministers' Fraternal of which he was the Chairman, and because there were more ex-LBC ministers in the Baptist Union than any other denomination he naturally had more contact with Baptist Union ministers than with others. Where men were baptistic and with no definite denominational affiliation, he did recommend those who sought his guidance to enter the Baptist ministry and seek accreditation with the Baptist Union – on some occasions putting pressure upon them to do so. There is no doubt Kevan felt that one way of overcoming the difficulties with the Union was to encourage men of quality and ability to serve in its churches and thus commend themselves and the College.

One of my friends whose 'memories of Kevan are overwhelmingly positive and characterised by gratitude' accepted a call to a Baptist Union church and sought Baptist Union ministerial recognition because of his encouragement. This led to ten very unhappy years 'caused by conflict with the other Baptist ministers' and to a period of 'real hardship characterised by isolation, loneliness and... poverty', when he eventually resigned. I know the names of others whose experiences were similar. Doubtless a lot depended on the sympathies of other Baptist ministers in the area.

I believe that it cost Kevan to leave the Strict Baptists and to become so involved in an interdenominational work. Kirby records: 'He did however remark on one occasion to a close friend that he felt at times that he was "nobody's child".'[13]

[13]Kirby, *Pastor and Principal*, p. 25.

That is a telling phrase. On the one hand he felt very much at home amongst the Strict Baptists, but he was also conscious of some of the weaknesses among them. He gave up the strict communion position and that became a matter of principle which would surely have led him out of their ranks at some point. On the other hand, trying to minister on a broad front as he did is not easy and at times he evidently felt that there was scarcely anywhere where he really belonged. Moreover after the war the consensus that there had been amongst evangelicals began to break down and gradually polarised, culminating later in Dr Lloyd-Jones' call for evangelicals to come together in some form of union free from liberalism. However, alleviating the situation was the fact that for twenty-one years Kevan was a member at Trinity Road Chapel and was extremely happy in this non-Baptist Union church. One of his last services to the church was to recommend to it the Rev. Kenneth Paterson who was firmly committed to the Fellowship of Independent Evangelical Churches.

18

The Wider Ministry
1949-1953

THE LAST FEW CHAPTERS have looked at Kevan almost exclusively within the London Bible College. Once the College began he gave himself unstintingly to its work and its students. Rowdon speaks of 'his single-hearted devotion to the work to which God had called him, he gave himself to the task of establishing the college on firm foundations.'[1] This meant that apart from preaching frequently on Sundays he did not have much time for the wider ministry which he might otherwise have exercised. Nevertheless, there are a number of other aspects of his life and ministry which need to be mentioned. This will also place the College in the context of the times and the developing evangelical scene.

In 1949 Kevan made a visit to the United States in order to let Christians there know about the work of the new college. His tour took him to many of the major American cities, including New York, Washington, Chicago, Philadelphia and Minneapolis and he greatly appreciated the generous hospitality which he received. He addressed students in the various colleges which he visited, and spoke at numerous luncheons and public meetings. He also gave a series of addresses at the well-known Winona Lake Conference Centre. However, as a typical Englishman he 'found it difficult to acclimatise himself to certain aspects of the American way of life'![2]

[1]Rowdon, *The First 25 Years*, p. 29.
[2]Kirby, *Pastor and Principal*, p. 39.

The Puritan and Reformed Studies Conference began in December 1950, originally under the auspices of the Tyndale Fellowship for Biblical Research. Over the years it became more generally known as the Puritan Conference and was held for many years in Westminster Chapel. In 1971 it was succeeded by the Westminster Conference. Its original purpose was to consider the teaching and practice of the seventeenth-century Puritans, but it gradually broadened to include historical and biographical papers beyond the Puritan period. Kevan was very likely present at the first Conference. He gave a paper at the second, and again in 1952 and 1954. The latter two were on *Antinomian Theology* and *The Life of the Believer in Relation to the Law*.[3] These three papers are only available now in brief note form; the latter two reveal a subject to which he was increasingly giving his attention.

1952 saw Kevan give the Annual Lecture of the Evangelical Library on 'The Puritan Doctrine of Conversion'.[4] This was thorough, containing many quotations and making demands on its listeners; it has principles in it that Christians in the twenty-first century need to hear. For example, he draws attention to 'Their Intellectual Presentation of the Truth':

> No-one can read the sermons of the Puritans, or study the vehemence of their 'Uses' and 'Applications', without being impressed by the way in which these Gospel preachers addressed themselves to man's *reason*. Sin and rebellion are regarded by them as utterly unreasonable, and so they employ the arguments of reason in their many endeavours for the conversion of men. [All emphases in original manuscript].

[3]*Puritan Principles*, 1951-54 Puritan Papers (Notes and Abstract). Available from Tentmaker Publications, 121 Hartshill Road, Stoke-on-Trent, Staffordshire, ST4 4LU, UK.

[4]As far as I know this is not available in printed form. I am grateful to the Rev. Alan Gibson for a duplicated copy of the manuscript.

Their reasoning, however, was based upon Scripture:

> The Puritans held to the belief in the perspicuity of Scripture, and they applied that belief to their preaching in the conviction that truth must convince the mind. They marshalled the evidence and piled up the arguments. They knew, of course, that argument ALONE could not avail to convert a man, but they strenuously believed that the enlightenment of the Holy Spirit came by God's grace and mercy through the reasoning that was based on Scripture.

Under the heading 'Their Belief in the Power of God', Kevan turns to their teaching on regeneration.

> Regeneration, then is that act of God by which the power to turn and come to Christ is imparted... 'In regeneration there is given a principle to turn; conversion is our actual turning... Conversion is related to regeneration, as the effect to the cause.'

Regeneration and conversion are far more than reformation; they result in reformation but are not constituted by it. This leads on to the Puritan 'Demand for Human Activity'.

> The sinner must 'seek', he must 'strive', he must 'forsake', he must 'apply himself', he must 'run', he must 'hide' – all these and many other such exhortations are found in the Puritan presentation of the Gospel call to conversion... Their Purpose in Formulating the Doctrine was clear: 'The reason for a right DOCTRINE of conversion was that the preacher might know how to LABOUR for conversion.'

As he draws to the end Kevan quotes this sobering passage from Baxter's *Treatise of Conversion*:

> I have delivered my message, and I hope God will not require your blood at my hands. You shall all be forced to bear me

> witness that I told you there was no salvation without conversion and that I manifested to you the reasonableness of the offers of God: and if you be not converted it is because you would not: and what a torment it will be everlastingly to your consciences to think that you wilfully damned yourselves, and to think that you wilfully refused your salvation; and that you might have been in heaven as well as others, if you had not wilfully and obstinately rejected it (VIII, p. 327).

Kevan's final paragraph leads him to this application:

> The conversion of sinners was the consuming purpose of the Puritans, and it is this purpose and this purpose alone that justifies us in having given our time to the study of their doctrine of it. For conversions we, too, must labour, and we must do so 'not in the words which man's wisdom teacheth, but which the Holy Ghost teacheth; comparing (or combining) spiritual things with spiritual' (*1 Cor.* 2:13).

The mention of regeneration and conversion in this paper recalls a very unfortunate incident that took place either in a meeting of the Westminster Fellowship or at the Puritan Conference, more likely the latter. Kevan took full part in discussion and debate, and sometimes he and Dr Lloyd-Jones engaged in repartee. The subject of discussion was regeneration, and at one point Kevan ventured to suggest that Saul of Tarsus, when he set out on the road to Damascus, was regenerate but just a babe in Christ. Quick as a flash, Lloyd-Jones replied, 'Yes, just breathing out threatenings and slaughter against the disciples of the Lord; some babe!' That, apparently, put an end to any discussion, which is a pity as Kevan must have had some reason for what he said. He was to repeat the same point about Saul in his book *Salvation*, published later in 1963.[5]

[5]Ernest Kevan, *Salvation* (Grand Rapids, MI: Baker Book House, 1963),

It is possible that it was his own childhood experience that influenced the way he spoke of regeneration and conversion in this case. In *Salvation* he says: 'It may thus also transpire that although regeneration occurs only once in the believer's experience he may many times be converted; that is to say, he may repent and turn round again and again.'[6] Here he is using the word 'conversion' in a broader sense than its more general usage. He has in mind the fluctuations of experience which people can go through, especially those brought up under a gospel ministry. They think they have believed; then they are not sure. They have a tentative assurance, and then feel convicted of sin once again. Such an experience may go on for some years, as it appears to have done in his case. If this is what he meant then he is speaking pastorally rather than theologically.

The point, however, might have been better illustrated with Peter in Luke 22:32, rather than Saul. Saul was 'kicking against the pricks', but this surely means pricks of conscience. It may well be that he began to experience conviction of sin with Stephen's martyrdom, for conviction generally precedes regeneration and conversion. It is hard to see how the Acts narrative can justify Kevan's understanding. What he was surely after was the need to understand, encourage and counsel those who really do not know where they stand spiritually, and that is very important. The irony is that both he and Dr Lloyd-Jones were past masters at giving such help.

---

p. 65. 'Saul of Tarsus found it hard "to kick against the pricks", Acts 9:5; 26:14, as all his old prejudices resisted the new life that was beginning to assert itself within him. Undoubtedly the Spirit of God began His work in Saul's heart at the time of Stephen's martyrdom and this was one of the effects.'

[6]Kevan, *Salvation*, p. 65.

The scholar

During this period Kevan also played a part in the wider arena of evangelical study and thought. In the July of 1952 he gave a paper at the Summer School at Tyndale House, Cambridge. Tyndale House began in 1944 as a residential research centre for biblical studies. Along with London Bible College it arose out of a desire to develop an evangelical scholarship.[7] His paper, entitled 'The Covenants and the Interpretation of the Old Testament', was published in *The Evangelical Quarterly* in 1954.[8]

His most important contribution in this connection was to come in the next year. In December 1953 the Inter-Varsity Fellowship published a landmark volume, *The New Bible Commentary*. At that time there was no up-to-date evangelical one-volume commentary on the whole Bible published in Britain and the initial printing of 30,000 sold out very rapidly. It was reprinted in the following March and a second, slightly revised, edition came out in the November. This went through nine reprints before a complete revision appeared in 1970. The main editor was Professor Francis Davidson, but he was assisted by Kevan and the Rev. Alan Stibbs. Considerable work was needed to produce a volume of this nature, and Kevan took his share of this.

One event, though not directly relevant to the story of Kevan's life, ought not to be omitted in connection with *The New Bible Commentary*. The commentary on the book of Psalms was entrusted to the Rev. Leslie McCaw, at that time the minister of West Street Baptist Church, Dunstable, in Bedfordshire. He was later to serve as Principal of All Nations

[7]Derek Tidball, *Who are the Evangelicals?* (London: Marshall Pickering, 1994), p. 51; Barclay, *Evangelicalism in Britain*, pp. 48-9, 55.

[8]*The Evangelical Quarterly*, 26:1 (1954), pp. 19-28. Available at www.biblicalstudies.org.uk/articles_evangelical_quarterly.php (accessed 9 Feb 2012).

Missionary College, and he wrote the correspondence course on 'The Poetic Books' for London Bible College. In the immediate post-war period typewriters were few and far between and as he did not own one he asked a young man, William Goode, if he would type up his commentary for him. In the course of doing this Bill was brought to saving faith in the Lord Jesus Christ. Later on, he became the part-time pastor of the Old Baptist Church, the Strict Baptist church in the town. So even before *The New Bible Commentary* was published it was used to bring a person to conversion and a life of service for Christ.

In addition to editorial work, Kevan wrote the commentary on Genesis and also a 'Note on the Resurrection Appearances of Our Lord'. The opening paragraph of his commentary on Genesis is typical of the man: 'The majestic language of the opening sentences of Genesis is indicative of the place which the Bible gives to God all through. Revelation places God in the centre, and its opening chapter yields not so much a doctrine of creation as the doctrine of the Creator. All things are shown in relation to God and in their dependence upon him.'

He does not come down definitely on any one understanding of the time element in the creation account of Genesis 1. He seems to lean towards the day/age view, which was almost standard among evangelicals at that time, but he adds: 'The revelation is put forward for the faith of the true worshipper. "Through faith we understand that the worlds were framed by the word of God, so that things which are seen were not made of things which do appear."'[9] Gradually commentaries on various books of the Bible written by evangelicals appeared during the fifties and sixties, but *The New Bible Commentary* was hugely influential and widely used in that period.

[9]*The New Bible Commentary* (London: Inter-Varsity Fellowship, 1953), pp. 76-7.

Some time in the next year or two he attended a World Evangelical Fellowship conference in Switzerland. Afterwards he was among several participants who met together to discuss contemporary Protestant theology. Out of these informal conversations came another significant volume, *Revelation and the Bible*, published by Tyndale Press in 1959. Edited by Carl Henry this was subtitled 'Contemporary Evangelical Thought'. Twenty four scholars covered twenty four subjects; Kevan writing the chapter on 'The Principles of Interpretation': 'After it has been established that the Bible is the Word of God, there can be no more important subject for consideration in Biblical studies than an enquiry into the principles, laws and methods of its interpretation.'[10]

Keswick

We have already seen that Kevan attended the Keswick Convention in his first year as a pastor. That he continued to do so is seen from the following letter in *The Gospel Herald* for September 1939:

> Dear Mr. Editor, – I believe it would be of interest to your readers to know of the good number of Strict Baptists who were at the Keswick Convention this year. It was good to meet so many of 'our own folk' about the town and in the meetings, and I am sure I am speaking for all when I say that the 'Keswick' message is one which we as a denomination love and appreciate. Its insistence upon the necessity for the power and grace of the Holy Spirit is a theme at which all our hearts rejoice. All cannot 'go to Keswick', but I would like to take this opportunity of urging one and all to a secret heart-searching and humbling before the Lord, so that we, by His precious cleansing blood, may be more

[10]Carl F. H. Henry (ed.), *Revelation and the Bible* (London: Tyndale Press, 1959), p. 285.

> usable for His glory. What about a 'S.B.' house-party at Keswick next year?
>
> Yours etc., Ernest F. Kevan

The first time that he actually spoke at Keswick was in 1953, the same year as the appearance of *The New Bible Commentary*. He had been invited to give the Bible Readings. In those days the convention lasted for a week, and the Bible Readings were a series of four Bible expositions given in the morning from Monday to Thursday. For his addresses Kevan chose to speak on a passage which was critical for what was, at that time, generally known as 'Keswick teaching': Romans 7:14 to 8:27. As was usual, these were published in the *Keswick Week* for 1953, and also separately as a slim book entitled *The Saving Work of the Holy Spirit* by Pickering and Inglis.

What is remarkable about his choice of passage is that in the previous year Rev. Graham Scroggie had given the Bible Readings, and he, too, had spoken from Romans, giving an overview of most of the book. His second and third messages covered chapters 6 to 8. In expounding chapters 7:14 to 8:1, he gave an exposition which clearly set out the usual understanding of 'Keswick teaching.' Kevan, a year later, contradicted this understanding of the passage, and gave the interpretation favoured by Calvinistic, or Reformed, Bible scholars. It is difficult to believe that Kevan did not know what Scroggie had said; it is probable that he was present to hear him. It is likely either that he had asked the committee responsible for planning the convention to give an alternative, or was approached by its members to do so.

Scroggie had divided up Romans 7:7 to 8:17 in this way:

> In ch. vii. 7-13 we are shown a '*natural man*'; in vii. 14-25, a '*carnal man*'; and in viii. 1-17, a '*spiritual man*'. In the

> first section the individual is in *Egypt*; in the second, he is in the *Wilderness*; and in the third, he is in the *Land*. The first is illustrated by Lazarus *dead in the grave*; the second, by Lazarus *alive, but bound* hand and foot with grave-clothes; and the third, by Lazarus *alive and free*.[11]

In describing the 'carnal man' he said: 'It is perilously possible for a Christian to stick *between Calvary and Pentecost*'. However, the key to becoming a 'spiritual man' lay in chapter 8:

> What the Apostle is here insisting upon is that a Power is given to us, the Holy Spirit, by Whom, if faith be present and continuous, the power of self is negatived; it is annulled, that is, it is put out of business... But victory is not inevitable... The Flesh and the Spirit cannot be on the throne of our life at the same time, but one or other of them *must* be, and our responsibility is to say which of them *shall* be.[12]

Kevan's approach was quite different. His heading for an exposition of Romans 7:14-25 was 'The Holy Spirit Provokes Conflict':

> What, then, is it that Paul is saying? He is opening up his heart to his readers concerning the increasing self-discoveries which any advance in the Christian life must necessarily bring. He has been learning the exceeding sinfulness of sin and the enormity of its hold upon him... It is quite true that the Holy Spirit is not mentioned by name in this immediate paragraph of the epistle, but His activity is everywhere evident... The more there is of the 'Spirit of life in Christ Jesus' in us, the more will the depths of inbred sin be discovered.[13]

[11]Graham Scroggie, *Salvation and Behaviour*, (London: Pickering and Inglis, 1952), p. 51.
[12]Scroggie, *Salvation*, pp. 51, 55-6.
[13]Ernest Kevan, *The Saving Work of the Holy Spirit*, (London: Pickering and Inglis, 1953), pp. 12-13.

> There is no question of an experimental "moving on" here from Romans vii into Romans viii. The *argument* moves on, it is true, but the *experience* with which the two chapters are concerned is the one and the same sanctifying work of the Holy Spirit. Romans viii takes the exposition forward and describes the all-sufficiency of the life of the indwelling Spirit of God; but the experiential knowledge of this will mean for the believer an increasing discovery of the depths of sinful corruption in his heart – a discovery that ever keeps pace with true advance in holiness. 'O wretched man that I am' is precisely the language which the apostle as a highly spiritual man might be expected to use.[14]

What explains this clear divergence of understanding, particularly in view of the fact that Scroggie's view could be described as 'Keswick teaching'? Kevan had attended Keswick during the inter-war years, during which Randall says: 'Keswick's message was subject to remoulding, but what remained central was a commitment to moderate views of "scriptural holiness"'.[15] The same writer also refers to a student leader who 'expressed the mood of the period well, querying in 1938 the idea of being changed instantaneously into a victorious Christian and suggesting rather that the call was to enter "Christ's school"'.[16] So it may be that Kevan is recalling a period when there was more divergence of message around the basic importance of holy living. He may have thought that too narrow a view of 'Keswick teaching' had become current.

Whether that is the case or not, it is probably true that some leaders involved in Keswick were also unhappy with the line that Scroggie and others were taking. Randall says that Kevan's 'theological standpoint contributed to the

[14]Kevan, *Holy Spirit*, pp. 23-24.
[15]Ian Randall, *Evangelical Experiences: A Study in the Spirituality of English Evangelicalism, 1918-39* (Carlisle: Paternoster, 1999), p. 14.
[16]Randall, *Evangelical Experiences*, p. 38.

convention's changing face... Council members defended his theological emphasis, and Kevan, especially in an article in 1957, attempted to show theologically how the spirituality of Keswick and the Puritans could be reconciled. For him, Keswick's call to accept Jesus "as Lord" was a summons to a new spiritual awareness.'[17] The article[18] Randall refers to is interesting and helpful up to a point, but it does not address the obvious difference between what he preached at Keswick and what others preached there. Kevan certainly helped to bring a different, more realistic and biblically based approach to the life of holiness. His willingness to attend Keswick and to speak at the convention gave him the opportunity for this.

At the same convention Kevan also spoke at the Ministers' Meeting. *The Keswick Week* reports:

> ...while disclaiming any desires to rebuke or scold, he appealed for searching of heart... He went on to apply the vivid imagery of Hosea concerning Ephraim: 'Strangers have devoured his strength and he knoweth it not: yea, grey hairs are here and there upon him, yet he knoweth it not' (7:9). Here was a solemn warning of spiritual decline. Decline was apparent when we permitted things we once religiously excluded... With increasing ability, official standing, and conscious seniority, pride might assert itself; we might become critical and 'bossy' toward others. Especially was it essential to maintain a humble attitude before God, otherwise we might lose our first love and a sense of awe in His presence. With the years we were tempted no longer to venture for Him. It was a word in season, and all the more impressive because delivered with such obvious sincerity.[19]

[17]Randall, *Educating Evangelicalism*, p. 73.

[18]Ernest Kevan, 'Holiness of Life', in *The Christian Graduate* (March 1957), pp. 12-21.

[19]*Keswick Week* (1953), p. 150.

19

The Wider Ministry 1954-1960

IN THE YEAR 1954, Billy Graham held his first crusade in Britain. This took place in north London in the Harringay arena, which was able to seat nearly 12,000 people. The crusade lasted for eleven weeks and created a considerable stir. The arena was crowded every evening, coaches came from near and far and people sang choruses on London Underground trains on their way home. The final Saturday saw 65,000 people at an afternoon rally at the White City, where the 1948 Olympic Games had been held. In the evening there were 120,000 at Wembley stadium. Harringay was followed up the next year by a shorter crusade using the vastly increased capacity of Wembley. These crusades resulted in many professions of conversions; over 37,000 came forward at Harringay to 'receive Christ' and were given counselling.

Graham was invited to Harringay by the Executive Committee of the Evangelical Alliance. Kevan made sure he did not get on to too many committees and councils, but he did serve on this one. He doubtless believed that Graham would do great good by his preaching; though he would not have believed that appealing for converts to come forward in the way that took place was the best way to help them. He preached the gospel himself of course, but there is no evidence of him calling people to the front. He was always glad to meet with anyone concerned for their spiritual need and may have stated his willingness to see them after a service on occasion.

He would never give people the impression that coming to the front at the end of a meeting was itself the way to become a Christian.

It was doubtless because of his position on the Committee that the following opportunities arose. The counsellors who were trained to speak with those who came forward at the meetings used a small booklet produced by the Navigators called *Beginning with Christ*. There was also a follow-up booklet to this called *Going on with Christ*. Kevan, however, was approached to write something more substantial for counsellors to use, perhaps to help further those whose commitment appeared genuine. So he wrote a course on basic Christian doctrines in eight brief booklets: God; Sin; The Lord Jesus Christ; The Atonement; Redemption; Salvation; The Holy Spirit; and Christian Behaviour. Each of these included a number of biblical references and with each, except the final booklet, there were thirty questions. The counsellor would go through a booklet each week with the new believer, who would answer the questions in readiness for meeting the counsellor the following week. This simply consisted of looking up in the Bible references already given in the booklet and writing the answer. Once the eighth and final week was reached they would no longer meet; so there were no questions in the last booklet. These booklets would prove to be very useful in the future.

Kevan was also commissioned to write a correspondence course for new Christians converted through the Billy Graham Harringay crusade. This was particularly focused on young people; some of whom had very little understanding of Christian truth and the Christian life. This course was issued by London Bible College as 'The Christian Life Course'. It consisted of twenty-two lessons with titles like 'What has happened?'; 'How can I be sure?' Going on through 'Should

I join a church?' to 'The next time men see Jesus', it covered many essential elements of the Christian life. By 1960, the whole print run of seven thousand sets had been sold. There were those who came forward at these crusades who soon gave evidence that they had not been converted, but over the next few years numbers of young people came for training to London Bible College for whom the Graham crusades had been highly significant in their spiritual pilgrimage.

The Law of God

In 1955, Kevan gave the Tyndale Lecture at Tyndale House. His subject was 'The Evangelical Doctrine of Law'. The following year this was published as a Tyndale Monograph. 1955 also saw him at Keswick to give the Bible Readings once again. This time his subject was 'The Law of God in Christian Experience: A Study in Galatians'. These addresses appear to have made a deep impression on those attending the convention; the *Keswick Week* for 1955 speaking of 'upward of 4,000 people, of all ages, listening intently to the closely reasoned studies of the Rev. E. F. Kevan.'[1]

We have already seen an evidence of his interest in the subject of God's law, and it was one to which he gave a great deal of thought and study. This was the theme of studies which later led to a Doctorate of Philosophy degree from London University. For this he chose to look at the subject historically from the teaching of the Puritans. Several of the tutors in the College studied for a doctorate at around this time. Both Dermot MacDonald and Donald Guthrie received their PhD before he did.

Kevan's choice of subject for his Bible Readings at Keswick raises the question whether he believed there was a particular need at that time to remind evangelicals of the law of God.

[1]*Keswick Week* (1955), p. 98.

There is some evidence to suggest that he did. 'Antinomianism' is the name given to the view that the law is not a guide for the life of the Christian. In the published version of his PhD thesis he wrote of 'the dispensationalist Antinomianism of certain schools of orthodoxy', and 'the evangelical Antinomianism of holiness movements'.[2] People influenced by dispensationalism and holding to varieties of holiness teaching were very likely to be present at Keswick.

In his second address, entitled, 'Wherefore then serveth the law?' he quoted from an older writer of the horrifying shock that the novelist George Eliot felt at the following incident. A woman, an evangelical, had told a lie and was confronted with it. '"Ah well," she replied, "*I do not feel that I have grieved the Spirit much.*"' Such an attitude was appalling to Kevan, too. He went on in his sermon to apply each of the ten commandments, in a sentence or two, very directly to his hearers. For example: 'What about our evangelical cliché, "God willing"? Do you mean it, or is this another taking of the name of God in vain?'[3]

It is, however, very important to understand precisely how he understood the believer's relation to the law. In his final address, 'So fulfil the law of Christ', he said:

> It cannot be said too often that law-keeping can never be the means of sanctification, but it will certainly be the result... The new life of the believer, expressed in a new and active obedience, is itself freedom. 'For freedom did Christ set us free.' 'Oh how I love Thy law,' cries the Christian. Love now binds him in a manner that legalism never could; but this 'bondage' is liberty itself. Love obligates him to an obedience to the will of God from which he has no desire to be released, and this is perfect freedom. As the liberty of a

[2]Kevan, *The Grace of Law*, p. 261.
[3]Ernest Kevan, *The Law of God in Christian Experience* (London: Pickering and Inglis, 1955), pp. 43-4.

railway train is that it should keep to the track, and to jump the rails would bring nothing but disaster, so the believer, constrained by the love of God will run in the way of his commandments (*Psa.* 119:32). The Christian now does as he likes, but he has such a new and powerful set of likes that he is held to his Lord and Master in mightier ways than ever he had been held in his slavery to sin. His spiritual freedom is such as the musician experiences when the scales and exercises have become easy, and work has turned to play. The rules are lost in the delight of musical satisfaction.[4]

Visit to India

Early in 1960 Kevan visited India at the invitation of the Evangelical Fellowship of India, visiting the 'Holy Land' on his way back. He addressed many meetings and conferences, including the Annual Conference of the Evangelical Fellowship, and his ministry was greatly blessed. He described his visit like this:

> In the course of my visit to India I travelled 18,500 miles in twenty different aeroplanes, as well as in trains and buses and motor cars and rickshaws. I slept in twenty-seven beds, but on five nights had no bed at all! Due to the extreme courtesies and attentions of the Indian and Lebanese airways I was privileged to have three breakfasts in one morning! I was nine weeks in India, during which time I gave eighty-three addresses, most of which were by interpretation, and I would like to say how helpful these interpreters were in their spiritual sympathy with the message.[5]

During this visit he also spent three weeks with the Strict Baptist Mission. Rowland Field was brought up in a Strict Baptist church in South London and as a young man was

[4]Kevan, *Christian Experience*, pp. 77-9.
[5]*College Review* (Spring 1960).

involved with the Strict Baptist Open Air Mission. He first heard Kevan while Kevan was still at Church Hill, and later he and his wife attended Evening Classes at London Bible College. Now out in India they 'had the privilege of welcoming our erstwhile Principal to our home and "station" in S. India.' He wrote:

> During his stay with us, I was deeply impressed by his very obvious spiritual distress and grief when we toured the area and he saw the Hindu temples with their blatant idolatry and superstition. I felt I had been shown my own hardened attitude to the way in which 'the heathen in his blindness bows down to wood and stone' and was helpfully reproved.[6]

Kevan himself was to refer to his experience in the first of his addresses on 'The Lord's Supper', given at Coonoor in February 1960, to the Conference of Missionaries and Pastors of the Strict Baptist Mission.

> This service is also a reminder of the historical basis of our faith... In my short journeys in India I had a number of conversations with educated Indian gentlemen, in the aeroplane and in the train, and one of the hardest things I found in these conversations was to get these men to admit the historical basis of our faith. They would say, 'everybody has his own ideas about religion.' My answer was to confront them with the facts, the historical facts of God incarnate in the person of Jesus Christ, who lived and suffered under Pontius Pilate. I tried to show them that the saving work of Christ is a thing that can be placed geographically, and can be pinpointed chronologically. They would then go off again on some philosophical discussion of religious abstractions.

This is a telling insight into his concern as he engaged in personal evangelism. And he goes on to make an important

[6]Personal communication between Rowland Field and the author.

point: 'Let us remember that our confidence is not merely the confidence of a book religion; valuable, authoritative, complete and final though this book is. It is in the historical fact of "God manifest in the flesh".'[7]

These addresses were recorded by John Appleby and typed up by his wife, Eileen. After Kevan had revised them to make them suitable for reading they were published in India in English. Later, in 1966, they were published in Britain by Evangelical Press under the title *The Lord's Supper*. This is a short book, in which Kevan considers the Lord's Supper under four headings: Remembrance; Covenant; Fellowship; and Hope. Early on he makes a very perceptive point:

> It is a remarkable thing, is it not, that the objects of the adversary's first attack on the gospel in the course of history have been the two material ordinances, baptism and the Lord's Supper. To corrupt either or both of these obscures, or even obliterates, the clear outlines of the gospel.[8]

In the opening chapter he also indicates his own approach to the Supper: 'The bread and wine, then, are *signs*, and in themselves they are nothing more. But let us be cautious. This does not mean that the service is nothing more.' A little later on he elaborates: 'I am convinced that what is often called the Zwinglian view of the Lord's Supper, that is, the commemorative view of the significance of the elements, is perfectly correct. But we rise above the elements. The service is not complete merely in bread and wine. The active faith of the believer in taking the elements is of immense significance. He is feeding upon the Lord Jesus Christ Himself. Thus, while the elements are mere representations, the service is more than representation.' He calls in the aid of C. H. Spurgeon in support

[7]Kevan, *The Lord's Supper*, p. 20.
[8]Kevan, *The Lord's Supper*, pp. 15-16.

of this and adds: 'Perhaps I may sum it up like this: the Lord's Supper is *a special means of grace, but not a means of special grace*.'[9] It would clarify things considerably if distinctions such as he draws were always kept in mind when believers discuss and debate the significance of the Lord's Supper.

There are some expressions that are both directly on the theme but also reveal the man: 'Unless there are right reasons for being absent, woe to us if we just walk out when the Lord's Table is set. How can we, for some flimsy domestic or social reason, leave the Lord's house when the Lord's Table is spread?' 'It is only those who love their sins, who cannot welcome the thought of the return of the Lord Jesus; but if you hate your sins and love the Saviour, then the prospect of His return can bring nothing but comfort, peace, and rest in your heart.'

> The Lord's Supper is a meal. All down the years, common meals have been occasions of conviviality and of friendship. A feast has been the method from time immemorial for expressing joy... In the Lord's Supper Christ is shown to be our peace offering. We enjoy Him as we feed on Him... 'What is the chief end of man?' asks the first question of the catechism. It is 'to glorify God and to enjoy Him for ever'; and the Lord's Supper is a feast of joy.[10]

[9]Kevan, *The Lord's Supper*, pp.17-19.
[10]Kevan, *The Lord's Supper*, pp. 14, 66, 41-2.

20

Glory

THE EARLY PART OF 1958 had been an extremely busy time for Ernest Kevan. Even before term began – indeed also in the last months of 1957 – preparations were taking place for the College to start the new term in January in the new building.[1] Once term had begun there must have been teething troubles to sort out and adaptations to be made. In May came the official opening of the College's new building with all the preparations that went with that. When Sports Day arrived he joined in the staff wheelbarrow race with gusto.

Once the summer term had ended Kevan went to Keswick to give three addresses at the convention. Near the middle of August when he was in Felixstowe, he had a severe attack of angina when walking up a hill. He went to see a doctor at once and visited his own doctor as soon as he returned home. The news came to Mr Baker, the college secretary from 1957 to 1970, in a handwritten letter:

> Both of these doctors confirm the same diagnosis and have indicated to me the serious nature of the warning I have received. They tell me, however, that though I may continue my normal programme of activities, I must avoid all physical exertion or hurried movement, and particularly stairs and hills. This means I have had to cancel my holiday to Switzerland. Both doctors explain that although, with care,

[1]See 'The Principal Writes...' in *College Review* (Spring Term 1958), p. 4.

I might continue to live as full a life as possible – fulfilling my duties at the College and my preaching ministry – there was at the same time the fairly definite certainty that I would not be able to go on as long as might otherwise have been the case. This grave news puts the whole of my life and my personal affairs into a new perspective, and I am indulging in the common feature of a 'go slow' method!! Mrs Kevan and I are joyfully trusting in the Lord about it all, and we believe His ways are perfect.

Kevan did begin to cut down his work load in lecturing; concern for his health was one of the reasons for Ralph Martin coming in September 1959 to lecture in Dogmatics. However, in spite of the warning, in other respects he seems to have been as busy as ever. Donald Baker had not met Kevan before applying for the post of secretary, but got to know him very well. Although Baker's work was behind the scenes, the College owed a great deal to his diligence and ability. It might be thought that the Principal and the secretary would not need to meet very often in the ordinary course of things, but with Kevan things were different. Baker wrote:

He was interested in every detail; he wanted to know every detail; he ferreted out every detail. He gave meticulous attention to every aspect of the work – not only to the students and their studies, but he was concerned that everything should be done decently and in order. He was an awful man for suggesting that even the most complicated exercises should be completed within 24 hours. My desk would be cleared for action, the light outside my door would indicate "Engaged", and my wife at home would be warned not to expect me before ten o'clock.

The fact was that the new building was outgrown almost as soon as it was occupied, so before long Kevan was on the lookout to expand further. 'There was a scheme for moving the College to the outskirts of London. We travelled miles together to places like Ruislip, Stanmore, Croydon, Worcester Park, Uxbridge, Surbiton, Mill Hill and Beckenham.' But there grew up another more personal side to the relationship between the Bakers and the Kevans. 'I came home from Crusaders one Sunday afternoon and found Mrs Kevan feeding our youngest with his bottle, and our eldest sitting on the floor with Dr Kevan, both realigning a collection of Dinky toys!'

During this time Kevan was also working on his thesis for a PhD and Jennie was busy too, typing it over twice in its preliminary stages. His studies for this were under the guidance of Professor G. F. Nuttall, himself an expert on Puritan thought. Nuttall's book, *The Holy Spirit in Puritan Faith and Experience*, first published in 1946 and reprinted by The University of Chicago Press in 1992, is described in the Introduction to the latter edition by Peter Lake as 'perhaps the best single account of English Puritan thought in the later 1640s and the 1650s'.[2] Kevan's work was very thorough; he reviewed 283 books from the Puritan era, with over 1,500 quotations from, and references to, these books. (See Appendix 1 for a brief synopsis of the book).

On Monday 14 May 1962, Kevan received his doctorate and the annual London Bible College publication, *The Story of the Year*, records the applause that greeted the announcement of this news by the College. However, it continues:

> But the joy following the award was turned to sorrow when three weeks later it became known that Dr Kevan had suffered a thrombosis and that he was taken to the Hampstead General Hospital. His condition was serious, but the Lord's people were praying. Old students around the world,

[2]Geoffrey F. Nuttall, *The Holy Spirit in Puritan Faith and Experience* (Chicago, IL: The University of Chicago Press, 1992), p. xxv.

> church members, friends of the Principal and the College, united in prayer that if it was the Lord's will, the Principal would be restored to health again. The first few days were critical, but gradually, in the Lord's goodness, Dr Kevan responded to medical care and skill. During the five weeks of hospital treatment both Dr and Mrs Kevan were very conscious of the volume of prayer made on their behalf, and it is now with thanksgiving that friends rejoice to know that the Principal has made steady progress, that as this burden was cast upon the Lord, so He sustained His servant. The Principal's doctors advise that his return to College should be delayed until 1st January, 1963; staff and students alike look forward to that time.

Back to the work

After leaving hospital Kevan spent a month recuperating in Bournemouth. He did not resume his work at the College until 1963, but towards the end of 1962 he did attend some Faculty and Board meetings, and kept in touch with all that was happening. Some, perhaps most, of the doctors that Kevan consulted recommended that he retire. They believed that in those circumstances he would have a reasonable expectation of another twelve years or more of life, but if he continued to carry on, his life might be extended by no more than two or three years. Kevan was determined to continue to fulfil his calling though the Governors went out of their way to urge him to take things more easily. How much he managed to 'go slow' as he said to Donald Baker is a matter of conjecture. When Baker was ill Kevan wrote to him: 'Just a love-note to say how sorry I am you are unwell and to add moral authority to Mrs Baker in keeping you under lock and key till you are *better*.' It may be doubted whether Mrs Kevan was able to keep him under lock and key! He did, however, take up some hobbies and other interests.

During 1963 two books appeared from his pen. *Salvation*, published by Baker in the United States, was based in part on some material from one of his correspondence courses. It is, of course, doctrinal, but there is application too, and, in places a real warmth:

> What then is grace? It is love in action, working for the sinner's salvation. It is not any sort of love, but the strong pure love of God Himself. It is an overflowing love that pours itself out in streams of mercy to the unworthy: it is a love that goes to all lengths, that gives to the uttermost and exceeds all the excesses of sin (*Rom.* 5:20) Contrasted with 'the wages of sin', it is 'the gift of God' (*Rom.* 6:23). It saves.[3]

The second book was also published in the United States. *The Moral Law*, based on a book by the Puritan Anthony Burgess, was produced by Sovereign Grace Publishers. It is on the theme that was close to his heart and is easier to read than the published version of his thesis. At much the same time, the eight brief booklets on basic Christian truth that he produced for the Billy Graham crusades were reprinted. They came without the questions, as individual tracts, published by Living Waters Missionary Union. They were subsidized and available at 3 pence per copy (that is 1.25p in present currency) 'or the equivalent in countries where other currencies are used'. It appears that they were used both in this country and a number of other countries as well.

In 1964 his PhD thesis was published by Carey Kingsgate Press and given the title *The Grace of Law*. This was later republished in the United States and is still available from Reformation Heritage Books. The same year saw the appearance of *The Christian Life Course* correspondence course in

[3]Kevan, *Salvation*, p. 29.

book form. Entitled *Going On – What a Christian believes and what he should do*, it was published by Marshall, Morgan and Scott. It was also translated into a number of foreign languages. Later it would be re-issued by Evangelical Press with the title *Now That I Am a Christian*.

Kevan was also still preaching in various parts of the country at the weekend. He was particularly in demand for Sunday School anniversaries and in 1964 he took thirteen anniversaries on consecutive Sundays. This must be something of a record for any minister, let alone a college principal. On one occasion he was invited by the Scripture Union to speak to a rally of children at Central Hall, Westminster and at the end of his address they broke out into spontaneous applause. The same happened at a children's rally at the Abinger Convention in Surrey.[4] David Kingdon was there and said that on a hot summer's afternoon in a large marquee he held a packed congregation of children spellbound as he spoke to them. It must also have been around this time that he was preparing a series of children's talks on the Bible for publication. *Let's Talk* came out in 1965; the last book he published would be for children.

Back to Wandsworth Common

The Kevans' home had been 8 Titchwell Road, Wandsworth Common, but some time in the fifties they sold this to a family belonging to Trinity Road Chapel. Mr and Mrs Walden had been both baptized and married by him, and had three children. Meanwhile the Kevans moved to a flat in Hampstead. In early 1965 they moved back to Wandsworth Common, three doors away from their old home, at number 14. One Sunday morning, late in 1964, Kevan had been taking the service at Trinity Road Chapel. When he spoke to the children he

[4]Kirby, *Pastor and Principal*, p. 22.

offered a copy of *Going On* to whoever best wrote the story of Paul and Silas in prison. Eleven year-old Mary Walden sent in her contribution and in January 1965 received a letter from him saying that so many had written such good stories that he wanted to give a book to everyone who had written. But unfortunately the book was delayed at the printers.

In their new home Kevan turned his attention to the garden, though he himself must only have pottered there. Jennie said of her husband that anything he turned his hand to he would work at until he did it well; he was never slipshod about anything. So he planned out the garden carefully, positioning the flowerbeds and plants appropriately, taking a particular interest in roses. He also took up playing the cello and after several months became reasonably proficient. More than once he played in a church hall along with a lad of only six years old, Stephen, the son of Mr Buckley, the College Extension Secretary.

On 14 August Kevan presided at the wedding of one of the college tutors. He and Jennie had picked up Mr Carey Oakley and taken him to the wedding in their car. They attended the reception and Kevan seemed in fine form, in one of his humorous moods. Afterwards they returned to Mr Oakley's home in St Albans, where they chatted for a while before returning home. On Sunday 22 August, 1965, Dr Kevan preached at Trinity Road Chapel. His text in the morning service was Isaiah 41:10: 'Fear thou not; for I am with thee'. In the evening he preached from Mark 2:17: 'When Jesus heard it, he saith unto them, They that are whole have no need of the physician, but they that are sick: I came not to call the righteous, but sinners to repentance'. Kirby says: 'He appeared to be in excellent health, and many who heard his messages on that day remarked on the power with which they were delivered'.[5]

[5]Kirby, *Pastor and Principal*, p. 45.

It was, of course, the vacation, but the following Friday afternoon he was at his desk in college as usual when he felt severe pain around his heart. He left the college and drove himself home. As he drew up outside his house, young Kath Walden, out on her bike, saw him arrive and waved to him as he went into the house. He went straight to bed and the doctor was called. Mrs Walden went round to spend the night with Mrs Kevan and in the small hours of Saturday 28 August he passed into the presence of the Lord whom he loved and served. In the words of Dr MacDonald at the Memorial Service: 'He left his work at the college on a Friday afternoon to take up a fuller service in the glory as a new day dawned on earth for us, and where a never-ending day was begun for him.'[6] Mrs Kevan clung for consolation to the text of his last Sunday morning sermon.

That same day the deacons of Trinity Road Chapel recorded:

> The deacons of Trinity Road Chapel have learned with great sorrow of the home-call of Dr. Ernest F. Kevan, their fellow-member for twenty-two years, and their one-time beloved minister. They wish to record their appreciation, and their thanks to God for the generosity of affection manifested towards their church by Dr. Kevan during many years, and for the wisdom of his counsel readily available and freely given whenever it was sought. They recall with esteem his distinguished scholarship and his strength of character, joined with a humility of spirit and a gracious personality, which endeared him to all who were privileged to know him.[7]

In his book *Salvation*, Kevan has a chapter entitled 'Final Preservation and Glory'. The last sentences of this chapter

[6]Annual Report of the Governors, 1965, p. 8.
[7]Kirby, *Pastor and Principal*, p. 27.

lead into a poem he was fond of quoting in sermons:

> The saving grace of God enlarges the spiritual capacity of the regenerate soul and increases the depth and the scope of its desires for heavenly things. The highest conception of the believer's full salvation is indicated by the word 'glory'. The Psalmist uses it when he says, 'Thou shalt guide me with thy counsel, and afterward receive me to glory' (*Psa.* 73:24). Its meaning is inconceivable.
>
> O think!
> To step on shore,
>   And that shore heaven!
> To take hold of a Hand,
>   And that God's Hand!
> To breathe a new air,
>   And find it celestial air;
> To feel invigorated,
>   And to know it immortality!
> O think!
> To pass from the storm and tempest
>   To one unbroken calm!
> To wake up,
>   And find it – GLORY![8]

On the Monday following Kevan's death, Mr Connell sent out a letter announcing the news and also indicating that a Service of Remembrance had been arranged for the coming Thursday, 2 September, at 2 p.m. at Trinity Road Chapel. The simple service was conducted by the Rev. Gilbert Kirby. Two tributes were given and Doreen Buckley played the organ. In spite of the shortness of notice five hundred people filled the chapel and its hall. Ernest Kevan was buried in Wandsworth cemetery, just a short distance from his home. On his

[8]Kevan, *Salvation*, pp. 101-2.

gravestone were engraved words from Psalm 21:2: 'Thou hast given him his heart's desire.' There was one hymn at this service which was also to be repeated at the later Memorial Service. By Joseph Irons, it recalls Kevan's Strict Baptist days and speaks not only of heaven but of heaven's joy over sinners who repent:

Hark! how the choir around the throne
  Adore their glorious King!
They drink full draughts of bliss unknown
  And hallelujah sing!

Another sinner born of God,
  Makes heaven's vast concave ring;
Again they Jesus' love record,
  And hallelujahs sing!

At last the ransomed throng complete,
  Is glorified throughout;
Again they bow at Jesus' feet,
  And hallelujah shout!

21

Strength and Gentleness

GILBERT KIRBY WROTE THAT Ernest Kevan wanted to die in harness and that he was quite sure that the right thing was to carry on while his strength allowed him. He adds: 'His heart was in the College, and while he was there he must give his full attention to it.'[1] This was undoubtedly true. Geoffrey Williams, Librarian and Organizing Secretary of The Evangelical Library, wrote in an obituary in its *Bulletin*: 'It is feared that he overtaxed his strength of constitution, but he used his gifts in the tasks he undertook in a manner beyond praise.'[2] Was Kevan unwise in not following the advice his doctors had given him? Would he have lived longer than sixty-two and done more, in a different way, if he had retired from London Bible College? It is worth noting that his father died at sixty-one years of age, his mother at sixty, his elder sister just one month short of that and his younger sister died at sixty-four. Such statistics prove nothing, but they are suggestive.

On Monday 13 September 1965, *The Times* carried the following obituary:

> Dr Ernest Kevan, who died at the age of 62, was the first principal of the London Bible College and the moving spirit in the establishment of the college in its present splendid building in the Marylebone Road. A convinced conservative

[1]Kirby, *Pastor and Principal*, p. 45.
[2]*The Evangelical Library Bulletin*, Autumn 1965, p. 20.

evangelical Ernest Kevan has been a Baptist minister in Walthamstow, New Cross and Upper Tooting before he ventured on the untried path of establishing in London a Bible college after the pattern of the famous ones in Glasgow and Chicago. He began with seven students in 1946 in a borrowed house in Highbury Park and each year since saw the college grow in numbers to over 200 with students from all parts of the world.

With no wealthy foundation behind him Kevan commended the college to hundreds of individual subscribers and was also able to secure sufficient financial support. His own scholarship was recognized by London University by the doctorate of philosophy for his book *The Grace of Law*.

The memorial service

A memorial service was arranged for Thursday 14 October at the Metropolitan Tabernacle. The *College Review* reported that some 1,500 people gathered. Twenty-two different societies, including a number of other colleges, were represented at the service. The closing sermon was given by the Rev. John Stott. If he had been unavailable the invitation would have gone to the Rev. George Bird, then minister at Bethesda Baptist Church, Ipswich. This alternative is interesting; it would have taken Kevan back to his Strict Baptist roots.

The first tribute at the service was given by Mr Philip Henman, the Chairman of the Board of Governors. In the course of his address he recalled the past, when he was honorary superintendent of a church in Surrey and Kevan used to pay occasional visits:

> ... his ministry was deeply appreciated by and greatly blessed to his hearers. These included children who loved his talks, and drank in his wise and winsome words. I remember, in those days, being concerned that the itinerant ministry

> of that church should not merely consist of a number of unconnected addresses Sunday by Sunday, and asking Dr Kevan's help to correct such a trend. In a very short space of time he sent me a masterly and comprehensive plan of Bible teaching covering the full scope of Christian faith and Bible truth which if followed met the need of the church.[3]

The Vice-Principal, Dr Dermot McDonald, spoke on behalf of the Faculty and Staff: 'He was a friend to us all – a brother beloved. He is remembered by us because of what he was, and yet he remains with us because of what he accomplished. For seventeen years, to introduce a personal note, I was in the closest association with him, and throughout that period no false note ever crept into our fellowship in the service of God in the work of the college.'[4] He spoke of Kevan as a man of greatness but he added: 'There is a sort of greatness which is cold and remote like the Himalayan heights which cannot be approached by ordinary folk. That was not his sort of greatness. Rather, his was the true biblical greatness: "Thy gentleness has made me great…" He was great in the gentleness of God. That is supreme greatness, approachable, understanding and caring.'[5] He went on to speak of Kevan as a man of grace and also a man of the gospel.

The Rev. John Stott preached from 2 Timothy 4:

> I charge you in the presence of God and of Christ Jesus who is to judge the living and the dead, and by his appearing and his kingdom: preach the word, be urgent in season and out of season, convince, rebuke, and exhort, be unfailing in patience and in teaching. For the time is coming when people will not endure sound teaching, but having itching ears they will accumulate for themselves teachers to suit

[3]Report of the Governors, 1965, p. 4.
[4]Report of the Governors, 1965, p. 5.
[5]Report of the Governors, 1965, p. 6.

> their own likings, and will turn away from listening to the truth and wander into myths. As for you, always be steady, endure suffering, do the work of an evangelist, fulfil your ministry (verses 1-5, RSV).

He began by saying:

> The background of this solemn charge of the Apostle Paul to Timothy is an anticipated time of theological flux. That time has come. We are living in just such a time today. The contemporary Christian Church is aptly described in verses three and four of this chapter.[6]

Against this background, and with the example of Dr Kevan in mind, he first focussed on 'Conviction'.

> The Church needs men and women of conviction today who (although allowing liberty on secondary matters) are firm as granite in the central doctrines of the Biblical faith. Men and women who in the midst of the prevailing confusion are steady and stand fast.[7]

His second word was 'Courage' and his final paragraph under this heading is well worth considering, and even more so forty years on:

> I want to suggest to you that these are the first two essentials in the work of God today – conviction and courage. Intellectual conviction and moral courage. They were very evident not only in the life of Ernest Kevan, but in the lives of the 16th century Reformers. One of the reasons why under God the Reformation bore such lasting fruit is that its pioneers were both scholars and martyrs. They knew what they believed and they were prepared to suffer and die for it. I cannot myself see any chance of winning the Church

[6]Report of the Governors, 1965, p. 11.
[7]Report of the Governors, 1965, p. 12.

> back to the truth of the Gospel until another generation of scholar-martyrs arises. We need men and women who know and believe the truth of the Gospel, and who are resolved to defend it and commend it both with all the godly scholarship which they can muster and (if necessary) with their tears and their blood, living behind the scene in obscurity, forgoing promotion, security and recognition for the sake of the Gospel of Jesus Christ.[8]

His third and final word was 'Courtesy', under which he also pointed out Paul's emphasis on gentleness in the Pastoral Epistles:

> The truth is that there are some of us who are not only rock-like in strength and steadfastness, but as hard and jagged as rock as well! Not Ernest Kevan. He was a most unusual combination of strength and gentleness. As Principal of the London Bible College, he was firm and immovable in his evangelical convictions, and yet he was as tender as a mother with little children. He could be wonderfully patient with backward, obtuse and unintelligent students; deeply sympathetic with those in trouble and sorrow; and very gracious towards his theological opponents.

Here are his concluding words:

> Paul's charge to Timothy is a charge to us. It was uttered with great solemnity in the presence of God and of Christ Jesus our Judge. It was grounded upon the certain appearing and coming kingdom of Jesus Christ. We need to live our lives, as Ernest Kevan lived his life, in the presence of God and in anticipation of the coming of Christ. Then by God's grace we shall grow in strong Biblical convictions, in the courage of our convictions, and in the gentle courtesy of Christ as we defend and proclaim our convictions.[9]

[8]Report of the Governors, 1965, pp. 12-13.
[9]Report of the Governors, 1965, p. 13.

Mrs Kevan

Those who were in contact with Jennie Kevan at that time tend to speak of her as being 'lost' in the early months after Dr Kevan's death. This is not at all surprising. In many ways hers was a supporting role to his ministry. He took all the major decisions and cared for her with tender love and after thirty-eight years of married life his passing was always going to be very difficult for her. But although there had been warning signs, when the end came it came with a suddenness for which she cannot have been prepared; in a few hours her world was turned upside down. Nevertheless, her confidence was in the Lord. Very soon letters of sympathy and appreciation of her husband began to arrive and, in time, she sent out a printed reply to all who had written to her.

> My dear Friend,
>
> The number of those who, in their great kindness, have written to me at this time is so great that it is impossible for me to write a personal reply to each. Will you please believe that this comes to you in true appreciation and gratitude.
>
> It is wonderful to know that my dear husband was so beloved. It is also a great comfort to know of those who have been blessed through his ministry. This would be his crowning joy.
>
> Less than a week before God took him he said, in conversation with a friend, "I do love to preach the Gospel". It was his constant delight to know that in so many parts of the world "his" students were making the Gospel known. And now he sees the face of the One he so longed to see and loved to uplift.
>
> The words which follow, I am sure, aptly express his heart's wish.
>
> Lord, when Thou seest my work is done,

Let me not linger on with failing powers
Adown the weary hours:
A workless worker in a world of work:
But with a word just bid me home,
And I will come right gladly,
Yes, right gladly will I come.

Yours so gratefully and sincerely,

Jane Kevan

By this time, Mrs Kevan was seventy years old and she had to consider her own future and where she was going to live. She received a sum of money from insurance on her husband's life and the College also contributed to her support, but to enable them to move back to Wandsworth Common Kevan had borrowed a sum from the College to purchase their house. This could now only be repaid by the sale of the house, and in any case Mrs Kevan needed a smaller place in which to live. Within a fairly short period she managed to sell the house (the College waived the interest which was due on the loan) and moved into a flat a little further out in the suburb of Sutton. One of her pleasant duties before she moved was to give out the copies of *Going On* to Mary Walden and the other young people who had written in response to Kevan's invitation. Inside Mary's copy were the words:

'The book promised to you by Dr Kevan. He prayed for you'. Those last words had a profound impression upon her: 'To think that he prayed for ME! It was a year later that I gave my life to the Lord.'[10]

It was Jennie Kevan who also wondered whether the short course of basic Christian truths that her husband had written for the Billy Graham crusade would be useful as a book.

[10]Personal communication between Mary Levell (*née* Walden) and the author.

Evangelical Press published it in 1966 with the title *What the Scriptures Teach*. There was a paperback version containing the text plus the questions; this was for those wanting a very basic introduction to Christian truth. A hardback version which included the answers was for anyone who led a group through the chapters. So, for example, when Pastor Phil Arthur was a young Christian, still a teenager, his first experience of Christian service came when his minister, Rev. David Jones of Sunderland, handed him the hardback copy and he led an after-church group of young people through the chapters, learning as well as teaching. The paperback version was kept in print by Evangelical Press until 2002. In 2007, Pastor Training International printed 5,000 copies which are used particularly for pastors in Africa who have had little or no previous training, especially in doctrine.

The early months after her husband's death were naturally very difficult for Mrs Kevan. In a letter to Donald Baker in January 1966, in reply to one which informed her that Gilbert Kirby had been appointed the next principal of the College, she wrote: 'Thank you for your letter r.e. Mr Kirby's appointment. I am, indeed, very thankful and have the first feeling of gladness in all these sad months.' Saturday 30 July 1966 was exactly eleven months after Kevan's death – but let Kath Paterson (*née* Walden) use her own words:

> I have two other memories as a ten year old. Mrs Kevan adored her budgie! The other memory was the afternoon of the 1966 World Cup. We'd been invited to tea but when we arrived she was *so* excited and asked if we could all watch the match together. So we sat and cheered England with her![11]

To start with, Jennie relied greatly on visits from friends

[11]Personal communication between Kath Paterson and the author.

from Trinity Road Chapel, but in due course she made friends at Cheam Baptist Church and enjoyed fellowship there. Donald Baker was Dr Kevan's executor and he and his wife were to be an enormous help and support to her through the years; later he received power of attorney for her and became her executor. She was to live on for another twenty-four years and his wisdom and care was crucial during all that time. In 1981 she wrote to him: 'Not the least of all [God's] goodness and mercy is all that you have been to me, and all that you have done in these past months. I can never fully express my gratitude but assure you it is very real and deep.'

As the years passed she moved into a care home, and later into a nursing home. Her letters to Donald Baker and his wife give some insight into her circumstances and illustrate her continuing faith. At the end of August 1966 she wrote:

> I do want to say a special 'thank you' for your great kindness in so especially remembering me while on your holiday. These days have been difficult, but the prayers of so many dear friends like yourselves are being answered… And now as a new academic year approaches with the coming of Mr Kirby my thoughts and prayers will be much with you, that you may find that the Lord has indeed gone before preparing the way, and that in His great goodness there may be great blessing. How strange that so soon there will be the second 'intake' since my beloved was called home, & very soon there will not be any students in the College who knew him. This great work, however, is the *Lord's* & I shall look forward to hearing of increasing growth and blessing.

After receiving a birthday card in 1984:

> If anybody wants to know my age I think I shall say 16 because that is what two eights (88) add up to!!! How good God has been to me in so many, many ways & still I am

> conscious of His loving care & praise Him for His provision for me still. I must admit that I often have a secret longing to be in my own home! Friends are very kind in visiting me, and I do appreciate it so much. When I used to spend so many afternoons visiting I sometimes wondered whether there would be anybody to visit me when need should arise. Now I know! And I am so thankful to them all.

On 1 February 1990, Jennie Kevan passed peacefully into the presence of her Lord; she was ninety-four. Donald Baker wrote: 'During 24 years of widowhood she had waited for this time: she had so often hoped to be released from her human frailty, and her prayer has now been answered.' Her times, like Dr Kevan's, were in the hands of her Lord and it was his will that she should see out many days and demonstrate her trust in him without the presence and support of her husband. Dr Kevan gave her a Bible on their twenty-fifth wedding anniversary and she appears to have continued to use it right up to the end, judging by its dilapidated condition. The funeral took place at Cheam Baptist Church; Rev. David Abernethie conducted it and Rev. Ken Paterson, Tim Buckley and Rev. Gilbert Kirby took part. Her body was laid to rest with that of her husband.

Some from Zion, New Cross, in 2009, still remembered Mrs Kevan as 'a lovely Christian lady, described as "nothing of self, entirely of the Lord"'. Moira Anderson wrote of the Kevans:

> No one could have chosen a more devoted, loyal and godly helpmeet, whose unobtrusive backing contributed greatly to his effectiveness as both Pastor and Principal, as well as keeping his renowned filing system in apple-pie order![12]

[12]From a tribute by Moira Anderson, presumably from the *College Review* in 1990.

22

In Retrospect

THE *College Review* FOR the Autumn term of 1965 was a special Memorial Edition. In looking over the tributes in it paid to Kevan by former students several features impress. The word 'shock' recurs again and again. David Appavoo, from India, wrote, 'It was indeed an unbearable shock to hear... that the beloved Principal has left the College at the call of the Master', and Jean-Marc Barral, from France: 'I am quite choked by the news of the passing of Dr Kevan'. Alan Perkins, who worked in Peru, wrote: 'I must confess that the sense of loss that I experienced with the knowledge of the passing of our beloved Principal was greater than I dreamed possible.' The sense of loss could express itself in some surprising ways. Bill Barkley, writing from Brazil, said, 'I was looking forward so much to seeing him next year and introducing Mary to him', and Emmi Muller from Japan: 'Just recently when it was decided that I shall go on furlough next year I thought that I would like to ask him a number of questions...'

Most of all there was the recognition of his personal interest in every student. Martha Hirsch wrote from Morocco, 'How privileged we were at LBC under his wise and levelheaded leadership and what a joy it was to go back and see him and to hear him calling us by our Christian names and know us and all about our present service.' Costas Kounadis, from Corfu, said, 'For me he was a good friend, a good teacher, a good father. I can't forget his sincere love not only to me but even to all. He was for me a living example of Christian character'. Of course, it was those who were most appreciative of Dr Kevan who wrote to the College, but I think it would be true that a large majority of students would identify with these sentiments.[1]

Of those who served with him, Frank Colquhoun said:

> He was beyond question one of the truly great Evangelicals of our day. Others will, I am sure, write more fully about him as scholar, teacher, administrator, and leader of men. For my part I like to recall that, with all his rich and varied gifts, he was at heart a very simple Christian believer, a humble man of God, and a most lovable and gracious friend.[2]

Donald Baker said: 'Ernest Kevan lived nearer to God than anyone I have ever known'.

Mr Carey Oakley paid his own tribute in the magazine of Trinity Road Chapel:

> Dr. Kevan's life and witness was based upon a personal experience of God's saving grace in Jesus Christ, a confidence in God's sovereignty, a fidelity to the Scriptures as God's word and a daily walk with God that made him the humble and gracious man that he was. To know him and to work with him was a privilege and an inspiration. His work lives on in the lives of countless men and women whose Christian character he helped to mould.[3]

From outside of the College, Dr George Beasley-Murray, the Principal of Spurgeon's College, said: 'Dr Kevan's passing is an incalculable loss to the whole Christian Church.' He

[1] *College Review*, Memorial Issue (Autumn Term 1965), pp. 10-12.
[2] *College Review*, Memorial Issue, p. 4.
[3] *College Review*, Memorial Issue, p. 27.

described him as: 'One of the most gracious men on earth who must have been held not only in esteem but in affection by a multitude.'[4]

Kevan's place in the twentieth century

Overall the twentieth century was a time of decline for evangelical Christianity in Great Britain. This decline was most obvious, of course, in the reduction of the number of churches and even more in the much smaller size of congregations for the churches that remained. The Christian faith came to have less and less influence on the wider society. Hand in hand with this went an increase in liberal theology and a much greater diversity amongst those who professed to be evangelicals.

But this was only the general trend; there were those who bucked the trend as well as those who buckled under it. There is no doubt that Kevan's ministry both as pastor and principal was blessed by God. His heritage, drawing as it did on the Puritans, was both doctrinal and experiential. He found clear truths in the Bible which were to be adhered to and affirmed, but he also knew the importance of a spiritual knowledge of God and sensitivity to his presence and guidance. His firm belief in the sovereignty of God, not only in salvation, but also in providence, carried him through the rigours of wartime. His consciousness of the grace of God towards him, and his understanding of it from the Scriptures, fashioned and moulded him into the man of grace that he became.

When the war ended he was able to play his part in bringing the best of true Calvinistic evangelicalism to the task of rebuilding the fortunes of the evangelical constituency and setting a firm foundation for the future years. The fact that his was an older evangelicalism, with deeper theological and spiritual roots, and that personally he was such a fine example

[4]Kirby, *Pastor and Principal*, p. 49.

and exponent of that tradition, enabled him to overcome all the difficulties that the immediate post-war period presented. Looking over his life it is possible to see how the early years prepared him for the considerable task which faced him when he was appointed to London Bible College. He was able to bring an almost unique blend of spiritual depth, wide pastoral experience, good scholarship and a remarkable capacity for work to his role as Principal.

As we have seen, in 1943 evangelical scholarship was at a low ebb. With the establishing of London Bible College, the Tyndale Fellowship, and Tyndale House, things gradually began to change. At the beginning Kevan was at the centre of things, but with the remarkable expansion of the College and with his health becoming more uncertain after 1958, he needed to concentrate his efforts upon the College. Moreover, he was always a preacher and had no interest in scholarship for its own sake or a merely theoretical theology. For him theology formed the heart of true preaching and also shaped the contours of the Christian life, both for the church and the individual. The Bible as a whole revealed a clear body of truth by which unbelievers would be brought to faith in Christ, the church and its members built up and its mission fulfilled in the world.

During the post-war period and especially the fifties there was something of a resurgence of evangelicalism. John Stott, who came to All Souls, Langham Place in London as curate in 1945, became Rector in due course and developed a powerful biblical and evangelistic teaching ministry. Interest in the Puritans led to the Puritan Conference with Dr Lloyd-Jones and Dr Packer as the most high-profile speakers. The theology that undergirded Kevan's ministry became much more influential and widespread than had been the case for many years.

Understandably the Graham crusades stand out as high points in the minds of many, but it is probably also true that they came at a time of spiritual opportunity. The war had had a sobering effect on many people; the old Christian certainties had carried many through the deprivations of those years. Children brought up under its shadow were growing up at a time when the Bible was still taught in schools. Many of these were looking for a sense of purpose in the new era opening up, and wanting to use their lives in productive and useful ways.

There was a great deal of evangelistic activity and if Haringay and Wembley were the venues that remained in people's minds, they were as much symbols of the time as specific events. No doubt in the evangelism of those times there was often a measure of superficiality, but Kevan and London Bible College were of strategic importance in providing solid biblical and doctrinal teaching in the capital city. In the late fifties significant numbers of students at the College had been converted through the Graham crusades, many going out to the foreign mission field. Rowdon writing of the first twenty-five years (up to 1968) said: 'Almost a hundred overseas students have returned to their home countries or become missionaries elsewhere, and have been joined by 194 who have gone abroad as missionaries.'[5]

In 1967 Kirby wrote: 'It was Dr Kevan's great concern that every student in the College should have a missionary vision whether he or she was destined to teach Scripture in schools or become a pastor in the homeland, or, of course, go overseas in missionary service. The College has never swerved from seeking to fulfil this ideal.'[6] The impetus for this concern of Kevan must surely have arisen from his own earlier desire

[5]Rowdon, *The First 25 Years*, p. 114.
[6]*College Review* (Autumn Term 1967), p. 5.

for missionary service. Instead of going to India himself with his wife, he was able to prepare many others who would take the gospel to every part of the globe.

Kevan was a pioneer in introducing a new level of scholarship and theological depth into Bible College training in the United Kingdom. Without demeaning the biblical training given and devotion shown by non-denominational Bible colleges before London Bible College began, he set a new standard. Although he wanted his students to do well in university exams and to be able to answer questions posed by liberalism, he was much more concerned that they were thoroughly grounded in the Scriptures and the doctrines these reveal. In the early days a number of those involved in other Bible colleges served on the London Bible College council, and this indicates a valuable spirit of co-operation and opportunity for cross-fertilisation.

One area which remains rather uncertain is Kevan's attitude to the church and denominationalism. Two things need to be kept in mind. Firstly, though he was brought up in what would be considered a very narrow churchmanship, from the early days he began to look beyond the Strict Baptists to the worldwide church of Jesus Christ. The trajectory of his life and ministry was very different from, for example, that of Dr Lloyd-Jones. Secondly, once he had accepted the call to the College he was, more or less, locked into an expression of evangelical co-operation and unity which accepted the denominations as they were and sent men and women out to serve where they believed they were being called. Probably his attitude was that he was called to serve in the situation as it was and he might have doubted the possibility of any radical alteration being possible.

It is probably true that Kevan's name began to be forgotten by most Christians as the years passed after his death, excepting those who had belonged to the churches he had pastored or who had been at London Bible College. There are several reasons for this. Firstly, once he left Zion, New Cross, he no longer had any real denominational affiliation, so he did not achieve prominence among any organized body of churches. Nor, of course, had he come through the ranks of the Inter-Varsity Fellowship. Secondly, on the one hand his commitment to the College left him little time for other Christian activities and on the other hand his ministry outside of the College was often to children and mainly in local churches. Apart from *The Grace of Law*, his books were generally written at a popular level; he was much more concerned to help new believers than to gain a reputation. Finally, though his character indicated someone to be reckoned with, his was not the sort of outgoing, charismatic personality that demands attention and easily impresses others.

The truth is, as the tributes paid to him at the time of his death make plain, that not only was Kevan a great and good man, he was a key figure in the immediate post-war period. His efforts and those of the faculty soon gained a reputation for London Bible College that brought remarkable growth and students from many different parts of the world. Before long, men and women were going into many different forms of Christian service, both at home and abroad, fired with a love for God, for his Word and for Gospel truth.

In his pastorates Kevan showed he was able to adapt to changes in society and was alive to the possibility of ministry in new ways, but by the time he died the larger shifts in attitudes in society that began in the sixties were getting beyond his capacity for flexibility. Committed as he was to the task in hand and with no children or grandchildren of his own to challenge his ideas, he and Mrs Kevan remained rather old-fashioned in their outlook. He would have found it very difficult to adapt to some of the cultural changes that were taking place. It was surely gracious of the Lord to take him when he did; he was the foundation-layer, it was left to others to build upon that foundation, seeking to maintain all that was truly biblical and godly but yet adapted to the fresh challenges that changing conditions were bringing.

Τα ανω φρονειτε - **'Set your affection on things above'**

When the College motto was changed, the opening words of Colossians 3:2 in Greek were chosen. This could be the motto for Kevan's life; summing up his attitude and purpose. These three terse Greek words are, of course, part of a larger whole: 'If then you were raised with Christ, seek those things which are above, where Christ is, sitting at the right hand of God. Set your mind on things above, not on things on the earth. For you died, and your life is hidden with Christ in God. When Christ who is our life appears, then you will also appear with him in glory.'

Here was Ernest Kevan's focus; it was in the light of these realities that he sought to live his life and set an example to those who, with all their faults and weaknesses, aspired to the same high calling. His life is a reminder of where the minds of Christian people ought to be set; not so much on the servants that God uses, however thankful we may be for them, but on Jesus Christ and the things that are above.

APPENDIX ONE

The Grace of Law

THE PUBLISHED VERSION OF Dr Kevan's thesis is a volume of just under three hundred pages. With its many quotations and footnotes it appears quite formidable. He goes into considerable detail and the reader is likely to concur with Francis Roberts, whom Kevan quotes, that the matter under discussion is 'a knotty and difficult question, and learned men have rendered it the more intricate, by their cross disputes about it.' Nevertheless it is an extremely valuable investigation of a vital subject. The issue is, in fact, of even greater importance in the present climate of opinion among evangelical Christians. The following is a very brief introduction, concentrating mainly on the positive teaching of the Puritans. In general one inverted comma indicates a quotation from Kevan, while two inverted commas introduce a quotation from a Puritan. I have, however, modernised the spelling, where necessary.

Kevan set out his purpose in this book in the following words: 'The object of this work is to explore the Puritan teaching on the place which the Law of God must take in the life of a believer and to examine it for the contribution that it may make towards a true understanding of the Christian doctrine of sanctification.' He says that among the Puritans: 'one of the most keenly debated questions was whether the Law still possessed commanding authority over the believer. The majority of the Puritans answered this question affirmatively, and it may, not unreasonably, be claimed that the authority of Law as the principle of the life of the believer was central to the distinctively Puritan concept of Christian experience.'

At this point it needs to be said that both sides in the debate accepted that the moral law of God was expressed in the Ten Commandments. Kevan, therefore, does not seek to justify this understanding in the book. The whole question at that time was whether these commandments still had commanding force when a person became a believer or whether the believer was set free from obedience to them as the way for Christians to live. A modern treatment of the same issue would need to consider this preliminary question. However, though the relationship of the Ten Commandments to the moral law and the Christian is of great importance, whether the Christian is obligated to obey the will of God revealed in Scripture or not actually goes beyond that.

Kevan reviews the controversy as it took place throughout virtually the whole of the seventeenth century. In speaking of the books that he used he says: 'In so far as the doctrine was a preached doctrine, and was one of immediate practical significance, only those writings which appeared in English, and for the guidance of the ordinary believer, are included'. This reminds us that the question was by no means a theoretical matter, nor simply a debate among theologians. The answers given directly impacted upon the congregation in the pew and shaped the lives of those who listened to the protagonists.

Those who did not believe in the continuing authority of the Law over believers were known as 'Antinomians' (from the Greek, 'against law'). Kevan speaks of the majority of Antinomians in this way: 'The main object of the moderate Antinomians was to glorify Christ; but failing to understand the true relation between "law" and "grace", they extolled the latter at the expense of the former. The issue raised by the Antinomians had its origin in the wide separation which they made between the Old and New Testaments... In some ways, it appears that the Antinomians brought themselves into difficulty by thinking of "Law" as if it were an entity to be done away, and of "Grace" as an entity taking its place.'

He acknowledges that many of them were 'strict in their church discipline and virtuous in their personal conduct' but adds this necessary caveat: 'It cannot be denied, however, that many fanatical persons were found among the Antinomians.' Moreover scholars and preachers whose own lives are unimpeachable may nevertheless present a message which leads to carelessness and disobedience on the part of those who listen to what they say.

Regrettably, the controversy led to some harsh and unfounded accusations, as all too frequently happens. 'There were many irresponsible accusations of heresy, joined with colourful language. There was much point-scoring which did not materially advance the discussion.' Both sides were guilty here. Thomas Edwards, for example, 'charges the Antinomians with one hundred and seventy-six errors, ranging from denial of the Trinity to eating black-puddings'!

The place and purpose of the law

Behind the law is the One who gave it, God in his majesty. 'God has the right to command, because He is the Source and End of all things. His sovereignty derives from the Creator-creature relation, and since man was made in the moral image of God "Moral obedience immediately becomes due, from such a creature to his Maker".' The law of God was written on man's heart from the very beginning and since the fall all human beings have a conscience which bears witness to their continuing sense of moral obligation.

Kevan points out that: 'It is one of the brighter aspects of the doctrinal outlook of the Puritans that they regarded the

Law, not as burdensome in its original purpose, but as the essence of man's delight... they were not aware of any extravagance when they affirmed that obedience to the Law of Nature was Adam's highest joy and good. They held that the Law was designed for the true well-being of man; it was his "way of life", and constituted his real liberty.' In the words of Richard Baxter: "God commands us a course of duty or right action to this end, that we may be happy in his love... His very law is a gift and a great benefit. Duty is the means to keep his first gifts and to receive more. The very doing of the duty is a receiving of the reward; the object of duty being felicitating... Holiness is happiness, in a large part."

To the Puritans the Law was 'nothing less than the very transcript of the glory of God... Man has been made in God's image, and so the moral Law written within him must be part of that very image itself... God could not be thought of as requiring from man anything less than that which accorded with the Divine character... The moral Law in man is a copy of the Divine nature, and what God wills in the moral Law is so "consonant to that eternal justice and goodness in himself", that any supposed abrogation of that Law would mean that God would "deny his own justice and goodness". "To find fault with the Law, were to find fault with God", for "the original draft is in God himself".'

The law, however, is not simply concerned with external behaviour; it is spiritual in its demands. This means that 'unless... the heart be right, the endeavour to obey God's Law is nothing more than a display of legalism. The words "before me" in the First Commandment indicate a worship that is "inward and spiritual before God".' This is crucial for the Puritan view. A believer has been set free from bondage to sin and now loves God in his heart and desires, out of gratitude and joy, to do all that pleases him.

This view of the law is fundamental to the Puritan – and to Kevan's – contention that the law still stands as the way in which the believer should walk. What is right and good in God's eyes does not change, nor does grace mean that the standard has been lowered or changed, the law is eternal. In the words of J. I. Packer: 'To orthodox Calvinism, the law of God is the permanent, unchanging expression of God's eternal and unchangeable holiness... God could not change this law, or set it aside, in His dealings with men, without denying Himself.'[1]

'No Moses now'

In Romans: Paul says that 'Christ is the end of the law for righteousness to every one that believeth'. The Antinomians took this verse, and other similar verses such as Romans 6:14, 'you are not under law but under grace', to mean that the law was abrogated for believers, a view that could be summed up by the phrase used by John Saltmarsh, "no Moses now"! Kevan points out that though 'the Antinomians made strong statements to the effect that the Law was abrogated... it is clear that, here and there, they qualified their assertions in ways that can be interpreted in a less unorthodox manner.' He says, 'They were most willing to concede the eternity of the matter of the Law, but they held that to serve God because of commandment to do so was legalistic and unspiritual.' They tended to be confused in their arguments and to confound 'the requirements of duty with the power to fulfil them'.

In general both the Antinomians and the Puritans held that Christ had fulfilled the law in two ways. Firstly, by what was termed his passive obedience he suffered death as the penalty of the law. Secondly, in his active obedience he obeyed his

[1]J. I. Packer, *The Redemption and Restoration of Man in the Thought of Richard Baxter*, Thesis for Oxford D.Phil, 1954, p. 304.

Father throughout his life, keeping the whole law perfectly and being in subjection to all that his Father willed for him. In Christ's passive obedience the sins of his elect were imputed to him and he bore the wrath of God against them, consequently delivering his elect from condemnation. The majority of the Puritans, and certainly the Antinomians, also held that the active obedience of Christ, that is his righteousness, was imputed to the elect. In part it was this that led the Antinomians to teach that the law was abrogated so far as believers were concerned. The reasoning here would go like this. If Christ has kept the law for Christians and they are righteous in him, what need is there then for them to keep the law, but rather simply to be led by the Spirit in their living.

The Puritans, however, were insistent that all human beings are under an obligation to obey God and thus to keep his commandments. Says John Barret: "But I should think that believers as they are creatures, are bound to obey God in all things, and that Christ came not to take off the obligation to duty and obedience, but to take off the obligation to wrath and punishment." Not only does obligation remain when people are converted but grace actually increases the sense of obligation. 'Our freedom and deliverance from the rigour and curse of the Law, binds us strongly to the service of God. The liberty of the Christian man is not a freedom from the obedience of the Law, but from the disobedience of it; for "to be free from obedience, is to be servants of sin."'

What the Antinomians so objected to, was the principle that 'duties are to be done because commanded'. Kevan quotes one of the Puritans who says that it is the Christian's "first virtue" when "we love, desire, and do any thing, especially because God commands" it. He continues: 'Anything less than obedience because commanded is not holiness... The insistence on this truth carries the subject into the very heart of the believer and into the citadel of his will. Only the heart that can say, "I delight to do thy will, O my God", can be adjudged to be truly converted and godly.' Duty and delight can belong together, and they do so in the life of the Christian.

'The Antinomians had a great distaste for the use of the Law as a rule of life and held that the only rule for the believer was the impulse of the Spirit within him through the inclination of his own heart.' Over against this the Puritans stressed the unity of Spirit and Word, the indwelling Spirit guides the believer through the Spirit-inspired written Word of God. Another bone of contention was the place of good works in assurance. 'The Antinomians denied the evidential value of good works and regarded "all notes and signs of a Christian estate" as "legal and unlawful". The believer must therefore obtain his assurance from the testimony of the Spirit who "gives such full and clear evidence" of his good estate that he has "no need to be tried by the fruits of sanctification"'. On the other hand the Puritans believed that obedience could have an evidential value. 'Thomas Goodwin charmingly says that the believer's graces and duties are "the daughters of faith", who "may in time of need indeed nourish their mother."'

Christian freedom and the law

The Puritans stressed that the law is written in the hearts of all the regenerate and this transforms the situation: 'The heart within echoes and answers to the commandments without... An obedient heart is like a crystal glass with a light in the midst, which shines forth through every part thereof. So that royal law that is written upon his heart shines forth into every parcel of his life; his outward works do echo to a law within.' There is nothing servile or legalistic about the believer's obedience, he 'is moved by a deep reverence for

God, without any trace of a servile spirit, or of being driven to obedience "with terrors". He keeps the Law, not "Legally" but "Evangelically", and finds nothing irksome in any of the commandments.'

'The Gospel... brings the spirit of power and life along with it; there goes a virtue together with the commands of the Gospel to strengthen the soul to obedience.' The believer is united to Jesus Christ, so Walter Marshal says: "Another great mystery in the Way of Sanctification, is the glorious Manner of our Fellowship with Christ in receiving an holy Frame of Heart from him; it is by our being in Christ, and having Christ himself in us." A Christian is indwelt by the Holy Spirit: 'Samuel Slater says that the difference between Law-obedience and Gospel-obedience is that the former is attempted by natural abilities, but the latter is performed in the "strength of a renewing Spirit".'

All this makes for a love for the law in the believer: 'It is part of the reconciling work of Christ that believers are made "friends" with the Law, for "after Christ has made agreement betwixt us and the Law, we delight to walk in it for the love of Christ".' This means that obedience becomes spontaneous: 'Love for God and His Law produces a new naturalness in obedience that amounts almost to spontaneity.' '"Faith makes the soul active... to run in the way of Gods Commandments... and... it cannot run too fast." Richard Sibbes says that a son does duties "out of nature" and like "water out of a spring"; they are not forced, but they have "a blessed freedom to all duties, an enlargement of heart to duties. God's people are a voluntary people."'

Conclusion

The Puritans held that Christian liberty freed the believer, not *from* the Law, but *for* the Law; so that although he is no longer *under* the Law, he is, nevertheless, still *in* the Law. This, they taught, was freedom itself. The Puritans believed that this freedom in the Law – a freedom dependent on the Law – was effected by the Holy Spirit who applied the saving merits of Christ's death to the believer and then wrote the Law within his heart. Love for the Law thus gave power to keep it.

[*The Grace of Law* was re-printed in 2011 by Reformation Heritage Books, Grand Rapids, Michigan, USA. ISBN: 978-1-87761-163-6.]

APPENDIX TWO

A Selection of Extracts from the Writings of Dr Kevan

For full details of works referred to, please see bibliography on page 285.

The Christian life

What a lovely life the real Christian life is, and it is all just beautifully natural. The roses in your garden do not have to try hard to look beautiful, nor do they have to struggle to be fragrant: it is just their nature. The musical song of the thrush or the blackbird is not a difficulty to the bird: it is its own nature. So it is with true goodness. I am perhaps going to give you a surprise in my next sentence. Well, here is what I am going to say very boldly. The real Christian *does as he likes*. Does that shock you? It will not shock you if you understand what it really is to be a Christian. The Christian is one who has been 'born again', that is to say, he has a new life with new 'likes'. Because of this new life, he likes to do the things that please God. 'Being good', then, is not really hard work at all when the love of God is in your heart.

Let's Talk, p. 147

Efficacious Grace

Efficacious Grace is the particular application of God's grace for a definite purpose. Efficacious Grace is saving grace... it is not just the benevolent wish of God who wants man to be saved 'if only they will let Him'... Efficacious Grace is successful in its purpose, it is 'invincible', for the victory belongs to the Holy Spirit; it is sovereign in its operations. It is bestowed at the sole will and good pleasure of God. Here God's mysterious and unfathomable purposes in Election and Predestination come into view, and the proper human reaction to such profound revelations is to say with the Apostle Paul, 'O the depth of the riches both of the wisdom and knowledge of God. How unsearchable are His judgments, and His ways past finding out' (*Rom.* 11:33).

The Gospel Herald, November 1943, pp. 166-7

Holiness and sanctification

There is no holiness where there is not subjection to God: all goodness must be for God's sake, not for its own. The good works of the believer are not merely good, they are good in that they are owed. The obligation of obedience is perpetual, and belongs to man's creaturely relation to God, and it is one of the richest fruits of grace that a regenerate soul is able to say, 'O how I love thy law!' (*Psa.* cxix. 97). The Biblical doctrine of sanctification, then, is not 'rely and relax' but 'trust and obey'. Puritan teaching avoids Pelagian activism on the one hand and Quietist passivism on the other, and in place of both of these it affirms the necessity for the obedience of faith.

The Moral Law, pp. 3-4

Legalism and law-keeping

In these days of evangelical uncertainty about the place of the Law in the life of the believer it is important that cries of 'Legalism!' shall not be irresponsibly raised, but that a clear distinction be kept between the legalism of unbelief and the Law-keeping of faith.

'Legalism: An Essay on the Views of Dr Brunner', in *Vox Evangelica* 2 (1963), p. 56

The Evangelical Library

The value of the Evangelical Library is that it preserves and makes available for us the convincing writings of the keen thinkers of the past. There is no more devastating criticism, for example, of Roman Catholic superstition than that which is contained in Book IV of Calvin's *Institutes of the Christian Religion*. These chapters meet the need of to-day just as clearly as they did those of the 16th century. It is humiliating sometimes to discover that what we imagine to be an original, forceful, and incontrovertible statement or defence of the truth was said by others before us, and said much better. But that this is the case can be proved over and over again. We shall need new books, of course, and the prayer of many is that God will raise up evangelical scholars of giant stature in our own day. It remains nevertheless true that the names appearing on the volumes on the shelves of the Evangelical Library are such as continue to demand our deepest respect. The monumental works of these writers challenge us still.

The Evangelical Quarterly, July 1946

The Lord's Supper

Now I know the doctrinal importance of preserving the Lord's Supper and preserving the church order which the New Testament teaches in the relation of baptism to the Lord's Supper, but there are some differences that we must sink in the presence of the Lord's Supper as fellowship. Mr Spurgeon once made the remark. 'I know many a brother with whom I cannot agree on certain points, but I can agree with him in remembering the Lord. I could not work with him in all he does, but if he wants to remember the Lord Jesus I can join him in that.' I do not quote this in any way of controversy, but what a good thing it would be if we could triumph over the barriers that come between fellow-believers. Some of these barriers have no reality in them, yet we allow them to cut us off from one another.

The Lord's Supper, p. 57

Sin and law

Near where I lived at one time there was an open common, through the middle of which there ran a busy main road. It was the custom of mothers to permit their little ones to play on the part of the common near their homes, but to forbid them to cross the busy road to the other section. The road was the boundary, and if a child crossed it in order to play in what seemed the more attractive part of the common, his action would be transgression – 'trans' (across) 'gression' (going). The drawing of the boundary line was not with the view to denying the child any pleasure; it was a boundary of loving wisdom. In the same way, the boundary of God's holy law, that has been put like a vast circle around our lives, is a limit of love drawn by infinitely wise and tender goodness in God. This boundary – the law of God – is nevertheless authoritative, just as the word of a parent to a little child, and the transgression of this boundary is a breaking of God's commandment.

What the Scriptures Teach, p. 15

Election

The things about which I want to speak to you now are taught to us by God after we have come to know Him. When we have entered into the joy of salvation through repentance and faith, God gives us a glimpse of His eternal plan. He wants us to know that our salvation was not something that happened on the spur of the moment: it was not left to chance or hazard. God tells us that we have come to love Him because of His everlasting love to us, and that we have chosen Him because He chose us long before we were born. We may find this difficult to grasp, but that is what we might expect with the deep mind of God.

In searching the Bible we come again and again upon the wonderful truth that wherever we find a sinner who trusts the Saviour, there too we see one who has been eternally chosen by God. Election to salvation and predestination into the family of God are great and comforting truths which God has revealed in the Bible. They are 'strong meat' on which we must feed our faith as we grow in grace. It is because God has chosen us to salvation, and because He is the One who began the good work in us, that we may be assured that we shall never perish (*Phil.* 1:6). Our Lord Jesus Christ brought all these deep truths together and put them in one sentence with the simple invitation of the gospel when He said, 'All that the Father giveth me shall come to me; and him that cometh to me I will in no wise cast out.'

What the Scriptures Teach, p. 48

Sanctification

In the discussion about 'perfection' and 'eradication' we have to remember that the 'old nature' or 'indwelling sin' is not a material thing of some sort which can be removed by a kind of surgical operation. The carnal mind is the sum of all those desires and thoughts of the sinner which are at enmity with God. In the sanctifying work of the Holy Spirit these desires and thoughts of the believer are transformed by the renewing of the mind (*Rom.* 12:1). Slightly changing the figure, this transformation of the believer's desires means that the sinful desires are displaced by a love for God. The beginning of this renewal is to be traced to the act of the Holy Spirit in regeneration, an act of God by which these new desires were first created in the believer. The continuance of this renewal is likewise the act of the Holy Spirit as he strengthens the new life and enables the believer to mortify the deeds of the body and to live unto righteousness.

'Holiness of Life', in *The Christian Graduate*, March 1957

Calvinism

A fifth good reason why the re-emergence of Calvinism need cause no surprise is that *Calvinism has room for the contradictions of life*. Life is a paradox, and Calvinism does not seek to impose an unreal unity upon it. Life is confronting many people today with its terrible contradictions. For the sake of liberty men put themselves in bondage. Civilisation is rising up in vigour to defend itself, yet in the very act is negating itself. The scientific progress of the last four decades has been phenomenal, yet man seems to be going backwards.

In spiritual things the paradox of life is acute. Man feels he is bound by the great invisible forces that are at work in the world; he feels he is a creature of circumstances in the iron chains of environment, upbringing and habit, but for all that he cannot bring himself to deny that he is free. The eternal contradiction of free-will and determinism is ever present. Man feels that he counts for nothing, and yet he cannot deny his own personal worth for that would mean the shattering of every noble purpose.

Because of these contradictions in life's deepest places man despises the facile solutions that are offered him. They are suspected because they are too easy. Man's thoughts, therefore, are again turned towards Calvinism despite, nay, because of, its self-confessed antinomies and its unresolved problem of grace and free-will. Men look to it because of its power to hold resolutely to the dual truth. The strength of Calvinism is just the room it has for the contradictions of life. Its own great doctrines contain within them this profound Yes and No, in which every affirmation is a denial and every denial carries with it an affirmation. To say this is not to mean that Calvinism is equivocal, but it is to say that it sees the truth and sees its depths.

'The Re-emergence of Calvinism', in
The Evangelical Quarterly, July 1943

Mortification

The mortification of sin is our own believing act through the indwelling Holy Spirit. The act most certainly is our own: that is to say, the Spirit does not do it for us. Not by an alleged masterly inactivity is the destruction of sin accomplished, but by the active prosecution of it. The verb 'mortify' is in the present tense: 'if by the Spirit you *are doing to death* the practices of the body, you will live'. Paul thus requires us to understand that the mortifying has to go on all the while that we are in the body. This is where the prayerfulness and the constant vigilance of the Christian life have their place.

The Saving Work of the Holy Spirit, p. 61

The resurrection of Christ

Nothing less than the actual rising again from the dead of the Lord Jesus Christ could possibly account for the transformation of the disciples and the faith of the Christian Church. The resurrection of the Lord Jesus Christ is demonstrated on the evidence of a three fold witness. The witnesses are unimpeachable, and the evidence is indestructible, and the conclusion is inevitable. The Acts, the Epistles, and the Gospels, each in their own way, proclaim the message, 'Now is Christ risen from the dead, and become the firstfruits of them that slept.' The empty tomb, the appearances of the living Christ, and the transformation of the disciples cry out with one triumphant voice, 'He is not here: for he is risen, as he said. Come, see the place where the Lord lay'.

The believer may lift up his head as the living Lord proclaims, 'Fear not; I am the first and the last: I am he that liveth, and was dead; and, behold, I am alive for evermore'.

The Resurrection of Christ
(Campbell Morgan Lecture, 1961), pp. 15-16

The Holy Spirit and preaching

The man who believes in this secret and invincible work of the Holy Spirit will preach with confidence. A conviction of the sovereignty of God in His saving grace and of the Spirit's re-creative power in the life of the soul will deliver us from that pathetic desperation with which some evangelistic appeals have been known to reach their climax. We shall preach in the deep knowledge that we are the servants of the most High God and the instruments of His saving love in the world. With our eyes opened to these things we shall know something of the experience of the missionary who once said that he had never preached the Gospel anywhere without finding that God had been there before him.

What shall we say to these things? We profess the high doctrine, but do we live there? How heart-searching is the doctrine of the Holy Spirit! Dare we go into the pulpit with contraband goods, with anything other than the sovereign Spirit purposes to give through us? If we truly believe that He has gone before us, we must seek Him for every word that we utter. It will not do for us simply to come before the people with what we believe to be a biblical message: we must have the very word for the very moment. Our doctrine of the Holy Spirit will fill us with the highest joy in the pulpit, but it will bring us to the lowest place in the humility and dependence of our prayers. This doctrine lays upon us the heaviest burden of spiritual responsibility that man can bear. So far from releasing us from any labour or care it demands the dedication of all our powers. Our doctrine of the Holy Spirit will compel us to think and to pray and to work.

The Doctrine of the Holy Spirit in Relation to our Preaching, pp. 19, 21

Sin

Sin therefore is a coming short of God's standard through a voluntary act which issues in a permanent state. In form, it is a failure to hit the mark; in substance, it is an attitude of resistance to God; in result, it is a state of moral perversion. All sin relates to God; it is not so much against law, but against God Himself. It is a rupture in personal relations: 'Against thee, thee only, have I sinned' (*Psa.* 51:4). The worst thing about sin is that it dishonours God and separates man from Him. 'Your iniquities have separated between you and your God, and your sins have hid his face from you, that he will not hear' (*Isa.* 59:2).

Sin is not a calamity that, having come upon man unawares, now spoils his happiness; rather it is an evil course which man has deliberately chosen to follow and which carries untold misery with it. It is not something passive, like a weakness, or a simple imperfection, but something active and opposed to God.

Man and his Nature, pp. 4-5

We must plead

Assured of the working of the Holy Spirit in our hearers we must therefore expose the sinner to the searching of the 'Eternal Light'; we must show him what he is; we must declare the doom of the impenitent. Together with this we must urge him with all earnestness and gravity at our command to repent and put his trust in Christ. With conversion as our aim, we must tell the sinner what God thinks of him, what God has done for him, and what God is able to do for him. Our preaching must be direct and challenging. We must hammer at his conscience, we must warn, we must alarm, and, like the apostle, we must even make Felix tremble. But we must also instruct and invite. Perhaps a simple quotation from the prince of British preachers may be employed here. 'Brethren', said Mr Spurgeon, 'we must plead. Entreaties and beseechings must blend with our instructions. Any and every appeal which will reach the conscience and move men to fly to Jesus we must perpetually employ, if by any means we may save some.'

The Doctrine of the Holy Spirit in Relation to our Preaching, p. 20

APPENDIX THREE

Documents

A transcription of a handout from one of Dr Kevan's lectures:

LONDON BIBLE COLLEGE

HOMILETICS

Lecture IX

THE FINISHING TOUCHES

I. Take Time

II. Meditate

III. Re-examine the Relation between Theme and Conclusion

IV. Review the Structure

V. Test the Cogency of the Argument

VI. Apply the Process of Elimination

a) Irrelevance
b) Flourishes
c) Complications
d) Disproportions
e) Repetitions

VII. Measure the "warmth" of the sermon

VIII. Write out the Sermon in Full

a) Write fully
b) Summarise
c) Outline

IX. Prepare yourself for the Preaching

X. Offer the work to God in Prayer and receive back just so much as He gives you.

An extract from an LBC exam paper in 1960:

LONDON BIBLE COLLEGE

Summer Term 1960 — PASTORAL THEOLOGY

Time Allowed: 2 hours — (Groups 4.8.)

Answer FOUR Questions

1. Why should a minister seek to live in accordance with higher standards than his people?

2. Write the following three specimen letters:-

   (a) In reply to a letter from a Missionary Society enquiring about the suitability of one of your young people for missionary work.

   (b) Answering a troubled parent who has written to you about their teenager son.

   (c) Ordering a supply of printed folders in connection with a Campaign.

3. What part should a minister take in the business and financial aspects of church life?

4. Discuss the minister's attitude to his home and family.

5. Exhibit the value of pastoral visitation.

6. How should a minister relate his ministry to his neighbourhood?

7. Explain the principles upon which an order of worship should be designed and give one or two illustrations of what you say.

Letter from Kevan to Lloyd-Jones regarding the latter speaking at the College on the subject of 'The Place of Theology in Practical Preaching':

LONDON BIBLE COLLEGE
19 Marylebone Road, N.W. 1
WELbeck 5850

From the Principal—
REV. ERNEST F. KEVAN, M.TH.
Private Telephone: WELbeck 9011

EFK/JW

20th January, 1948.

The Rev. Dr. D. Martyn Lloyd-Jones,
39 Mount Park Crescent,
Ealing, W.5.

My dear Dr. Lloyd-Jones,

There are just one or two things upon which I wanted to write to you. The first is to say how exceedingly sorry I am that on the occasion of your visit to the L.I.F.C.U. Conference on Saturday 7th February I have to be away speaking at two meetings at Southend-on-Sea. I fear that this means I shall not be able to see you at all; I do trust the occasion may be one of blessing, but I felt I wanted to express to you my real regret about my absence on the day of your visit.

I trust you will forgive my constant importunity, but our men equally with myself are insistent that we do wish you to pay us a visit as a College. I realise that Monday mornings are not the best time for you after your heavy day on the Sunday. At the end of every term, however, on the last two days we have special visitors to deal with topics which are somewhat outside the ordinary run of the curriculum. The last two days of this term are Thursday and Friday 11th and 12th March. Do you think you could come on Thursday 11th March at 11.30 a.m. to give the men a talk on the subject "The Place of Theology in Pastoral Preaching"? You would have a whole hour for this, and then nothing would please our men more than to have the opportunity of your presence with them at the College lunch immediately following. If this particular day is not convenient to you then as an alternative there is a session on Friday 12th March at 9.30. I do hope you will be able to come on one or other of these dates.

It was a joy to be in Westminster Chapel on Sunday and I received blessing in the worship.

With my kindest regards in which Mrs. Kevan joins me.

Yours most sincerely,

Ernest F. Kevan
Principal.

Letter from Kevan to Lloyd-Jones with invitation to tea with himself and Mrs Kevan, before a meeting of the Evangelical Library committee:

LONDON BIBLE COLLEGE
19 Marylebone Road, N.W. 1
WELbeck 5850

From the Principal—
REV. ERNEST F. KEVAN, M.TH.
Private Telephone: WELbeck 9011

EFK/JW 2nd July, 1948.

Dr. D. Martyn Lloyd-Jones,
39 Mount Park Crescent,
Ealing, W.5.

My dear Dr. Lloyd Jones,

I expect you have heard that owing to the large number of friends who indicated their desire to come to our Prize Day we had to transfer the meeting from Livingstone Hall to your own Church. Thank you for allowing us to come at such short notice. You will be delighted to know that we had an immense company of people and well filled the floor of the Chapel. This was astonishing to us as the meeting had been advertised in so limited a way. We are much looking forward to our Annual Meeting on October 5th when, if all goes well, we shall have an even larger attendance.

The special purpose of my writing to you is to ask whether you could find the time to come in and have a cup of tea with Mrs. Kevan and myself on Friday 9th July just prior to the Committee Meeting of the Evangelical Library. The meeting is at 4.15, and if you could be here between 3.30 and 3.35 we should be so glad. This will give me the opportunity of a few moments with you which I would very much prize to talk over one or two matters connected both with the Library and with the College.

With my kindest regards and every good wish.

Yours most cordially,

Ernest F. Kevan

Principal.

Letter from Kevan to Lloyd-Jones requesting the latter's help and advice on the publication of a reworking of an item of Puritan literature:

London Bible College

19 MARYLEBONE ROAD
LONDON, N.W.1.

WELbeck 5850

From the Principal—
REV. ERNEST F. KEVAN, M.TH.

EFK/JW

22nd November, 1956.

Dr. D.M. Lloyd-Jones,
39 Mount Park Crescent,
Ealing, W.5.

My dear Dr. Lloyd-Jones,

I am now almost ready with the typescript of the "translation" that I have made of John Ball, "A Treatise of the Covenant of Grace". You will remember I talked to you about this last year at our Puritan Conference.

It makes such a difference in negotiation with possible publishers if an introduction to the right person can be obtained. I am wondering, therefore, whether through your contacts you could give me any introductions to publishers, either in Great Britain or in the U.S.A., who might be willing to sponsor Puritan literature. The work would not be very large, probably about 120 pages by the time it was prepared, and so should not be too great a strain on the resources of British publishers. I would greatly prefer the book to be published in this country by one of the reputable houses, but if this is not possible then maybe the United States is the direction in which I must look, though I fear that there again such publishers will be more interested in American authors than in British.

The last few pages of my typescript are now being finished, and I would greatly value your judgment on the work if it were at all possible for you to find time to read it through. I am not dreaming, therefore, of sending this to you without your kind permission as I know that your days and hours are far too full. If however you felt you could do this for me I think you know how grateful I would be. Perhaps you would either telephone me or drop me a line about any suggestions that you could kindly make.

With my warmest regards,

Yours as ever,

Ernest F. Kevan

Principal.

Letter from Kevan to Lloyd-Jones detailing the forthcoming dedication of the new college building:

London Bible College

τὰ ἄνω φρονεῖτε

19 MARYLEBONE ROAD
LONDON, N.W.

[redacted]
WELbeck 2315

From the Principal—
REV. ERNEST F. KEVAN, M.TH.

EFK/JW

23rd April, 1958.

Dr. D.M. Lloyd-Jones,
39 Mount Park Crescent,
Ealing, W.5.

My dear Dr. Lloyd-Jones,

The time of the Opening and Dedication of the new building of the College is fast drawing near, and the enclosed invitation will give you some idea of what is being sent out to our prayerful friends. On an attached sheet I am setting out the Order of Service as it is being printed on a special programme now in the hands of the printer. From this you will see that after the President's welcome and a statement by the Treasurer Mr. Laing will formally declare the building open. As a kind of addendum to what Mr. Laing has said Mr. Stevenson, the editor of The Life of Faith, will in a very short speech "present" the large Lecture Hall which was paid for by the gifts of readers of The Life of Faith and is to be known as the "Life of Faith Lecture Hall". Immediately following upon this you will please lead us in the prayer dedicating the entire place and work to the glory of God. After further acts of worship we shall then look forward to a sermon from you, and pray that God may give you His message for this occasion.

It is impossible for us to forecast how many people will be present, but it is quite conceivable that there might easily be 2,000. By a public address system which is installed in the College the entire proceedings will be relayed over the whole building and also on some supplementary loud-speakers into the open car park behind the College. Seats are being reserved for a large number of friends, and I am hoping that Mrs. Lloyd-Jones may be able to accompany you; a place will, of course, be reserved for her.

I think I mentioned that the B.B.C. are coming with a recording apparatus, and they have promised to give some excerpts from the proceedings on the Church Programme on the following Wednesday.

If by any chance you have any spare moments between now and May 10th so that I may show you the building in greater comfort to yourself, and you may thus be able to take in the significance of it, do please be assured of the great pleasure that it will give to me to be able to welcome you at any time. I observe that the Westminster Fellowship meets on Tuesday, May 6th. Would you care to come up here at about 12.30 p.m. so that I could show you the College, and you could then have lunch with us before proceeding to Westminster for the meeting?

One further thought occurs to me while writing to you, and it relates to Professor Young's four Lectures that he is to give at the College on the following Monday to Thursday. Would it be too great a breach of the necessary regulations governing outside meetings at Westminster Chapel if you were able to draw attention to these Lectures. As you know, we are bringing Dr. Young over by air specially for these four evenings, and we would like him to have as worthy an audience as possible. The College is planning to print these Lectures in a book, and Messrs. James Clark have agreed to publish it at 10/6d. We hope that this book will thus prove something of a manifesto concerning our conservative attitude to the Bible and thus prove a testimony.

I desire to keep you as little burdened as possible with the affairs of the College, but if there is anything I can tell you at any time please never hesitate to ring me or drop me a line.

With my very warm affection,

Yours most cordially,

Ernest F. Kevan

Principal.

Select Bibliography

Books by Ernest Kevan, in order of publication:

London's Oldest Baptist Church (London: The Kingsgate Press, 1933).

The Saving Work of the Holy Spirit (London: Pickering & Inglis, 1953).*

The Law of God in Christian Experience: A Study in the Epistle to the Galatians (London: Pickering & Inglis, 1955).*

Salvation (Grand Rapids, MI: Baker Book House, 1963).

The Moral Law (n.p., Sovereign Grace Publishers, 1963).

Going On: What a Christian Believes and What He Should Do (London: Marshall, Morgan & Scott, 1964); later republished as *Now That I Am a Christian* (London: Evangelical Press, 1966).

The Grace of Law (London: Carey Kingsgate Press, 1964).

Let's Talk: Talks About the Bible (London: Henry E. Walter, 1965).

The Lord's Supper (London: Evangelical Press, 1966).

What the Scriptures Teach (London: Evangelical Press, 1966).

*These two publications were originally given as Bible readings at Keswick and therefore also appear in *The Keswick Week* for 1953 and 1955 respectively. Three addresses on Ephesians were also published in the 1958 edition of *Keswick Week*.

Booklets and articles by Ernest Kevan, in order of publication:

Doctrine and Development, 1938.

The Faith and Practice of the Church Worshipping in Trinity Road Chapel, Upper Tooting, 1944.

'The Re-emergence of Calvinism', in *The Evangelical Quarterly* 15 (July 1943), pp. 216-23.

'The Evangelical Library', in *The Evangelical Quarterly* 17 (July 1945). pp. 221-5 (with D. M. Lloyd-Jones).

'The Person and Work of Christ', in *The Evangelical Quarterly* 23:3 (1951), pp. 213-18.

'The Doctrine of the Holy Spirit in Relation to Our Preaching', in *The Story of the Year* (London Bible College), 1952.

The Puritan Doctrine of Conversion (Annual Lecture of the Evangelical Library), 1952.

'The Covenants and Interpretation of the Old Testament', in *The Evangelical Quarterly* 26:1 (1954), pp. 19-28.

The Evangelical Doctrine of Law (The Tyndale Biblical Theology Lecture), 1955.

The Law and the Covenants: A Study in John Ball (Puritan Conference paper), 1956.

'Holiness of Life: A Survey of Several Lines of Teaching', in *The Christian Graduate* 10:1 (1957).

Man and His Nature, a Crusade 'School of Faith' booklet, 1959.

The Resurrection of Christ (The Campbell Morgan Memorial Lecture), 1961.

'Legalism: An Essay on the Views of Dr Brunner', in *Vox Evangelica* 2 (1963).

Keep His Commandments, 1964.

'The Moral Law and its Relation to Believers', in *Reformed Perspectives*, 10:30 (2008).*

'The Moral Law', in *Reformed Perspectives* 11:22 (2009).*

*The above two online articles are chapters 8 and 10 of *The Moral Law* (1963) respectively.

* * *

Works relating to Ernest Kevan: his life-time, work, and religious background:

Oliver Barclay, *Evangelicalism in Britain, 1935-1995* (Leicester: IVP, 1997).

John Brencher, *Martyn Lloyd-Jones (1899-1981) and Twentieth-Century Evangelicalism* (Carlisle: Paternoster, 2002).

H. Carey Oakley, *From the First Day Until Now 1870-1970, being a record of the church worshipping at Trinity Road Chapel, Upper Tooting, London, S.W.17, from its foundation in 1870 to its centenary.* (Trinity Road Chapel, 1970).

Kenneth Dix, *Strict and Particular* (Didcot: The Baptist Historical Society, 2001).

Timothy Dudley-Smith, *John Stott: The Making of a Leader* (Leicester: IVP, 1999).

Gilbert Kirby, *Ernest Kevan: Pastor and Principal* (Eastbourne: Victory Press, 1968).

Iain H. Murray, *D. Martyn Lloyd-Jones: The Fight of Faith, 1939-1981* (Edinburgh: Banner of Truth Trust, 1990).

John J. Murray, *Catch the Vision: Roots of the Reformed Recovery* (Darlington: Evangelical Press, 2007).

Robert Oliver, *From John Spilsbury to Ernest Kevan*, The 1984 Annual Lecture of the Evangelical Library (London: Grace Publications Trust, 1984).

Robert Oliver, *History of the English Calvinistic Baptists, 1771-1892*, (Edinburgh: Banner of Truth Trust, 2006).

Ian M. Randall, *Educating Evangelicalism: The Origin, Development and Impact of London Bible College* (Carlisle: Paternoster, 2000).

Ian M. Randall, *The English Baptists of the Twentieth Century* (Didcot: Baptist Historical Society, 2005).

Ian M. Randall, *Evangelical Experiences: A Study in the Spirituality of English Evangelicalism, 1918-1939* (Carlisle: Paternoster, 1999).

Harold Rowdon, *London Bible College: The First 25 Years* (London: Henry E. Walter, 1968).

Geoffrey Thomas, 'Ernest Kevan', in *The Banner of Truth* 271 (April 1986), pp. 8-13 and Issue 272 (May 1986), pp. 4-11.

Derek J. Tidball, *Who Are the Evangelicals?* (London: Marshall Pickering, 1994).

Index

Aberneithie, David, 248
Abinger Convention, 234
Aldis, W. H., 113, 145
Alliance of Honour, 29
Am I Ready for Training?, 171
Anderson, Moira, 181, 248
Antinomians, 258-9, 261-3
Areopagus, 157
Ash, Raymond, 144
Association of Grace Baptist Churches, South East, 6

Bachelor of Divinity (BD), 62, 86-7, 140, 153, 187-98
Back, Mrs., 10
Bairns, 78
Baker, Donald, 230, 232, 241, 247-8, 250
Baker, W. S., 75
Baptist Confessions, 64
Baptist Union, 15n, 22n, 36, 44, 68, 91, 99, 111, 118-19, 182, 199-202, 203, 205-7
—Examination, 91, 202
Recognition Committee, 202
Baptist Times, 111
Barret, John, 262
Basham, Jane (see Kevan, Mrs)
Battersea, 1, 3, 4, 10
Battersea Grammar School, 10
Battle of Britain, 106
Baxter, Richard, 7, 211, 260, 261n
Beasley-Murray, Dr George, 250
Bethesda Baptist Church, Ipswich, 240
Billy Graham crusades, 233, 245
Bird, George, 59, 75, 112, 240
Boorne, Mr, 127-8
Booth, Abraham, 65-7
Bowen's Chemical Works, 4
Bralwright, Mr & Mrs, 2
Brand, Paul, 79
Bray, Dr Gerald, 95
British Empire, xvi, 26, 93
Brown, Alice, 105
Brown, Bill, 82, 102, 111
Buckley, Doreen, 133, 237
Buckley, Timothy, xi, 22n, 133, 235, 248

Cairns, D. S., 105
Calvinism, 16, 64, 98n, 110, 123, 187, 204, 261, 272-3
Cambridgeshire and East Midlands Union, 17, 78
Campaigners, 78
Campen, Bob, 167
Certificate of Proficiency in Religious Knowledge, 136, 190-1
Chapman, Mr, 102
Charismatic renewal, 156
Chatham Road Chapel, 21
Cheam Baptist Church, 247-8
Children's ministry, xvi, xvii, 8, 39, 44-6, 51, 77-8, 92, 130, 168, 234, 240, 255

Chiltern Hall, 145
Chilvers, H. Tydeman, 19, 58
China Inland Mission, 105, 139, 143
Chisnall, W., 21
Church Hill Baptist Church, xii, xv, 33-42, 45-51, 53, 68, 70-74, 85, 226
Church of England, 29, 59-60, 110, 204-5
Christian Endeavour, 17, 46, 58
Christian Life course, 222, 233
Christian's Pathway, 16, 69-70
Clapham Junction, 3, 31
Clarke, O. F., 128
College Diploma, 136
College Review, 77n, 136n, 140n, 144n, 149n, 157, 167n, 168, 181n, 225n, 229n, 240, 248n, 249, 250n, 253n
Collin, J. B., 59, 75, 87
Colnbrook, 2-3
Communion, 15-17, 45, 69-70, 86, 122, 131, 185, 207
Connell, J. C., 148, 168, 192
Conscientious objectors, 83, 108
Cooper, Miss, 108
Colquhoun, Canon Frank, 135, 250
Correspondence courses
—Strict Baptist, 76, 108
—London Bible College, 116, 137-8, 202, 215, 222, 233
Council for National Academic Awards (CNAA), 197
Crees, Percy, 79
Cudmore, Ezra, 67
Cudmore, Frank, 38

Deptford, 73, 85-6, 110-12
Dix, Dr Kenneth, xii, 16n, 287
Doctorate, 223, 231, 240
Downgrade Controversy, 118
Dulwich College, xii, 11-12, 24, 83, 87
Duty-faith, 69-70, 121

Earthen Vessel, 16
East London Tabernacle, 16, 29
Education Act 1944, 194
Edwards, Brian, xii
Edwards, Thomas, 259
Ellison, H. L., 150-53
Evangelical Alliance, 221
Evangelical Fellowship of India, 225, 105
Evangelical Library, 110, 143, 210, 239, 269, 280, 286, 288
Evangelical Quarterly, 110, 150, 151, 214, 269, 286
Evans, Percy, 201
Ewing, J. W., 135
Eyers, John, 152
Eyers, P. G., 137

Faculty, 79, 122, 133-6, 147-8, 150, 152-4, 156, 158, 175, 177, 188-90, 196, 197, 200, 232, 241, 255
Fellowship of Independent Evangelical Churches (FIEC), 182, 207
Fellowship of Youth, 79, 104
Fox, William, 67
Free churches, 28, 62
Free Churches Council, 45
Free offer of the gospel, 121

George VI, 92-3
Gibson, Alan, xii, 184-5, 210n
Gill, Dr, 66
Going On, 19, 20n, 234-5, 245, 285

Gordon, Murdo, 140
Gospel Herald, xii, 3n, 5, 6n, 16, 39, 50-52, 75, 79n, 80-81, 94, 101, 103-5, 107n, 108, 127
Gospel Standard, 16-17
Grace Baptist Mission, 6
Grace of Law, The, xv, 9n, 194, 224n, 233, 240, 255, 257-65, 285
Guthrie, Dr Donald, 148, 223

Hainault Road Church, 54
Halstead, 3
Hammond, T. C., 116, 172
Hampstead, 181, 231, 234
Handbook of the London Bible College, 175, 179, 180-81, 203
Harringay Arena, 221-2, 253
Heddle, Edmund, 183
Held-Out-Hand, 51, 53, 75, 83, 162, 167
Helwys, Thomas, 35
Henman, Philip, 240
Herriot, Miss, 65
Highbury New Park, 139-40, 143
Hills, Leonard, 73, 77, 84
Home & Colonial Stores, 24, 40
Homework Fund, 202
Howden, J. Russell, 113, 190n, 195
Hughes, Betty, 80
Hyper-Calvinism, 16, 204

India, 5, 48, 65, 79, 104-5, 158, 168, 225-7, 249, 254
Inskip, Bishop J. T., 60
Inter-Varsity Fellowship, 113, 214, 255
Irons, Joseph, 238

Jacob-Lathrop-Jessey Church, 36
Johnson, Dr Douglas, 113-14, 195n
Jones, I. L., 69
'Just War' theory, 84

Kentish Town, 185
Kentish Mercury, 76, 84, 85, 111, 112n
Keswick Convention, 40, 68, 216-20, 223-4, 229, 285
Kevan, Mrs Ann, 2
KEVAN, ERNEST FREDERICK,
—Author, xv, xvi, 8, 19-20, 60, 62, 76, 94, 110, 121, 214, 217, 220, 222-3, 227, 233-4, 240, 246, 255
—Called to ministry, 30-31, 33-9
—Childhood, 1-13, 17, 213
—Conversion, 18-22, 23
—Degrees, 62, 86, 109, 193, 223
—Illness and death, 43-4, 236-8, 231-2
—Invitation to London Bible College, 116, 122, 252
—Lecturer, 135-8, 158-65
—Marriage, 40-42, 43, 76
—Principal of London Bible College, xv, 115, 122, 147-65, 168, 170, 180-1, 197, 243, 249, 252
Kevan, Ethel, 1, 9, 37
Kevan, Frederick W., 1-6, 24-5, 37, 48, 62, 81-2, 87
Kevan, Hilda, 1, 6, 9, 37
Kevan (*née* Basham), Mrs Jane, 40-42, 43, 47-8, 74, 76-7, 80, 87, 107, 128-9, 141, 144, 181, 183-4, 185, 186, 230, 231, 232, 235, 236, 244, 245, 246, 248, 255, 280
Kevan, Mrs Kate, 6, 7, 23, 26, 37,

47, 75, 87, 101, 106
Kevan, Samuel, 2, 3
Kingdon, David, 234
Kirby, Gilbert, xi, 9n, 13n, 18n, 20, 24n, 25, 30n, 40, 41n, 52, 53, 54n, 57, 58n, 77, 79n, 85n, 86n, 120n, 126, 127, 129n, 130, 131, 140n, 141, 142, 147, 161n, 168n, 169n, 171, 204n, 207, 209n, 234n, 235, 236, 237, 239, 246, 247, 248, 251n, 253, 287
Knibb, William, 61

Laing House, 174
Laing, Sir John, 113, 143
Lake District, 40
Law of God in Christian Experience, The, 223
Lay Preachers' Federation, 202
Leng, George, 103
Let's Talk, xvi, 8, 10n, 12n, 54, 55n, 93n, 234, 267, 285
Liberal Evangelicalism, 111
Lloyd-Jones, Dr D. M., 98n, 109, 113, 116, 121, 128, 135, 151, 162, 187-8, 189n, 190-91, 196-7, 207, 212-13, 252, 254, 279-83, 287
London, xv, xvi, 1, 6, 16, 23-4, 26-31, 35, 47, 49, 50, 61-2, 64, 66, 102-4, 106, 110, 113, 129, 139, 143, 169, 180, 185, 221, 226, 231
London Bible College, xi, xii, xv, 25n, 114-16, 120, 122, 126-7, 131-3, 135-45, 147, 149, 153, 155-6, 159, 167, 172, 175, 181-2, 184, 186, 190-91, 195-207, 209, 214-15, 222-3, 226, 231, 239, 243, 252-3, 254-5, 277, 286, 288
London Bible College Baptist Ministers' Fraternal, 206
London's Oldest Baptist Church, 35n, 60-68, 285
London University, 86, 109, 113, 136, 187-8, 190, 193-4, 223, 240
Long, Mr, 120
Lord's Supper, The, 20, 227-8, 269-70, 285
Lord's Table/Supper, 15-16, 20, 69-70, 104, 117, 122, 226-8, 269-70, 285
Lynn, John Hunt, 38

MacDonald, Dr H. D., 148, 169, 223, 236
Madsen, John, 180
Manchester University, 154
Manton, Margaret, 149, 161
Martin, Mr, 103
Martin, Dr Ralph P., xi, 153-4, 158, 230
Mason, Kate (See Kevan, Mrs Kate)
Memorial Service, 236, 238, 240-43
Metropolitan Association, 5-6, 16-17, 29, 36, 45, 48, 50, 59, 73, 78, 91, 94, 99, 101, 122, 128, 194
Metropolitan Tabernacle, 5, 19, 29, 58, 116-17, 118n, 240
Meyer, F. B., 29
Middlesex University, 197
Ministry of Education, 195
Moral Law, The, 285
Modernism, 91, 94, 106
Moore College, 116
Murray, Iain H., xi, 187n, 189-90, 196, 199, 201, 287
Muswell Hill Baptist Church, 119

New Bible Commentary, 76, 214-15, 217
New Bible Dictionary, 140
New Cross, xii, xv, 61, 73-89, 108n, 110, 112, 117, 204, 240, 248, 255
Nonconformity, 28, 59, 118n
North Chingford (church plant), 50-51, 68-71
Now That I Am a Christian, 19, 234, 285
Nuttall, Professor G. F., 231

Oak Hill College, 135
Oakley, Henry, 118, 132-3
Oakley, H. Carey, 117n, 119n, 129n, 132n, 133, 158n, 235, 250, 287
Oram, William, 140, 144

Paedobaptist, 204
Packer, Dr J. I., 197, 252, 261
Park, R. J., 119
Parker, Dr, 95
Parker, Miss R., 149
Paterson, Kath (*née* Walden), xii, 236, 246
Paterson, Kenneth, 132, 207, 248
Payne, Ernest A., 62, 203
Payne, William, 62
Peace Pledge Union, 83-4, 108
Pentecostalism, 156
Poole-Connor, E. J., 46, 135
Presbyterians, 58, 64, 202
Price-Lewis, Mr, 132
Puritans, 194, 210-12, 220, 223, 251, 252, 257-65
Puritan Conference, 197, 210, 212, 252, 286

Randall, Dr Ian, xi, 29n, 40n, 44, 111n, 114n, 148-53, 155, 156, 190, 192, 199, 200n, 201-2, 219, 220, 288
Religious Education, 195
Re-emergence of Calvinism, The, 110, 272-3, 286
Reformers, 242
Regents Park College, 67
Restricted communion (see also Lord's Table/Supper), 15-16, 122
Reynolds, Philip, 38-9
Rhone, Mrs, 61
Richardson, Samuel, 64
Robinson, R.,
Romanism, 106-7
Rose, E., 6
Rowdon, Dr Harold, xi, 114n, 115n, 135, 137n, 143n, 154n, 148-9, 152, 192-3, 195n, 196, 204, 209, 253

Salvation, 121, 122n, 186, 212-13, 233, 236, 237n, 285
Saltmarsh, John, 261
Scripture Union, 234
Scroggie, Dr Graham, 40, 116, 135, 217, 218n, 219
Seed Thoughts, 6, 26, 78, 82
Sharpe, J., 39
Shawcross, William, 93n, 103n
Sibbes, Richard, 264
Slater, Samuel, 264
South India Strict Baptist Missionary Society, 5
South Wales Bible College, 153
Southwark, 2,
Spanish Gospel Mission, 105
Spilsbury, John, 35, 64, 288
Spiritism, 106-7
Sport, 10-11, 168, 177, 229
Spurgeon, C. H., 5, 117-18,

130-31, 171, 228, 269, 276
Spurgeon, C. &. T., 5
Spurgeon's College, 201, 250
St. Andrew's Church, Holborn, 137
Story of the Year, 231, 286
Stovel, Charles, 36, 61-2, 65
Strict Baptists, xii, 2, 5, 7, 15-18, 21, 23, 28, 30-31, 33-4, 36, 40, 45, 48-50, 58-9, 61, 64, 67-71, 77-8, 82, 87-91, 95-7, 99, 104-5, 109-10, 112, 118, 120-22, 131-2, 162, 185, 199, 205-7, 215-16, 225-6, 238, 240, 254
Strict Baptist Bible Institute, 34n, 59, 69, 87n, 205
Strict Baptist Mission, 5-6, 21, 48, 87, 105, 225-6
Strict Baptist National Sunday School Association, 78
Strict Baptist Open Air Mission, 23, 226
Strict and Particular Baptists, 15-16, 69-70
Stringer, Harry, 149
Suffolk and Norfolk Association, 78
Swanage, 80
Systematic Theology, 148, 160

Teacher's Supplementary Courses, 195
The Saving Work of the Holy Spirit, 217, 218n, 273, 285
Thiselton, Professor Anthony, xii
Thomas, Owen, 148
Thomas, Dr W. H. Griffith, 29
Thompson, R., 3
Times Furnishing Company, 145
Times, obituary, 239
Tooting, xv, 117-19, 128, 185, 240, 286, 287
Torquay, 107, 129
Trinity Road Chapel, xii, xv, 117-20, 123, 125-33, 138, 207, 234-7, 247, 250, 286-7
Trussler, Norman, 76, 77n
Tye, Tommie, 51-2, 54
Tyndale Fellowship, 210, 214, 223, 252, 286

United States, 209, 233

Vereker, A. J., 113
Victoria, 144

Waite, J. C. J., 153
Walden, Mr & Mrs, 234
Walthamstow, xii, xv, 33-42, 46, 50-51, 59-60, 62, 68-70, 75, 240
Walthamstow Guardian, 33n, 38, 39, 40, 45, 46, 52, 53n, 60, 71
Wandsworth, 1-5, 30, 35, 117, 125, 128, 130, 162, 234, 237, 245
Wapping, 36
Waterside, 3
Welford, C. J., 38